My Days of Adventure

Ernest Alfred Vizetelly

Contents

THE PEOPLE'S WAR 7
PREFACE 8
I INTRODUCTORY--SOME EARLY RECOLLECTIONS 11
II THE OUTBREAK OF THE FRANCO-GERMAN WAR 28
III ON THE ROAD TO REVOLUTION 43
IV FROM REVOLUTION TO SIEGE 69
V BESIEGED 82
VI MORE ABOUT THE SIEGE DAYS 106
VII FROM PARIS TO VERSAILLES 121
VIII FROM VERSAILLES TO BRITTANY 135
IX THE WAR IN THE PROVINCES 151
X WITH THE "ARMY OF BRITTANY" 167
XI BEFORE LE MANS 182
XII LE MANS AND AFTER 196
XIII THE BITTER END 225

MY DAYS OF ADVENTURE

BY

Ernest Alfred Vizetelly

THE PEOPLE'S WAR

O husbandmen of hill and dale,
  O dressers of the vines,
O sea-tossed fighters of the gale,
  O hewers of the mines,
O wealthy ones who need not strive,
  O sons of learning, art,
O craftsmen of the city's hive,
  O traders of the man,
Hark to the cannon's thunder-call
  Appealing to the brave!
Your France is wounded, and may fall
  Beneath the foreign grave!
Then gird your loins! Let none delay
  Her glory to maintain;
Drive out the foe, throw off his sway,
  Win back your land again!

1870. E.A.V.

PREFACE

While this volume is largely of an autobiographical character, it will be found to contain also a variety of general information concerning the Franco-German War of 1870-71, more particularly with respect to the second part of that great struggle--the so-called "People's War" which followed the crash of Sedan and the downfall of the Second French Empire. If I have incorporated this historical matter in my book, it is because I have repeatedly noticed in these later years that, whilst English people are conversant with the main facts of the Sedan disaster and such subsequent outstanding events as the siege of Paris and the capitulation of Metz, they usually know very little about the manner in which the war generally was carried on by the French under the virtual dictatorship of Gambetta. Should England ever be invaded by a large hostile force, we, with our very limited regular army, should probably be obliged to rely largely on elements similar to those which were called to the field by the French National Defence Government of 1870 after the regular armies of the Empire had been either crushed at Sedan or closely invested at Metz. For that reason I have always taken a keen interest in our Territorial Force, well realizing what heavy responsibilities would fall upon it if a powerful enemy should obtain a footing in this country. Some indication of those responsibilities will be found in the present book.

Generally speaking, however, I have given only a sketch of the latter part of the Franco-German War. To have entered into details on an infinity of matters would have necessitated the writing of a very much longer work. However, I have supplied, I think, a good deal of precise information respecting the events which I actually witnessed, and in this connexion, perhaps, I may have thrown some useful sidelights on the war generally; for many things akin to those which I saw, occurred under more or less similar circumstances in other parts of France.

People who are aware that I am acquainted with the shortcomings of the French in those already distant days, and that I have watched, as closely as most foreigners can watch, the evolution of the French army in these later times, have often asked me what, to my thinking, would be the outcome of another Franco-German War. For many years I fully anticipated another struggle between the two Powers, and held myself in readiness to do duty as a war-correspondent. I long thought, also, that the signal for that struggle would be given by France. But I am no longer of that opinion. I fully believe that all French statesmen worthy of the name realize that it would be suicidal for France to provoke a war with her formidable neighbour. And at the same time I candidly confess that I do not know what some journalists mean by what they call the "New France." To my thinking there is no "New France" at all. There was as much spirit, as much patriotism, in the days of MacMahon, in the days of Boulanger, and at other periods, as there is now. The only real novelty that I notice in the France of to-day is the cultivation of many branches of sport and athletic exercise. Of that kind of thing there was very little indeed when I was a stripling. But granting that young Frenchmen of to-day are more athletic, more "fit" than were those of my generation, granting, moreover, that the present organization and the equipment of the French army are vastly superior to what they were in 1870, and also that the conditions of warfare have greatly changed, I feel that if France were to engage, unaided, in a contest with Germany, she would again be worsted, and worsted by her own fault.

She fully knows that she cannot bring into the field anything like as many men as Germany; and it is in a vain hope of supplying the deficiency that she has lately reverted from a two to a three years' system of military service. The latter certainly gives her a larger effective for the first contingencies of a campaign, but in all other respects it is merely a piece of jugglery, for it does not add a single unit to the total number of Frenchmen capable of bearing arms. The truth is, that during forty years of prosperity France has been intent on racial suicide. In the whole of that period only some 3,500,000 inhabitants have been added to her population, which is now still under 40 millions; whereas that of Germany has increased by leaps and bounds, and stands at about 66 millions. At the present time the German birth-rate is certainly falling, but the numerical superiority which Germany has acquired over

France since the war of 1870 is so great that I feel it would be impossible for the latter to triumph in an encounter unless she should be assisted by powerful allies. Bismarck said in 1870 that God was on the side of the big battalions; and those big battalions Germany can again supply. I hold, then, that no such Franco-German war as the last one can again occur. Europe is now virtually divided into two camps, each composed of three Powers, all of which would be more or less involved in a Franco-German struggle. The allies and friends on either side are well aware of it, and in their own interests are bound to exert a restraining influence which makes for the maintenance of peace. We have had evidence of this in the limitations imposed on the recent Balkan War.

On the other hand, it is, of course, the unexpected which usually happens; and whilst Europe generally remains armed to the teeth, and so many jealousies are still rife, no one Power can in prudence desist from her armaments. We who are the wealthiest nation in Europe spend on our armaments, in proportion to our wealth and our population, less than any other great Power. Yet some among us would have us curtail our expenditure, and thereby incur the vulnerability which would tempt a foe. Undoubtedly the armaments of the present day are great and grievous burdens on the nations, terrible impediments to social progress, but they constitute, unfortunately, our only real insurance against war, justifying yet to-day, after so many long centuries, the truth of the ancient Latin adage-- ***Si vis pacem, para bellum***.

It is, I think, unnecessary for me to comment here on the autobiographical part of my book. It will, I feel, speak for itself. It treats of days long past, and on a few points, perhaps, my memory may be slightly defective. In preparing my narrative, however, I have constantly referred to my old diaries, note-books and early newspaper articles, and have done my best to abstain from all exaggeration. Whether this story of some of my youthful experiences and impressions of men and things was worth telling or not is a point which I must leave my readers to decide.

E.A.V.
London, *January* 1914.

I
INTRODUCTORY--SOME EARLY RECOLLECTIONS

The Vizetelly Family--My Mother and her Kinsfolk--The *Illustrated Times* and its Staff--My Unpleasant Disposition--Thackeray and my First Half-Crown--School days at Eastbourne--Queen Alexandra--Garibaldi--A few old Plays and Songs--Nadar and the "Giant" Balloon--My Arrival in France-- My Tutor Brossard--Berezowski's Attempt on Alexander II--My Apprenticeship to Journalism--My first Article--I see some French Celebrities--Visits to the Tuileries--At Compiegne--A few Words with Napoleon III--A "Revolutionary" Beard.

This is an age of "Reminiscences," and although I have never played any part in the world's affairs, I have witnessed so many notable things and met so many notable people during the three-score years which I have lately completed, that it is perhaps allowable for me to add yet another volume of personal recollections to the many which have already poured from the press. On starting on an undertaking of this kind it is usual, I perceive by the many examples around me, to say something about one's family and upbringing. There is less reason for me to depart from this practice, as in the course of the present volume it will often be necessary for me to refer to some of my near relations. A few years ago a distinguished Italian philosopher and author, Angelo de Gubernatis, was good enough to include me in a dictionary of writers belonging to the Latin races, and stated, in doing so, that the Vizetellys were of French origin. That was a rather curious mistake on the part of an Italian writer, the truth being that the family originated at Ravenna, where some members of it held various offices in the Middle Ages. Subsequently, after dabbling in a conspiracy, some of the Vizzetelli fled to Venice and took to glass-making there, until at last Jacopo, from whom I am descended, came to England in the spacious days of Queen Elizabeth. From that time until my own the men of my family invariably married English women, so that very little Italian blood can flow in my veins.

Matrimonial alliances are sometimes of more than personal interest. One point has particularly struck me in regard to those contracted by members of my own family, this being the diversity of English counties from which the men have derived their wives and the women their husbands. References to Cheshire, Lancashire, Yorkshire, Staffordshire, Warwickshire, Leicestershire, Berkshire, Bucks, Suffolk, Kent, Surrey, Sussex, and Devonshire, in addition to Middlesex, otherwise London, appear in my family papers. We have become connected with Johnstons, Burslems, Bartletts, Pitts, Smiths, Wards, Covells, Randalls, Finemores, Radfords, Hindes, Pollards, Lemprieres, Wakes, Godbolds, Ansells, Fennells, Vaughans, Edens, Scotts, and Pearces, and I was the very first member of the family (subsequent to its arrival in England) to take a foreigner as wife, she being the daughter of a landowner of Savoy who proceeded from the Tissots of Switzerland. My elder brother Edward subsequently married a Burgundian girl named Clerget, and my stepbrother Frank chose an American one, *nee* Krehbiel, as his wife, these marriages occurring because circumstances led us to live for many years abroad.

Among the first London parishes with which the family was connected was St. Botolph's, Bishopsgate, where my forerunner, the first Henry Vizetelly, was buried in 1691, he then being fifty years of age, and where my father, the second Henry of the name, was baptised soon after his birth in 1820. St. Bride's, Fleet Street, was, however, our parish for many years, as its registers testify, though in 1781 my great-grandfather was resident in the parish of St. Ann's, Blackfriars, and was elected constable thereof. At that date the family name, which figures in old English registers under a variety of forms--Vissitaler, Vissitaly, Visataly, Visitelly, Vizetely, etc.--was by him spelt Vizzetelly, as is shown by documents now in the Guildhall Library; but a few years later he dropped the second z, with the idea, perhaps, of giving the name a more English appearance.

This great-grandfather of mine was, like his father before him, a printer and a member of the Stationers' Company. He was twice married, having by his first wife two sons, George and William, neither of whom left posterity. The former, I believe, died in the service of the Honourable East India Company. In June, 1775, however, my great-grandfather married Elizabeth, daughter of James Hinde, stationer, of Little Moorfields, and had by her, first, a daughter Elizabeth, from whom some of the Burslems and Godbolds are descended; and, secondly, twins, a boy and a girl, who were respectively christened James Henry and Mary Mehetabel. The former became my grandfather. In August, 1816, he married, at St. Bride's, Martha Jane Vaughan, daughter of a stage-coach proprietor of Chester, and had by her a daughter, who died unmarried, and four sons--my father, Henry Richard, and my uncles James, Frank, and Frederick Whitehead Vizetelly.

Some account of my grandfather is given in my father's "Glances Back through Seventy Years," and I need not add to it here. I will only say that, like his immediate forerunners, James Henry Vizetelly was a printer and freeman of the city. A clever versifier, and so able as an amateur actor that on certain occasions he replaced Edmund Kean on the boards when the latter was hopelessly drunk, he died in 1840, leaving his two elder sons, James and Henry, to carry on the printing business, which was then established in premises occupying the site of the ***Daily Telegraph*** building in Fleet Street.

In 1844 my father married Ellen Elizabeth, only child of John Pollard, M.D., a member of the ancient Yorkshire family of the Pollards of Bierley and Brunton, now chiefly represented, I believe, by the Pollards of Scarr Hall. John Pollard's wife, Charlotte Maria Fennell, belonged to a family which gave officers to the British Navy--one of them serving directly under Nelson--and clergy to the Church of England. The Fennells were related to the Bronte sisters through the latter's mother; and one was closely connected with the Shackle who founded the original ***John Bull*** newspaper. Those, then, were my kinsfolk on the maternal side. My mother presented my father with seven children, of whom I was the sixth, being also the fourth son. I was born on November 29, 1853, at a house called Chalfont Lodge in Campden House Road, Kensington, and well do I remember the great conflagration which destroyed the fine old historical mansion built by Baptist Hicks, sometime a mercer in Cheapside and ultimately Viscount Campden. But another scene which has more particularly haunted me all through my life was that of my mother's sudden death in a saloon carriage of an express train on the London and Brighton line. Though she was in failing health, nobody thought her end so near; but in the very midst of a journey to London, whilst the train was rushing on at full speed, and no help could be procured, a sudden weakness came over her, and in a few minutes she passed away. I was very young at the time, barely five years old, yet everything still rises before me with all the vividness of an imperishable memory. Again, too, I see that beautiful intellectual brow and those lustrous eyes, and hear that musical voice, and feel the gentle touch of that loving motherly hand. She was a woman of attainments, fond of setting words to music, speaking perfect French, for she had been partly educated at Evreux in Normandy, and having no little knowledge of Greek and Latin literature, as was shown by her annotations to a copy of Lempriere's "Classical Dictionary" which is now in my possession.

About eighteen months after I was born, that is in the midst of the Crimean War, my father founded, in conjunction with David Bogue, a well-known publisher of the time, a journal called the ***Illustrated Times***, which for several years competed successfully with the ***Illustrated London News***. It was issued at threepence per copy, and an old memorandum of the printers now lying before me shows that in the paper's earlier years the average printings were 130,000 copies weekly--a notable figure for that period, and one which was considerably exceeded when any really important event occurred. My father was the chief editor and manager, his leading coadjutor being Frederick Greenwood, who afterwards founded the ***Pall Mall Gazette***. I do not think that Greenwood's connection with the ***Illustrated Times*** and with my father's other journal, the ***Welcome Guest***, is mentioned in any of the accounts of his career. The literary staff included four of the Brothers Mayhew-- Henry, Jules, Horace, and Augustus, two of whom, Jules and Horace, became godfathers to my father's first children by his second wife. Then there were also William and Robert Brough, Edmund Yates, George Augustus Sala, Hain Friswell, W.B. Rands, Tom Robertson, Sutherland Edwards, James Hannay, Edward Draper, and Hale White (father of "Mark Rutherford"), and several artists and engravers, such as Birket Foster, "Phiz." Portch, Andrews, Duncan, Skelton, Bennett, McConnell, Linton, London, and Horace Harrall. I saw all those men in my early years, for my father was very hospitably inclined, and they were often guests at Chalfont Lodge.

After my mother's death, my grandmother, *nee* Vaughan, took charge of the establishment, and I soon became the terror of the house, developing a most violent temper and acquiring the vocabulary of the roughest market porter. My wilfulness was probably innate (nearly all the Vizetellys having had impulsive wills of their own), and my flowery language was picked up by perversely loitering to listen whenever there happened to be a street row in Church Lane, which I had to cross on my way to or from Kensington Gardens, my daily place of resort. At an early age I started bullying my younger brother, I defied my grandmother, insulted the family doctor because he was too fond of prescribing grey powders for my particular benefit, and behaved abominably to the excellent Miss Lindup of Sheffield Terrace, who endeavoured to instruct me in the rudiments of reading, writing, and arithmetic. I frequently astonished or appalled the literary men and artists who were my father's guests. I hated being continually asked what I should like to be when I grew up, and the slightest chaff threw me into a perfect paroxysm of passion. Whilst, however, I was resentful of the authority of others, I was greatly inclined to exercise authority myself--to such a degree, indeed, that my father's servants generally spoke of me as "the young master," regardless of the existence of my elder brothers.

Having already a retentive memory, I was set to learn sundry "recitations," and every now and then was called upon to emerge from behind the dining-room curtains and repeat "My Name is Norval" or "The Spanish Armada," for the delectation of my father's friends whilst they lingered over their wine. Disaster generally ensued, provoked either by some genial chaff or well-meant criticism from such men as Sala and Augustus Mayhew, and I was ultimately carried off--whilst venting incoherent protests--to be soundly castigated and put to bed.

Among the real celebrities who occasionally called at Chalfont Lodge was Thackeray, whom I can still picture sitting on one side of the fireplace, whilst my father sat on the other, I being installed on the hearthrug between them. Provided that I was left to myself, I could behave decently enough, discreetly preserving silence, and, indeed, listening intently to the conversation of my father's friends, and thereby picking up a very odd mixture of knowledge. I was, I believe, a pale little chap with lank fair hair and a wistful face, and no casual observer would have imagined that my nature was largely compounded of such elements as enter into the composition of Italian brigands, Scandinavian pirates, and wild Welshmen. Thackeray, at all events, did not appear to think badly of the little boy who sat so quietly at his feet. One day, indeed, when he came upon me and my younger brother Arthur, with our devoted attendant Selina Horrocks, in Kensington Gardens, he put into practice his own dictum that one could never see a schoolboy without feeling an impulse to dip one's hand in one's pocket. Accordingly he presented me with the first half-crown I ever possessed, for though my father's gifts were frequent they were small. It was understood, I believe, that I was to share the aforesaid half-crown with my brother Arthur, but in spite of the many remonstrances of the faithful Selina--a worthy West-country woman, who had largely taken my mother's place--I appropriated the gift in its entirety, and became extremely ill by reason of my many indiscreet purchases at a tuck-stall which stood, if I remember rightly, at a corner of the then renowned Kensington Flower Walk. This incident must have occurred late in Thackeray's life. My childish recollection of him is that of a very big gentleman with beaming eyes.

My grandmother's reign in my father's house was not of great duration, as in February, 1861, he contracted a second marriage, taking on this occasion as his wife a "fair maid of Kent," [Elizabeth Anne Ansell, of Broadstairs; mother of my stepbrother, Dr. Frank H. Vizetelly, editor of the "Standard Dictionary," New York.] to whose entry into our home I was at first violently opposed, but who promptly won me over by her unremitting affection and kindness, eventually becoming the best and truest friend of my youth and early manhood. My circumstances changed, however, soon after that marriage, for as I was now nearly eight years old it was deemed appropriate that I should be sent to a boarding-school, both by way of improving my mind and of having some nonsense knocked out of me, which, indeed, was promptly accomplished by the pugnacious kindness of my schoolfellows. Among the latter was one, my senior by a few years, who became a very distinguished journalist. I refer to the late Horace Voules, so long associated with Labouchere's journal, *Truth*. My brother Edward was also at the same school, and my brother Arthur came there a little later.

It was situated at Eastbourne, and a good deal has been written about it in recent works on the history of that well-known watering-place, which, when I was first sent there, counted less than 6000 inhabitants. Located in the old town or village, at a distance of a mile or more from the sea, the school occupied a building called "The Gables," and was an offshoot of a former ancient school connected with the famous parish church. In my time this "academy" was carried on as a private venture by a certain James Anthony Bown, a portly old gentleman of considerable attainments.

I was unusually precocious in some respects, and though I frequently got into scrapes by playing impish tricks--as, for instance, when I combined with others to secure an obnoxious French master to his chair by means of some cobbler's wax, thereby ruining a beautiful pair of peg-top trousers which he had just purchased--I did not neglect my lessons, but secured a number of "prizes" with considerable facility. When I was barely twelve years old, not one of my schoolfellows--and some were sixteen and seventeen years old--could compete with me in Latin, in which language Bown ended by taking me separately. I also won three or four prizes for "excelling" my successive classes in English grammar as prescribed by the celebrated Lindley Murray.

In spite of my misdeeds (some of which, fortunately, were never brought home to me), I became, I think, somewhat of a favourite with the worthy James Anthony, for he lent me interesting books to read, occasionally had me to supper in his own quarters, and was now and then good enough to overlook the swollen state of my nose or the blackness of one of my eyes when I had been having a bout with a schoolfellow or a young clodhopper of the village. We usually fought with the village lads in Love Lane on Sunday evenings, after getting over the playground wall. I received firstly the nickname of Moses, through falling among some rushes whilst fielding a ball at cricket; and secondly, that of Noses, because my nasal organ, like that of Cyrano de Bergerac, suddenly grew to huge proportions, in such wise that it embodied sufficient material for two noses of ordinary dimensions. Its size was largely responsible for my defeats when fighting, for I found it difficult to keep guard over such a prominent organ and prevent my claret from being tapped.

Having generations of printers' ink mingled with my blood, I could not escape the unkind fate which made me a writer of articles and books. In conjunction with a chum named Clement Ireland I ran a manuscript school journal, which included stories of pirates and highwaymen, illustrated with lurid designs in which red ink was plentifully employed in order to picture the gore which flowed so freely through the various tales. My grandmother Vaughan was an inveterate reader of the ***London Journal*** and the ***Family Herald***, and whenever I went home for my holidays I used to pounce upon those journals and devour some of the stories of the author of "Minnegrey," as well as Miss Braddon's "Aurora Floyd" and "Henry Dunbar." The perusal of books by Ainsworth, Scott, Lever, Marryat, James Grant, G. P. R. James, Dumas, and Whyte Melville gave me additional material for storytelling; and so, concocting wonderful blends of all sorts of fiction, I spun many a yarn to my schoolfellows in the dormitory in which I slept--yarns which were sometimes supplied in instalments, being kept up for a week or longer.

My summer holidays were usually spent in the country, but at other times I went to London, and was treated to interesting sights. At Kensington, in my earlier years, I often saw Queen Victoria and the Prince Consort with their children, notably the Princess Royal (Empress Frederick) and the Prince of Wales (Edward VII). When the last-named married the "Sea-King's daughter from over the sea"--since then our admired and gracious Queen Alexandra--and they drove together through the crowded streets of London on their way to Windsor, I came specially from Eastbourne to witness that triumphal progress, and even now I can picture the young prince with his round chubby face and little side-whiskers, and the vision of almost tearfully-smiling beauty, in blue and white, which swept past my eager boyish eyes.

During the Easter holidays of 1864 Garibaldi came to England. My uncle, Frank Vizetelly, was the chief war-artist of that period, the predecessor, in fact, of the late Melton Prior. He knew Garibaldi well, having first met him during the war of 1859, and having subsequently accompanied him during his campaign through Sicily and then on to Naples--afterwards, moreover, staying with him at Caprera. And so my uncle carried me and his son, my cousin Albert, to Stafford House (where he had the *entrée*), and the grave-looking Liberator patted us on the head, called us his children, and at Frank Vizetelly's request gave us photographs of himself. I then little imagined that I should next see him in France, at the close of the war with Germany, during a part of which my brother Edward acted as one of his orderly officers.

My father, being at the head of a prominent London newspaper, often received tickets for one and another theatre. Thus, during my winter holidays, I saw many of the old pantomimes at Drury Lane and elsewhere. I also well remember Sothern's "Lord Dundreary," and a play called "The Duke's Motto," which was based on Paul Feval's novel, "Le Bossu." I frequently witnessed the entertainments given by the German Reeds, Corney Grain, and Woodin, the clever quick-change artist. I likewise remember Leotard the acrobat at the Alhambra, and sundry performances at the old Pantheon, where I heard such popular songs as "The Captain with the Whiskers" and "The Charming Young Widow I met in the Train." Nigger ditties were often the "rage" during my boyhood, and some of them, like "Dixie-land" and "So Early in the Morning," still linger in my memory. Then, too, there were such songs as "Billy Taylor," "I'm Afloat," "I'll hang my Harp on a Willow Tree," and an inane composition which contained the lines--

"When a lady elopes
Down a ladder of ropes,
She may go, she may go,
She may go to--Hongkong--for me!"

In those schoolboy days of mine, however, the song of songs, to my thinking, was one which we invariably sang on breaking up for the holidays. Whether it was peculiar to Eastbourne or had been derived from some other school I cannot say. I only know that the last verse ran, approximately, as follows:

"Magistrorum is a borum,
  Hic-haec-hoc has made his bow.
Let us cry: 'O cockalorum!'
  That's the Latin for us now.
Alpha, beta, gamma, delta,
  Off to Greece, for we are free!
Helter, skelter, melter, pelter,
  We're the lads for mirth and spree!"

For "cockalorum," be it noted, we frequently substituted the name of some particularly obnoxious master.

To return to the interesting sights of my boyhood, I have some recollection of the Exhibition of 1862, but can recall more vividly a visit to the Crystal Palace towards the end of the following year, when I there saw the strange house-like oar of the "Giant" balloon in which Nadar, the photographer and aeronaut, had lately made, with his wife and others, a memorable and disastrous aerial voyage. Readers of Jules Verne will remember that Nadar figures conspicuously in his "Journey to the Moon." Quite a party of us went to the Palace to see the "Giant's" car, and Nadar, standing over six feet high, with a great tangled mane of frizzy flaxen hair, a ruddy moustache, and a red shirt *a la* Garibaldi, took us inside it and showed us all the accommodation it contained for eating, sleeping and photographic purposes. I could not follow what he said, for I then knew only a few French words, and I certainly had no idea that I should one day ascend into the air with him in a car of a very different type, that of the captive balloon which, for purposes of military observation, he installed on the Place Saint Pierre at Montmartre, during the German siege of Paris.

A time came when my father disposed of his interest in the **Illustrated Times** and repaired to Paris to take up the position of Continental representative of the **Illustrated London News**. My brother Edward, at that time a student at the Ecole des Beaux Arts, then became his assistant, and a little later I was taken across the Channel with my brother Arthur to join the rest of the family. We lived, first, at Auteuil, and then at Passy, where I was placed in a day-school called the Institution Nouissel, where lads were prepared for admission to the State or municipal colleges. There had been some attempt to teach me French at Eastbourne, but it had met with little success, partly, I think, because I was prejudiced against the French generally, regarding them as a mere race of frog-eaters whom we had deservedly whacked at Waterloo. Eventually my prejudices were in a measure overcome by what I heard from our drill-master, a retired non-commissioned officer, who had served in the Crimea, and who told us some rousing anecdotes about the gallantry of "our allies" at the Alma and elsewhere. In the result, the old sergeant's converse gave me "furiously to think" that there might be some good in the French after all.

At Nouissel's I acquired some knowledge of the language rapidly enough, and I was afterwards placed in the charge of a tutor, a clever scamp named Brossard, who prepared me for the Lycee Bonaparte (now Condorcet), where I eventually became a pupil, Brossard still continuing to coach me with a view to my passing various examinations, and ultimately securing the usual *baccalaureat*, without which nobody could then be anything at all in France. In the same way he coached Evelyn

Jerrold, son of Blanchard and grandson of Douglas Jerrold, both of whom were on terms of close friendship with the Vizetellys. But while Brossard was a clever man, he was also an unprincipled one, and although I was afterwards indebted to him for an introduction to old General Changarnier, to whom he was related, it would doubtless have been all the better if he had not introduced me to some other people with whom he was connected. He lived for a while with a woman who was not his wife, and deserted her for a girl of eighteen, whom he also abandoned, in order to devote himself to a creature in fleshings who rode a bare-backed steed at the Cirque de l'Imperatrice. When I was first introduced to her "behind the scenes," she was bestriding a chair, and smoking a pink cigarette, and she addressed me as ***mon petit***. Briefly, the moral atmosphere of Brossard's life was not such as befitted him to be a mentor of youth.

Let me now go back a little. At the time of the great Paris Exhibition of 1867 I was in my fourteenth year. The city was then crowded with royalties, many of whom I saw on one or another occasion. I was in the Bois de Boulogne with my father when, after a great review, a shot was fired at the carriage in which Napoleon III and his guest, Alexander II of Russia, were seated side by side. I saw equerry Raimbeaux gallop forward to screen the two monarchs, and I saw the culprit seized by a sergeant of our Royal Engineers, attached to the British section of the Exhibition. Both sovereigns stood up in the carriage to show that they were uninjured, and it was afterwards reported that the Emperor Napoleon said to the Emperor Alexander: "If that shot was fired by an Italian it was meant for me; if by a Pole, it was meant for your Majesty." Whether those words were really spoken, or were afterwards invented, as such things often are, by some clever journalist, I cannot say; but the man proved to be a Pole named Berezowski, who was subsequently sentenced to transportation for life.

It was in connection with this attempt on the Czar that I did my first little bit of journalistic work. By my father's directions, I took a few notes and made a hasty little sketch of the surroundings. This and my explanations enabled M. Jules Pelcoq, an artist of Belgian birth, whom my father largely employed on behalf of the ***Illustrated London News***, to make a drawing which appeared on the first page of that journal's next issue. I do not think that any other paper in the world was able to supply a pictorial representation of Berezowski's attempt.

I have said enough, I think, to show that I was a precocious lad, perhaps, indeed, a great deal too precocious. However, I worked very hard in those days. My hours at Bonaparte were from ten to twelve and from two to four. I had also to prepare home-lessons for the Lycee, take special lessons from Brossard, and again lessons in German from a tutor named With. Then, too, my brother Edward ceasing to act as my father's assistant in order to devote himself to journalism on his own account, I had to take over a part of his duties. One of my cousins, Montague Vizetelly (son of my uncle James, who was the head of our family), came from England, however, to assist my father in the more serious work, such as I, by reason of my youth, could not yet perform. My spare time was spent largely in taking instructions to artists or fetching drawings from them. At one moment I might be at Mont-martre, and at another in the Quartier Latin, calling on Pelcoq, Anastasi, Janet Lange, Gustave Janet, Pauquet, Thorigny, Gaildrau, Deroy, Bocourt, Darjou, Lix, Moulin, Fichot, Blanchard, or other artists who worked for the ***Illustrated London News***. Occasionally a sketch was posted to England, but more frequently I had to despatch some drawing on wood by rail. Though I have never been anything but an amateurish draughtsman myself, I certainly developed a critical faculty, and acquired a knowledge of different artistic methods, during my intercourse with so many of the ***dessinateurs*** of the last years of the Second Empire.

By-and-by more serious duties were allotted to me. The "Paris Fashions" design then appearing every month in the ***Illustrated London News*** was for a time prepared according to certain dresses which Worth and other famous costumiers made for empresses, queens, princesses, great ladies, and theatrical celebrities; and, accompanying Pelcoq or Janet when they went to sketch those gowns (nowadays one would simply obtain photographs), I took down from ***la premiere***, or sometimes from Worth himself, full particulars respecting materials and styles, in order that the descriptive letterpress, which was to accompany the illustration, might be correct.

In this wise I served my apprenticeship to journalism. My father naturally revised my work. The first article, all my own, which appeared in print was one on that notorious theatrical institution, the Claque. I sent it to ***Once a Week***, which E. S. Dallas then edited, and knowing that he was well acquainted with my father, and feeling very diffident respecting the merits of what I had written, I assumed a ***nom*** *de plume* ("Charles Ludhurst") for the occasion, Needless to say that I was delighted when I saw the article in print, and yet more so when I received for it a couple of guineas, which I speedily expended on gloves, neckties, and a walking-stick. Here let me say that we were rather swagger young fellows at Bonaparte. We did not have to wear hideous ill-fitting uniforms like other Lyceens, but endeavoured to present a very smart appearance. Thus we made it a practice to wear gloves and to carry walking-sticks or canes on our way to or from the Lycee. I even improved on that by buying "button-holes" at the flower-market beside the Madeleine, and this idea "catching on," as the phrase goes, quite a commotion occurred one morning when virtually half my classmates were found wearing flowers--for it happened to be La Saint Henri, the *fete*-day of the Count de Chambord, and both our Proviseur and our professor imagined that this was, on our part, a seditious Legitimist demonstration. There were, however, very few Legitimists among us, though Orleanists and Republicans were numerous.

I have mentioned that my first article was on the Claque, that organisation established to encourage applause in theatres, it being held that the Parisian spectator required to be roused by some such method. Brossard having introduced me to the *sous-chef* of the Claque at the Opera Comique, I often obtained admission to that house as a *claqueur*. I even went to a few other theatres in the same capacity. Further, Brossard knew sundry authors and journalists, and took me to the Cafe de Suede and the Cafe de Madrid, where I saw and heard some of the celebrities of the day. I can still picture the great Dumas, loud of voice and exuberant in gesture whilst holding forth to a band of young "spongers," on whom he was spending his last napoleons. I can also see Gambetta--young, slim, black-haired and bearded, with a full sensual underlip--seated at the same table as Delescluze, whose hair and beard, once red, had become a dingy white, whose figure was emaciated and angular, and whose yellowish, wrinkled face seemed to betoken that he was possessed by some fixed idea. What that idea was, the Commune subsequently showed. Again, I can see Henri Rochefort and Gustave Flourens together: the former straight and sinewy, with a great tuft of very dark curly hair, flashing eyes and high and prominent cheekbones; while the latter, tall and bald, with long moustaches and a flowing beard, gazed at you in an eager imperious way, as if he were about to issue some command.

Other men who helped to overthrow the Empire also became known to me. My father, whilst engaged in some costly litigation respecting a large castellated house which he had leased at Le Vesinet, secured Jules Favre as his advocate, and on various occasions I went with him to Favre's residence. Here let me say that my father, in spite of all his interest in French literature, did not know the language. He could scarcely express himself in it, and thus he always made it a practice to have one of his sons with him, we having inherited our mother's linguistic gifts. Favre's command of language was great, but his eloquence was by no means rousing, and I well remember that when he pleaded for my father, the three judges of the Appeal Court composed themselves to sleep, and did not awaken until the counsel opposed to us started banging his fist and shouting in thunderous tones. Naturally enough, as the judges never heard our side of the case, but only our adversary's, they decided against us.

Some retrenchment then became necessary on my father's part, and he sent my step-mother, her children and my brother Arthur, to Saint Servan in Brittany, where he rented a house which was called "La petite Amelia," after George III's daughter of that name, who, during some interval of peace between France and Great Britain, went to stay at Saint Servan for the benefit of her health. The majority of our family having repaired there and my cousin Monty returning to England some time in 1869, I remained alone with my father in Paris. We resided in what I may call a bachelor's flat at No. 16, Rue de Miromesnil, near the Elysee Palace. The principal part of the house was occupied by the Count and Countess de Chateaubriand and their daughters. The Countess was good enough to take some notice of me, and subsequently, when she departed for Combourg at the approach of the German siege, she gave me full permission to make use, if necessary, of the coals and wood left in the Chateaubriand cellars.

In 1869, the date I have now reached, I was in my sixteenth year, still studying, and at the same time giving more and more assistance to my father in connection with his journalistic work. He has included in his "Glances Back" some account of the facilities which enabled him to secure adequate pictorial delineation of the Court life of the Empire. He has told the story of Moulin, the police-agent, who frequently watched over the Emperor's personal safety, and who also supplied sketches of Court functions for the use of the *Illustrated London News*. Napoleon

III resembled his great-uncle in at least one respect. He fully understood the art of advertisement; and, in his desire to be thought well of in England, he was always ready to favour English journalists. Whilst a certain part of the London Press preserved throughout the reign a very critical attitude towards the Imperial policy, it is certain that some of the Paris correspondents were in close touch with the Emperor's Government, and that some of them were actually subsidized by it.

The best-informed man with respect to Court and social events was undoubtedly Mr. Felix Whiteburst of *The Daily Telegraph*, whom I well remember. He had the *entree* at the Tuileries and elsewhere, and there were occasions when very important information was imparted to him with a view to its early publication in London. For the most part, however, Whitehurst confined himself to chronicling events or incidents occurring at Court or in Bonapartist high society. Anxious to avoid giving offence, he usually glossed over any scandal that occurred, or dismissed it airily, with the *desinvolture* of a *roue* of the Regency. Withal, he was an extremely amiable man, very condescending towards me when we met, as sometimes happened at the Tuileries itself.

I had to go there on several occasions to meet Moulin, the detective-artist, by appointment, and a few years ago this helped me to write a book which has been more than once reprinted. [Note] I utilized in it many notes made by me in 1869-70, notably with respect to the Emperor and Empress's private apartments, the kitchens, and the arrangements made for balls and banquets. I am not aware at what age a young fellow is usually provided with his first dress-suit, but I know that mine was made about the time I speak of. I was then, I suppose, about five feet five inches in height, and my face led people to suppose that I was eighteen or nineteen years of age.

[Note: The work in question was entitled "The Court of the Tuileries, 1852-1870," by "Le Petit Homme Rouge"--a pseudonym which I have since used when producing other books. "The Court of the Tuileries" was founded in part on previously published works, on a quantity of notes and memoranda made by my father, other relatives, and myself, and on some of the private papers of one of my wife's kinsmen, General Mollard, who after greatly distinguishing himself at the Tchernaya and Magenta, became for a time an aide-de-camp to Napoleon III.]

In the autumn of 1869, I fell rather ill from over-study--I had already begun to read up Roman law--and, on securing a holiday, I accompanied my father to Compiegne, where the Imperial Court was then staying. We were not among the invited guests, but it had been arranged that every facility should be given to the ***Illustrated London News*** representatives in order that the Court ***villegiatura*** might be fully depicted in that journal. I need not recapitulate my experiences on this occasion. There is an account of our visit in my father's "Glances Back," and I inserted many additional particulars in my "Court of the Tuileries." I may mention, however, that it was at Compiegne that I first exchanged a few words with Napoleon III.

One day, my father being unwell (the weather was intensely cold), I proceeded to the chateau [We slept at the Hotel de la Cloche, but had the ***entree*** to the chateau at virtually any time.] accompanied only by our artist, young M. Montbard, who was currently known as "Apollo" in the Quartier Latin, where he delighted the ***habitues*** of the Bal Bullier by a style of choregraphy in comparison with which the achievements subsequently witnessed at the notorious Moulin Rouge would have sunk into insignificance. Montbard had to make a couple of drawings on the day I have mentioned, and it so happened that, whilst we were going about with M. de la Ferriere, the chamberlain on duty, Napoleon III suddenly appeared before us. Directly I was presented to him he spoke to me in English, telling me that he often saw the ***Illustrated London News***, and that the illustrations of French life and Paris improvements (in which he took so keen an interest) were very ably executed. He asked me also how long I had been in France, and where I had learnt the language. Then, remarking that it was near the ***dejeuner*** hour, he told M. de la Ferriere to see that Montbard and myself were suitably entertained.

I do not think that I had any particular political opinions at that time. Montbard, however, was a Republican--in fact, a future Communard--and I know that he did not appreciate his virtually enforced introduction to the so-called "Badinguet." Still, he contrived to be fairly polite, and allowed the Emperor to inspect the sketch he was making. There was to be a theatrical performance at the chateau that evening, and it had already been arranged that Montbard should witness it. On hearing, however, that it had been impossible to provide my father and myself with seats, on account of the great demand for admission on the part of local magnates and the officers of the garrison, the Emperor was good enough to say, after I had explained that my father's indisposition would prevent him from attending: "Voyons, vous pourrez bien trouver une petite place pour ce jeune homme. Il n'est pas si grand, et je suis sur que cela lui fera plaisir." M. de la Ferriere bowed, and thus it came to pass that I witnessed the performance after all, being seated on a stool behind some extremely beautiful women whose white shoulders repeatedly distracted my attention from the stage. In regard to Montbard there was some little trouble, as M. de la Ferriere did not like the appearance of his "revolutionary-looking beard," the sight of which, said he, might greatly alarm the Empress. Montbard, however, indignantly refused to shave it off, and ten months later the "revolutionary beards" were predominant, the power and the pomp of the Empire having been swept away amidst all the disasters of invasion.

II
THE OUTBREAK OF THE FRANCO-GERMAN WAR

Napoleon's Plans for a War with Prussia--The Garde Mobile and the French Army generally--Its Armament--The "White Blouses" and the Paris Riots--The Emperor and the Elections of 1869--The Troppmann and Pierre Bonaparte Affairs--Captain the Hon. Dennis Bingham--The Ollivier Ministry--French Campaigning Plans--Frossard and Bazaine--The Negotiations with Archduke Albert and Count Vimeroati--The War forced on by Bismarck--I shout "A Berlin!"--The Imperial Guard and General Bourbaki--My Dream of seeing a War--My uncle Frank Vizetelly and his Campaigns--"The Siege of Pekin"-- Organization of the French Forces--The Information Service--I witness the departure of Napoleon III and the Imperial Prince from Saint Cloud.

There was no little agitation in France during the years 1868 and 1869. The outcome first of the Schleswig-Holstein war, and secondly of the war between Prussia and Austria in 1866, had alarmed many French politicians. Napoleon III had expected some territorial compensation in return for his neutrality at those periods, and it is certain that Bismarck, as chief Prussian minister, had allowed him to suppose that he would be able to indemnify himself for his non-intervention in the afore-mentioned contests. After attaining her ends, however, Prussia turned an unwilling ear to the French Emperor's suggestions, and from that moment a Franco-German war became inevitable. Although, as I well remember, there was a perfect "rage" for Bismarck "this" and Bismarck "that" in Paris--particularly for the Bismarck colour, a shade of Havana brown--the Prussian statesman, who had so successfully "jockeyed" the Man of Destiny, was undoubtedly a well hated and dreaded individual among the Parisians, at least among all those who thought of the future of Europe. Prussian policy, however, was not the only cause of anxiety in France, for at the same period the Republican opposition to the Imperial authority was steadily gaining strength in the great cities, and the political concessions by which Napoleon III sought to disarm it only emboldened it to make fresh demands.

In planning a war on Prussia, the Emperor was influenced both by national and by dynastic considerations. The rise of Prussia--which had become head of the North German Confederation--was without doubt a menace not only to French ascendency on the Continent, but also to France's general interests. On the other hand, the prestige of the Empire having been seriously impaired, in France itself, by the diplomatic defeats which Bismarck had inflicted on Napoleon, it seemed that only a successful war, waged on the Power from which France had received those successive rebuffs, could restore the aforesaid prestige and ensure the duration of the Bonaparte dynasty.

Even nowadays, in spite of innumerable revelations, many writers continue to cast all the responsibility of the Franco-German War on Germany, or, to be more precise, on Prussia as represented by Bismarck. That, however, is a great error. A trial of strength was regarded on both sides as inevitable, and both sides contributed to bring it about. Bismarck's share in the conflict was to precipitate hostilities, selecting for them what he judged to be an opportune moment for his country, and thereby preventing the Emperor Napoleon from maturing his designs. The latter did not intend to declare war until early in 1871; the Prussian statesman brought it about in July, 1870.

The Emperor really took to the war-path soon after 1866. A great military council was assembled, and various measures were devised to strengthen the army. The principal step was the creation of a territorial force called the Garde Mobile, which was expected to yield more than half a million men. Marshal Niel, who was then Minister of War, attempted to carry out this scheme, but was hampered by an insufficiency of money. Nowadays, I often think of Niel and the Garde Mobile when I read of Lord Haldane, Colonel Seely, and our own "terriers." It seems to me, at times, as if the clock had gone back more than forty years.

Niel died in August, 1869, leaving his task in an extremely unfinished state, and Marshal Le Boeuf, who succeeded him, persevered with it in a very faint-hearted way. The regular army, however, was kept in fair condition, though it was never so strong as it appeared to be on paper. There was a system in vogue by which a conscript of means could avoid service by supplying a *remplacant*. Originally, he was expected to provide his *remplacant* himself; but, ultimately, he only had to pay a sum of money to the military authorities, who undertook to find a man to take his place. Unfortunately, in thousands of instances, over a term of some years, the *remplacants* were never provided at all. I do not suggest that the money was absolutely misappropriated, but it was diverted to other military purposes, and, in the result, there was always a considerable shortage in the annual contingent.

The creature comforts of the men were certainly well looked after. My particular chum at Bonaparte was the son of a general-officer, and I visited more than one barracks or encampment. Without doubt, there was always an abundance of good sound food. Further, the men were well-armed. All military authorities are agreed, I believe, that the Chassepot rifle--invented in or about 1866--was superior to the Dreyse needle-gun, which was in use in the Prussian army. Then, too, there was Colonel de Reffye's machine-gun or *mitrailleuse*, in a sense the forerunner of the Gatling and the Maxim. It was first devised, I think, in 1863, and, according to official statements, some three or four years later there were more than a score of *mitrailleuse* batteries. With regard to other ordnance, however, that of the French was inferior to that of the Germans, as was conclusively proved at Sedan and elsewhere. In many respects the work of army reform, publicly advised by General Trochu in a famous pamphlet, and by other officers in reports to the Emperor and the Ministry of War, proceeded at a very slow pace, being impeded by a variety of considerations. The young men of the large towns did not take kindly to the idea of serving in the new Garde Mobile. Having escaped service in the regular army, by drawing exempting "numbers" or by paying for *remplacants*, they regarded it as very unfair that they should be called upon to serve at all, and there were serious riots in various parts of France at the time of their first enrolment in 1868. Many of them failed to realize the necessities of the case. There was no great wave of patriotism sweeping through the country. The German danger was not yet generally apparent. Further, many upholders of the Imperial authority shook their heads in deprecation of this scheme of enrolling and arming so many young men, who might suddenly blossom into revolutionaries and turn their weapons against the powers of the day.

There was great unrest in Paris in 1868, the year of Henri Rochefort's famous journal **La Lanterne**. Issue after issue of that bitterly-penned effusion was seized and confiscated, and more than once did I see vigilant detectives snatch copies from people in the streets. In June, 1869, we had general elections, accompanied by rioting on the Boulevards. It was then that the "White Blouse" legend arose, it being alleged that many of the rioters were ***agents provocateurs*** in the pay of the Prefecture of Police, and wore white blouses expressly in order that they might be known to the sergents-de-ville and the Gardes de Paris who were called upon to quell the disturbances. At first thought, it might seem ridiculous that any Government should stir up rioting for the mere sake of putting it down, but it was generally held that the authorities wished some disturbances to occur in order, first, that the middle-classes might be frightened by the prospect of a violent revolution, and thereby induced to vote for Government candidates at the elections; and, secondly, that some of the many real Revolutionaries might be led to participate in the rioting in such wise as to supply a pretext for arresting them.

I was with my mentor Brossard and my brother Edward one night in June when a "Madeleine-Bastille" omnibus was overturned on the Boulevard Montmartre and two or three newspaper kiosks were added to it by way of forming a barricade, the purpose of which was by no means clear. The great crowd of promenaders seemed to regard the affair as capital fun until the police suddenly came up, followed by some mounted men of the Garde de Paris, whereupon the laughing spectators became terrified and suddenly fled for their lives. With my companions I gazed on the scene from the *entresol* of the Cafe Mazarin. It was the first affair of the kind I had ever witnessed, and for that reason impressed itself more vividly on my mind than several subsequent and more serious ones. In the twinkling of an eye all the little tables set out in front of the cafes were deserted, and tragi-comical was the sight of the many women with golden chignons scurrying away with their alarmed companions, and tripping now and again over some fallen chair whilst the pursuing cavalry clattered noisily along the foot-pavements. A Londoner might form some idea of the scene by picturing a charge from Leicester Square to Piccadilly Circus at the hour when Coventry Street is most thronged with undesirables of both sexes.

The majority of the White Blouses and their friends escaped unhurt, and the police and the guards chiefly expended their vigour on the spectators of the original disturbance. Whether this had been secretly engineered by the authorities for one of the purposes I previously indicated, must always remain a moot point. In any case it did not incline the Parisians to vote for the Government candidates. Every deputy returned for the city on that occasion was an opponent of the Empire, and in later years I was told by an ex-Court official that when Napoleon became acquainted with the result of the pollings he said, in reference to the nominees whom he had favoured, "Not one! not a single one!" The ingratitude of the Parisians, as the Emperor styled it, was always a thorn in his side; yet he should have remembered that in the past the bulk of the Parisians had seldom, if ever, been on the side of constituted authority.

Later that year came the famous affair of the Pantin crimes, and I was present with my father when Troppmann, the brutish murderer of the Kinck family, stood his trial at the Assizes. But, quite properly, my father would not let me accompany him when he attended the miscreant's execution outside the prison of La Roquette. Some years later, however, I witnessed the execution of Prevost on the same spot; and at a subsequent date I attended both the trial and the execution of Caserio--the assassin of President Carnot--at Lyons. Following Troppmann's case, in the early days of 1870 came the crime of the so-called Wild Boar of Corsica, Prince Pierre Bonaparte (grandfather of the present Princess George of Greece), who shot the young journalist Victor Noir, when the latter went with Ulrich de Fonvielle, aeronaut as well as journalist, to call him out on behalf of the irrepressible Henri Rochefort. I remember accompanying one of our artists, Gaildrau, when a sketch was made of the scene of the crime, the Prince's drawing-room at Auteuil, a peculiar semi-circular, panelled and white-painted apartment furnished in what we should call in England a tawdry mid-Victorian style. On the occasion of Noir's funeral my father and myself were in the Champs Elysees when the tumultuous revolutionary procession, in which Rochefort figured conspicuously, swept down the famous avenue along which the victorious Germans were to march little more than a year afterwards. Near the Rond-point the *cortege* was broken up and scattered by the police, whose violence was extreme. Rochefort, brave enough on the duelling-ground, fainted away, and was carried off in a vehicle, his position as a member of the Legislative Body momentarily rendering him immune from arrest.

Within a month, however, he was under lock and key, and some fierce rioting ensued in the north of Paris.

During the spring, my father went to Ireland as special commissioner of the *Illustrated London News* and the *Pall Mall Gazette*, in order to investigate the condition of the tenantry and the agrarian crimes which were then so prevalent there. Meantime, I was left in Paris, virtually "on my own," though I was often with my elder brother Edward. About this time, moreover, a friend of my father's began to take a good deal of interest in me. This was Captain the Hon. Dennis Bingham, a member of the Clanmorris family, and the regular correspondent of the *Pall Mall Gazette* in Paris. He subsequently became known as the author of various works on the Bonapartes and the Bourbons, and of a volume of recollections of Paris life, in which I am once or twice mentioned. Bingham was married to a very charming lady of the Laoretelle family, which gave a couple of historians to France, and I was always received most kindly at their home near the Arc de Triomphe. Moreover, Bingham often took me about with him in my spare time, and introduced me to several prominent people. Later, during the street fighting at the close of the Commune in 1871, we had some dramatic adventures together, and on one occasion Bingham saved my life.

The earlier months of 1870 went by very swiftly amidst a multiplicity of interesting events. Emile Ollivier had now become chief Minister, and an era of liberal reforms appeared to have begun. It seemed, moreover, as if the Minister's charming wife were for her part intent on reforming the practices of her sex in regard to dress, for she resolutely set her face against the extravagant toilettes of the ladies of the Court, repeatedly appearing at the Tuileries in the most unassuming attire, which, however, by sheer force of contrast, rendered her very conspicuous there. The patronesses of the great *couturiers* were quite irate at receiving such a lesson from a *petite bourgeoise*; but all who shared the views expressed by President Dupin a few years previously respecting the "unbridled luxury of women," were naturally delighted.

Her husband's attempts at political reform were certainly well meant, but the Republicans regarded him as a renegade and the older Imperialists as an intruder, and nothing that he did gave satisfaction. The concession of the right of public meeting led to frequent disorders at Belleville and Montmartre, and the increased freedom of the Press only acted as an incentive to violence of language. Nevertheless, when there came a Plebiscitum--the last of the reign--to ascertain the country's opinion respecting the reforms devised by the Emperor and Ollivier, a huge majority signified approval of them, and thus the "liberal Empire" seemed to be firmly established. If, however, the nation at large had known what was going on behind the scenes, both in diplomatic and in military spheres, the result of the Plebiscitum would probably have been very different.

Already on the morrow of the war between Prussia and Austria (1866) the Emperor, as I previously indicated, had begun to devise a plan of campaign in regard to the former Power, taking as his particular ***confidants*** in the matter General Lebrun, his ***aide-de-camp***, and General Frossard, the governor of the young Imperial Prince. Marshal Niel, as War Minister, was cognizant of the Emperor's conferences with Lebrun and Frossard, but does not appear to have taken any direct part in the plans which were devised. They were originally purely defensive plans, intended to provide for any invasion of French territory from across the Rhine. Colonel Baron Stoffel, the French military *attache* at Berlin, had frequently warned the War Office in Paris respecting the possibility of a Prussian attack and the strength of the Prussian armaments, which, he wrote, would enable King William (with the assistance of the other German rulers) to throw a force of nearly a million men into Alsace-Lorraine. Further, General Ducrot, who commanded the garrison at Strasburg, became acquainted with many things which he communicated to his relative, Baron de Bourgoing, one of the Emperor's equerries.

There is no doubt that these various communications reached Napoleon III; and though he may have regarded both the statements of Stoffel and those of Ducrot as exaggerated, he was certainly sufficiently impressed by them to order the preparation of certain plans. Frossard, basing himself on the operations of the Austrians in December, 1793, and keeping in mind the methods by which Hoche, with the Moselle army, and Pichegru, with the Rhine army, forced them back from the French frontier, drafted a scheme of defence in which he foresaw the battle of Woerth, but, through following erroneous information, greatly miscalculated the probable number of combatants. He set forth in his scheme that the Imperial Government could not possibly allow Alsace-Lorraine and Champagne to be invaded without a trial of strength at the very outset; and Marshal Bazaine, who, at some period or other, annotated a copy of Frossard's scheme, signified his approval of that dictum, but added significantly that good tactical measures should be adopted. He himself demurred to Frossard's plans, saying that he was no partisan of a frontal defence, but believed in falling on the enemy's flanks and rear. Yet, as we know, MacMahon fought the battle of Woerth under conditions in many respects similar to those which Frossard had foreseen.

However, the purely defensive plans on which Napoleon III at first worked, were replaced in 1868 by offensive ones, in which General Lebrun took a prominent part, both from the military and from the diplomatic standpoints. It was not, however, until March, 1870, that the Archduke Albert of Austria came to Paris to confer with the French Emperor. Lebrun's plan of campaign was discussed by them, and Marshal Le Boeuf and Generals Frossard and Jarras were privy to the negotiations. It was proposed that France, Austria, and Italy should invade Germany conjointly; and, according to Le Boeuf, the first-named Power could place 400,000 men on the frontier in a fortnight's time. Both Austria and Italy, however, required forty-two days to mobilize their forces, though the former offered to provide two army corps during the interval. When Lebrun subsequently went to Vienna to come to a positive decision and arrange details, the Archduke Albert pointed out that the war ought to begin in the spring season, for, said he, the North Germans would be able to support the cold and dampness of a winter campaign far better than the allies. That was an absolutely correct forecast, fully confirmed by all that took place in France during the winter of 1870-1871.

But Prussia heard of what was brewing. Austria was betrayed to her by Hungary; and Italy and France could not come to an understanding on the question of Rome. At the outset Prince Napoleon (Jerome) was concerned in the latter negotiations, which were eventually conducted by Count Vimercati, the Italian military *attache* in Paris. Napoleon, however, steadily refused to withdraw his forces from the States of the Church and to allow Victor Emmanuel to occupy Rome. Had he yielded on those points Italy would certainly have joined him, and Austria--however much Hungarian statesmen might have disliked it--would, in all probability, have followed suit. By the policy he pursued in this matter, the French Emperor lost everything, and prevented nothing. On the one hand, France was defeated and the Empire of the Bonapartes collapsed; whilst, on the other, Rome became Italy's true capital.

Bismarck was in no way inclined to allow the negotiations for an anti-Prussian alliance to mature. They dragged on for a considerable time, but the Government of Napoleon III was not particularly disturbed thereat, as it felt certain that victory would attend the French arms at the outset, and that Italy and Austria would eventually give support. Bismarck, however, precipitated events. Already in the previous year Prince Leopold of Hohenzollern-Sigmaringen had been a candidate for the throne of Spain. That candidature had been withdrawn in order to avert a conflict between France and Germany; but now it was revived at Bismarck's instigation in order to bring about one.

I have said, I think, enough to show--in fairness to Germany--that the war of 1870 was not an unprovoked attack on France. The incidents--such as the Ems affair--which directly led up to it were after all only of secondary importance, although they bulked so largely at the time of their occurrence. I well remember the great excitement which prevailed in Paris during the few anxious days when to the man in the street the question of peace or war seemed to be trembling in the balance, though in reality that question was already virtually decided upon both sides. Judging by all that has been revealed to us during the last forty years, I do not think that M. Emile Ollivier, the Prime Minister, would have been able to modify the decision of the fateful council held at Saint Cloud even if he had attended it. Possessed by many delusions, the bulk of the imperial councillors were too confident of success to draw back, and, besides, Bismarck and Moltke were not disposed to let France draw back. They were ready, and they knew right well that opportunity is a fine thing.

It was on July 15 that the Duc de Gramont, the Imperial Minister of Foreign Affairs, read his memorable statement to the Legislative Body, and two days later a formal declaration of war was signed. Paris at once became delirious with enthusiasm, though, as we know by all the telegrams from the Prefects of the departments, the provinces generally desired that peace might be preserved.

Resident in Paris, and knowing at that time very little about the rest of France--for I had merely stayed during my summer holidays at such seaside resorts as Trouville, Deauville, Beuzeval, St. Malo, and St. Servan--I undoubtedly caught the Parisian fever, and I dare say that I sometimes joined in the universal chorus of

"A Berlin!" Mere lad as I was, in spite of my precocity, I shared also the universal confidence in the French army. In that confidence many English military men participated. Only those who, like Captain Hozier of *The Times*, had closely watched Prussian methods during the Seven Weeks' War in 1866, clearly realized that the North German kingdom possessed a thoroughly well organized fighting machine, led by officers of the greatest ability, and capable of effecting something like a revolution in the art of war.

France was currently thought stronger than she really was. Of the good physique of her men there could be no doubt. Everybody who witnessed the great military pageants of those times was impressed by the bearing of the troops and their efficiency under arms. And nobody anticipated that they would be so inferior to the Germans in numbers as proved to be the case, and that the generals would show themselves so inferior in mental calibre to the commanders of the opposing forces. The Paris garrison, it is true, was no real criterion of the French army generally, though foreigners were apt to judge the latter by what they saw of it in the capital. The troops stationed there were mostly picked men, the garrison being very largely composed of the Imperial Guard. The latter always made a brilliant display, not merely by reason of its somewhat showy uniforms, recalling at times those of the First Empire, but also by the men's fine *physique* and their general military proficiency. They certainly fought well in some of the earlier battles of the war. Their commander was General Bourbaki, a fine soldierly looking man, the grandson of a Greek pilot who acted as intermediary between Napoleon I and his brother Joseph, at the time of the former's expedition to Egypt. It was this original Bourbaki who carried to Napoleon Joseph's secret letters reporting Josephine's misconduct in her husband's absence, misconduct which Napoleon condoned at the time, though it would have entitled him to a divorce nine years before he decided on one.

With the spectacle of the Imperial Guard constantly before their eyes, the Parisians of July, 1870, could not believe in the possibility of defeat, and, moreover, at the first moment it was not believed that the Southern German States would join North Germany against France. Napoleon III and his confidential advisers well knew, however, what to think on that point, and the delusions of the man in the street departed when, on July 20, Bavaria, Wuertemberg, Baden, and Hesse-Darmstadt announced their intention of supporting Prussia and the North German Confederation. Still, this did not dismay the Parisians, and the shouts of "To Berlin! To Berlin!" were as frequent as ever.

It had long been one of my dreams to see and participate in the great drama of war. All boys, I suppose, come into the world with pugnacious instincts. There must be few, too, who never "play at soldiers." My own interest in warfare and soldiering had been steadily fanned from my earliest childhood. In the first place, I had been incessantly confronted by all the scenes of war depicted in the ***Illustrated Times*** and the ***Illustrated London News***, those journals being posted to me regularly every week whilst I was still only a little chap at Eastbourne. Further, the career of my uncle, Frank Vizetelly, exercised a strange fascination over me. Born in Fleet Street in September, 1830, he was the youngest of my father's three brothers. Educated with Gustave Doré, he became an artist for the illustrated Press, and, in 1850, represented the ***Illustrated Times*** as war-artist in Italy, being a part of the time with the French and at other moments with the Sardinian forces. That was the first of his many campaigns. His services being afterwards secured by the ***Illustrated London News***, he next accompanied Garibaldi from Palermo to Naples. Then, at the outbreak of the Civil War in the United States, he repaired thither with Howard Russell, and, on finding obstacles placed in his way on the Federal side, travelled "underground" to Richmond and joined the Confederates. The late Duke of Devonshire, the late Lord Wolseley, and Francis Lawley were among his successive companions. At one time he and the first-named shared the same tent and lent socks and shirts to one another.

Now and again, however, Frank Vizetelly came to England after running the blockade, stayed a few weeks in London, and then departed for America once more, yet again running the blockade on his way. This he did on at least three occasions. His next campaign was the war of 1866, when he was with the Austrian commander Benedek. For a few years afterwards he remained in London assisting his eldest brother James to run what was probably the first of the society journals, ***Echoes of the Clubs***, to which Mortimer Collins and the late Sir Edmund Monson largely contributed. However, Frank Vizetelly went back to America once again, this time with Wolseley on the Red River Expedition. Later, he was with Don Carlos in Spain and with the French in Tunis, whence he proceeded to Egypt. He died on the field of duty, meeting his death when Hicks Pasha's little army was annihilated in the denies of Kashgil, in the Soudan.

Now, in the earlier years, when Frank Vizetelly returned from Italy or America, he was often at my father's house at Kensington, and I heard him talk of Napoleon III, MacMahon, Garibaldi, Victor Emmanuel, Cialdini, Robert Lee, Longstreet, Stonewall Jackson, and Captain Semmes. Between-times I saw all the engravings prepared after his sketches, and I regarded him and them with a kind of childish reverence. I can picture him still, a hale, bluff, tall, and burly-looking man, with short dark hair, blue eyes and a big ruddy moustache. He was far away the best known member of our family in my younger days, when anonymity in journalism was an almost universal rule. In the same way, however, as everybody had heard of Howard Russell, the war correspondent of the *Times*, so most people had heard of Frank Vizetelly, the war-artist of the *Illustrated*. He was, by-the-by, in the service of the *Graphic* when he was killed.

I well remember being alternately amused and disgusted by a French theatrical delineation of an English war correspondent, given in a spectacular military piece which I witnessed a short time after my first arrival in Paris. It was called "The Siege of Pekin," and had been concocted by Mocquard, the Emperor Napoleon's secretary. All the "comic business" in the affair was supplied by a so-called war correspondent of the *Times*, who strutted about in a tropical helmet embellished with a green Derby veil, and was provided with a portable desk and a huge umbrella. This red-nosed and red-whiskered individual was for ever talking of having to do this and that for "the first paper of the first country in the world," and, in order to obtain a better view of an engagement, he deliberately planted himself between the French and Chinese combatants. I should doubtless have derived more amusement from his tomfoolery had I not already known that English war correspondents did not behave in any such idiotic manner, and I came away from the performance with strong feelings of resentment respecting so outrageous a caricature of a profession counting among its members the uncle whom I so much admired.

Whatever my dreams may have been, I hardly anticipated that I should join that profession myself during the Franco-German war. The Lycees "broke up" in confusion, and my father decided to send me to join my stepmother and the younger members of the family at Saint Servan, it being his intention to go to the front with my elder brother Edward. But Simpson, the veteran Crimean War artist, came over to join the so-called Army of the Rhine, and my brother, securing an engagement from the *New York Times*, set out on his own account. Thus I was promptly recalled to Paris, where my father had decided to remain. In those days the journey from Brittany to the capital took many long and wearisome hours, and I made it in a third-class carriage of a train crowded with soldiers of all arms, cavalry, infantry, and artillery. Most of them were intoxicated, and the grossness of their language and manners was almost beyond belief. That dreadful night spent on the boards of a slowly-moving and jolting train, [There were then no cushioned seats in French third-class carriages.] amidst drunken and foul-mouthed companions, gave me, as it were, a glimpse of the other side of the picture--that is, of several things which lie behind the glamour of war.

It must have been about July 25 when I returned to Paris. A decree had just been issued appointing the Empress as Regent in the absence of the Emperor, who was to take command of the Army of the Rhine. It had originally been intended that there should be three French armies, but during the conferences with Archduke Albert in the spring, that plan was abandoned in favour of one sole army under the command of Napoleon III. The idea underlying the change was to avoid a superfluity of staff-officers, and to augment the number of actual combatants. Both Le Boeuf and Lebrun approved of the alteration, and this would seem to indicate that there were already misgivings on the French side in regard to the inferior strength of their effectives. The army was divided into eight sections, that is, seven army corps, and the Imperial Guard. Bourbaki, as already mentioned, commanded the Guard, and at the head of the army corps were (1) MacMahon, (2) Frossard, (3) Bazaine, (4) Ladmerault, (5) Failly, (6) Canrobert, and (7) Felix Douay. Both Frossard and Failly, however, were at first made subordinate to Bazaine. The head of the information service was Colonel Lewal, who rose to be a general and Minister of War under the Republic, and who wrote some commendable works on tactics; and immediately under him were Lieut.-Colonel Fay, also subsequently a well-known general, and Captain Jung, who is best remembered perhaps by his inquiries into the mystery of the Man with the Iron Mask. I give those names because, however distinguished those three men may have become in later years, the French intelligence service at the outset of the war was without doubt extremely faulty, and responsible for some of the disasters which occurred.

On returning to Paris one of my first duties was to go in search of Moulin, the detective-artist whom I mentioned in my first chapter. I found him in his somewhat squalid home in the Quartier Mouffetard, surrounded by a tribe of children, and he immediately informed me that he was one of the "agents" appointed to attend the Emperor on the campaign. The somewhat lavish Imperial ***equipage***, on which Zola so frequently dilated in "The Downfall," had, I think, already been despatched to Metz, where the Emperor proposed to fix his headquarters, and the escort of Cent Gardes was about to proceed thither. Moulin told me, however, that he and two of his colleagues were to travel in the same train as Napoleon, and it was agreed that he should forward either to Paris or to London, as might prove most convenient, such sketches as he might from time to time contrive to make. He suggested that there should be one of the Emperor's departure from Saint Cloud, and that in order to avoid delay I should accompany him on the occasion and take it from him. We therefore went down together on July 28, promptly obtained admittance to the chateau, where Moulin took certain instructions, and then repaired to the railway-siding in the park, whence the Imperial train was to start.

Officers and high officials, nearly all in uniform, were constantly going to and fro between the siding and the chateau, and presently the Imperial party appeared, the Emperor being between the Empress and the young Imperial Prince. Quite a crowd of dignitaries followed. I do not recollect seeing Emile Ollivier, though he must have been present, but I took particular note of Rouher, the once all-powerful minister, currently nicknamed the Vice-Emperor, and later President of the Senate. In spite of his portliness, he walked with a most determined stride, held his head very erect, and spoke in his customary loud voice. The Emperor, who wore the undress uniform of a general, looked very grave and sallow. The disease which eventually ended in his death had already become serious, [I have given many particulars of it in my two books, "The Court of the Tuileries, 1862-1870" (Chatto and Windus), and "Republican France, 1870-1912" (Holden and Hardingham).] and only a few days later, that is, during the Saarbrucken affair (August 2), he was painfully affected by it. Nevertheless, he had undertaken to command the Army of France! The Imperial Prince, then fourteen years of age, was also in uniform, it having been arranged that he should accompany his father to the front, and he seemed to be extremely animated and restless, repeatedly turning to exchange remarks with one or another officer near him. The Empress, who was very simply gowned, smiled once or twice in response to some words which fell from her husband, but for the most part she looked as serious as he did. Whatever Emile Ollivier may have said about beginning this war with a light heart, it is certain that these two sovereigns of France realized, at that hour of parting, the magnitude of the issues at stake. After they had exchanged a farewell kiss, the Empress took her eager young son in her arms and embraced him fondly, and when we next saw her face we could perceive the tears standing in her eyes. The Emperor was already taking his seat and the boy speedily sprang after him. Did the Empress at that moment wonder when, where, and how she would next see them again? Perchance she did. Everything, however, was speedily in readiness for departure. As the train began to move, both the Emperor and the Prince waved their hands from the windows, whilst all the enthusiastic Imperial dignitaries flourished their hats and raised a prolonged cry of "Vive l'Empereur!" It was not, perhaps, so loud as it might have been; but, then, they were mostly elderly men. Moulin, during the interval, had contrived to make something in the nature of a thumb-nail sketch; I had also taken a few notes myself; and thus provided I hastened back to Paris.

III
ON THE ROAD TO REVOLUTION

First French Defeats--A Great Victory rumoured--The Marseillaise, Capoul and Marie Sass--Edward Vizetelly brings News of Forbach to Paris--Emile Ollivier again--His Fall from Power--Cousin Montauban, Comte de Palikao-- English War Correspondents in Paris--Gambetta calls me "a Little Spy"-- More French Defeats--Palikao and the Defence of Paris--Feats of a Siege-- Wounded returning from the Front--Wild Reports of French Victories--The Quarries of Jaumont--The Anglo-American Ambulance--The News of Sedan-- Sala's Unpleasant Adventure--The Fall of the Empire.

It was, I think, two days after the Emperor's arrival at Metz that the first Germans--a detachment of Badeners--entered French territory. Then, on the second of August came the successful French attack on Saarbrucken, a petty affair but a well-remembered one, as it was on this occasion that the young Imperial Prince received the "baptism of fire." Appropriately enough, the troops, whose success he witnessed, were commanded by his late governor, General Frossard. More important was the engagement at Weissenburg two days later, when a division of the French under General Abel Douay was surprised by much superior forces, and utterly overwhelmed, Douay himself being killed during the fighting. Yet another two days elapsed, and then the Crown Prince of Prussia--later the Emperor Frederick--routed MacMahon at Woerth, in spite of a vigorous resistance, carried on the part of the French Cuirassiers, under General the Vicomte de Bonnemains, to the point of heroism. In later days the general's son married a handsome and wealthy young lady of the bourgeoisie named Marguerite Crouzet, whom, however, he had to divorce, and who afterwards became notorious as the mistress of General Boulanger.

Curiously enough, on the very day of the disaster of Woerth a rumour of a great French victory spread through Paris. My father had occasion to send me to his bankers in the Rue Vivienne, and on making my way to the Boulevards, which I proposed to follow, I was amazed to see the shopkeepers eagerly setting up the tricolour flags which they habitually displayed on the Emperor's fete-day (August 15). Nobody knew exactly how the rumours of victory had originated, nobody could give any precise details respecting the alleged great success, but everybody believed in it, and the enthusiasm was universal. It was about the middle of the day when I repaired to the Rue Vivienne, and after transacting my business there, I turned into the Place de la Bourse, where a huge crowd was assembled. The steps of the exchange were also covered with people, and amidst a myriad eager gesticulations a perfect babel of voices was ascending to the blue sky. One of the green omnibuses, which in those days ran from the Bourse to Passy, was waiting on the square, unable to depart owing to the density of the crowd; and all at once, amidst a scene of great excitement and repeated shouts of "La Marseillaise!" "La Marseillaise!" three or four well-dressed men climbed on to the vehicle, and turning towards the mob of speculators and sightseers covering the steps of the Bourse, they called to them repeatedly: "Silence! Silence!" The hubbub slightly subsided, and thereupon one of the party on the omnibus, a good-looking slim young fellow with a little moustache, took off his hat, raised his right arm, and began to sing the war-hymn of the Revolution. The stanza finished, the whole assembly took up the refrain.

Since the days of the Coup d'Etat, the Marseillaise had been banned in France, the official imperial air being "Partant pour la Syrie," a military march composed by the Emperor's mother, Queen Hortense, with words by Count Alexandre de Laborde, who therein pictured a handsome young knight praying to the Blessed Virgin before his departure for Palestine, and soliciting of her benevolence that he might "prove to be the bravest brave, and love the fairest fair." During the twenty years of the third Napoleon's rule, Paris had heard the strains of "Partant pour la Syrie" many thousand times, and, though they were tuneful enough, had become thoroughly tired of them. To stimulate popular enthusiasm in the war the Ollivier Cabinet had accordingly authorized the playing and singing of the long-forbidden "Marseillaise," which, although it was well-remembered by the survivors of '48, and was hummed even by the young Republicans of Belleville and the Quartier Latin, proved quite a novelty to half the population, who were destined to hear it again and again and again from that period until the present time.

The young vocalist who sang it from the top of a Passy-Bourse omnibus on that fateful day of Woerth, claimed to be a tenor, but was more correctly a tenorino, his voice possessing far more sweetness than power. He was already well-known and popular, for he had taken the part of Romeo in Gounod's well-known opera based on the Shakespearean play. Like many another singer, Victor Capoul might have become forgotten before very long, but a curious circumstance, having nothing to do with vocalism, diffused and perpetuated his name. He adopted a particular way of dressing his hair, "plastering" a part of it down in a kind of semi-circle over the forehead; and the new style "catching on" among young Parisians, the "coiffure Capoul" eventually went round the world. It is exemplified in certain portraits of King George V.

In those war-days Capoul sang the "Marseillaise" either at the Opera Comique or the Theatre Lyrique; but at the Opera it was sung by Marie Sass, then at the height of her reputation. I came in touch with her a few years later when she was living in the Paris suburbs, and more than once, when we both travelled to the city in the same train, I had the honour of assisting her to alight from it--this being no very easy matter, as la Sass was the very fattest and heaviest of all the ***prime donne*** that I have ever seen.

On the same day that MacMahon was defeated at Woerth, Frossard was badly beaten at Forbach, an engagement witnessed by my elder brother Edward, [Born January 1, 1847, and therefore in 1870 in his twenty-fourth year.] who, as I previously mentioned, had gone to the front for an American journal. Finding it impossible to telegraph the news of this serious French reverse, he contrived to make his way to Paris on a locomotive- engine, and arrived at our flat in the Rue de Miromesnil looking as black as any coal-heaver. When he had handed his account of the affair to Ryan, the Paris representative of the ***New York Times***, it was suggested that his information might perhaps be useful to the French Minister of War. So he hastened to the Ministry, where the news he brought put a finishing touch to the dismay of the officials, who were already staggering under the first news of the disaster of Woerth.

Paris, jubilant over an imaginary victory, was enraged by the tidings of Woerth and Forbach. Already dreading some Revolutionary enterprise, the Government declared the city to be in a state of siege, thereby placing it under military authority. Although additional men had recently been enrolled in the National Guard the arming of them had been intentionally delayed, precisely from a fear of revolutionary troubles, which the *entourage* of the Empress-Regent at Saint Cloud feared from the very moment of the first defeats. I recollect witnessing on the Place Venddme one day early in August a very tumultuous gathering of National Guards who had flocked thither in order to demand weapons of the Prime Minister, that is, Emile Ollivier, who in addition to the premiership, otherwise the "Presidency of the Council," held the offices of Keeper of the Seals and Minister of Justice, this department then having its offices in one of the buildings of the Place Vendome. Ollivier responded to the demonstration by appearing on the balcony of his private room and delivering a brief speech, which, embraced a vague promise to comply with the popular demand. In point of fact, however, nothing of the kind was done during his term of office.

Whilst writing these lines I hear that this much-abused statesman has just passed away at Saint Gervais-les-Bains in Upper Savoy (August 20, 1913). Born at Marseilles in July, 1825, he lived to complete his eighty-eighth year. His second wife (nee Gravier), to whom I referred in a previous chapter, survives him. I do not wish to be unduly hard on his memory. He came, however, of a very Republican family, and in his earlier years he personally evinced what seemed to be most staunch Republicanism. When he was first elected as a member of the Legislative Body in 1857, he publicly declared that he would appear before that essentially Bonapartist assembly as one of the spectres of the crime of the Coup d'Etat. But subsequently M. de Morny baited him with a lucrative appointment connected with the Suez Canal. Later still, the Empress smiled on him, and finally he took office under the Emperor, thereby disgusting nearly every one of his former friends and associates.

I believe, however, that Ollivier was sincerely convinced of the possibility of firmly establishing a liberal-imperialist *regime*. But although various reforms were carried out under his auspices, it is quite certain that he was not allowed a perfectly free hand. Nor was he fully taken into confidence with respect to the Emperor's secret diplomatic and military policy. That was proved by the very speech in which he spoke of entering upon the war with Prussia "with a light heart"; for in his very next sentences he spoke of that war as being absolutely forced upon France, and of himself and his colleagues as having done all that was humanly and honourably possible to avoid it. Assuredly he would not have spoken quite as he did had he realized at the time that Bismarck had merely forced on the war in order to defeat the Emperor Napoleon's intention to invade Germany in the ensuing spring. The public provocation on Prussia's part was, as I previously showed, merely her reply to the secret provocation offered by France, as evidenced by all the negotiations with Archduke Albert on behalf of Austria, and with Count Vimercati on behalf of Italy. On all those matters Ollivier was at the utmost but very imperfectly informed. Finally, be it remembered that he was absent from the Council at Saint Cloud at which war was finally decided upon.

At a very early hour on the morning of Sunday, August 7--the day following Woerth and Forbach--the Empress Eugenie came in all haste and sore distress from Saint Cloud to the Tuileries. The position was very serious, and anxious conferences were held by the ministers. When the Legislative Body met on the morrow, a number of deputies roundly denounced the manner in which the military operations were being conducted. One deputy, a certain Guyot-Montpeyroux, who was well known for the outspokenness of his language, horrified the more devoted Imperialists by describing the French forces as an army of lions led by jackasses. On the following day Ollivier and his colleagues resigned office. Their position had become untenable, though little if any responsibility attached to them respecting the military operations. The Minister of War, General Dejean, had been merely a stop-gap, appointed to carry out the measures agreed upon before his predecessor, Marshal Le Boeuf, had gone to the front as Major General of the army.

It was felt; however, among the Empress's *entourage* that the new Prime Minister ought to be a military man of energy, devoted, moreover, to the Imperial *regime*. As the marshals and most of the conspicuous generals of the time were already serving in the field, it was difficult to find any prominent individual possessed of the desired qualifications. Finally, however, the Empress was prevailed upon to telegraph to an officer whom she personally disliked, this being General Cousin-Montauban, Comte de Palikao. He was certainly, and with good reason, devoted to the Empire, and in the past he had undoubtedly proved himself to be a man of energy. But he was at this date in his seventy-fifth year--a fact often overlooked by historians of the Franco-German war--and for that very reason, although he had solicited a command in the field at the first outbreak of hostilities, it had been decided to decline his application, and to leave him at Lyons, where he had commanded the garrison for five years past.

Thirty years of Palikao's life had been spent in Algeria, contending, during most of that time, against the Arabs; but in 1860 he had been appointed commander of the French expedition to China, where with a small force he had conducted hostilities with the greatest vigour, repeatedly decimating or scattering the hordes of Chinamen who were opposed to him, and, in conjunction with the English, victoriously taking Pekin. A kind of stain rested on the expedition by reason of the looting of the Chinese Emperor's summer-palace, but the entire responsibility of that affair could not be cast on the French commander, as he only continued and completed what the English began. On his return to France, Napoleon III created him Comte de Palikao (the name being taken from one of his Chinese victories), and in addition wished the Legislative Body to grant him a ***dotation***. However, the summer-palace looting scandal prevented this, much to the Emperor's annoyance, and subsequent to the fall of the Empire it was discovered that, by Napoleon's express orders, the War Ministry had paid Palikao a sum of about L60,000, diverting that amount of money (in accordance with the practices of the time) from the purpose originally assigned to it in the Estimates.

This was not generally known when Palikao became Chief Minister. He was then what might be called a very well preserved old officer, but his lungs had been somewhat affected by a bullet-wound of long standing, and this he more than once gave as a reason for replying with the greatest brevity to interpellations in the Chamber. Moreover, as matters went from bad to worse, this same lung trouble became a good excuse for preserving absolute silence on certain inconvenient occasions. When, however, Palikao was willing to speak he often did so untruthfully, repeatedly adding the ***suggestio falsi*** to the ***suppressio veri***. As a matter of fact, he, like other fervent partisans of the dynasty, was afraid to let the Parisians know the true state of affairs. Besides, he himself was often ignorant of it. He took office (he was the third War Minister in fifty days) without any knowledge whatever of the imperial plan of campaign, or the steps to be adopted in the event of further French reverses, and a herculean task lay before this septuagenarian officer, who by experience knew right well how to deal with Arabs and Chinamen, but had never had to contend with European troops. Nevertheless, he displayed zeal and activity in his new semi-political and semi-military position. He greatly assisted MacMahon to reconstitute his army at Chalons, he planned the organization of three more army corps, and he started on the work of placing Paris in a state of defence, whilst his colleague, Clement Duvernois, the new Minister of Commerce, began gathering flocks and herds together, in order that the city, if besieged, might have the necessary means of subsistence.

At this time there were quite a number of English "war" as well as "own" correspondents in Paris. The former had mostly returned from Metz, whither they had repaired at the time of the Emperor's departure for the front. At the outset it had seemed as though the French would allow foreign journalists to accompany them on their "promenade to Berlin," but, on reverses setting in, all official recognition was denied to newspaper men, and, moreover, some of the representatives of the London Press had a very unpleasant time at Metz, being arrested there as spies and subjected to divers indignities. I do not remember whether they were ordered back to Paris or whether they voluntarily withdrew to the capital on their position with the army becoming untenable; but in any case they arrived in the city and lingered there for a time, holding daily symposiums at the Grand Cafe at the corner of the Rue Scribe, on the Boulevards.

From time to time I went there with my father, and amongst, this galaxy of journalistic talent I met certain men with whom I had spoken in my childhood. One of them, for instance, was George Augustus Sala, and another was Henry Mayhew, the famous author of "London Labour and the London Poor," he being accompanied by his son Athol. Looking back, it seems to me that, in spite of all their brilliant gifts, neither Sala nor Henry Mayhew was fitted to be a correspondent in the field, and they were certainly much better placed in Paris than at the headquarters of the Army of the Rhine. Among the resident correspondents who attended the gatherings at the Grand Cafe were Captain Bingham, Blanchard (son of Douglas) Jerrold, and the jaunty Bower, who had once been tried for his life and acquitted by virtue of the "unwritten law" in connection with an ***affaire passionelle*** in which he was the aggrieved party. For more than forty years past, whenever I have seen a bluff looking elderly gentleman sporting a buff-waistcoat and a white-spotted blue necktie, I have instinctively thought of Bower, who wore such a waistcoat and such a necktie, with the glossiest of silk hats and most shapely of patent-leather boots, throughout the siege of Paris, when he was fond of dilating on the merits of boiled ostrich and stewed elephant's foot, of which expensive dainties he partook at his club, after the inmates of the Jardin des Plantes had been slaughtered.

Bower represented the *Morning Advertiser*. I do not remember seeing Bowes of the *Standard* at the gatherings I have referred to, or Crawford of the *Daily News*, who so long wrote his Paris letters at a little cafe fronting the Bourse. But it was certainly at the Grand Cafe that I first set eyes on Labouchere, who, like Sala, was installed at the neighbouring Grand Hotel, and was soon to become famous as the *Daily News*' "Besieged Resident." As for Mr. Thomas Gibson Bowles, who represented the *Morning Post* during the German Siege, I first set eyes on him at the British Embassy, when he had a beautiful little moustache (which I greatly envied) and wore his hair nicely parted down the middle. *Eheu! fugaces labuntur anni*.

Sala was the life and soul of those gatherings at the Grand Cafe, always exuberantly gay, unless indeed the conversation turned on the prospects of the French forces, when he railed at them without ceasing. Blanchard Jerrold, who was well acquainted with the spy system of the Empire, repeatedly warned Sala to be cautious--but in vain; and the eventual result of his outspokenness was a very unpleasant adventure on the eve of the Empire's fall. In the presence of all those distinguished men of the pen, I myself mostly preserved, as befitted my age, a very discreet silence, listening intently, but seldom opening my lips unless it were to accept or refuse another cup of coffee, or some *sirop de groseille* or *grenadine*. I never touched any intoxicant excepting claret at my meals, and though, in my Eastbourne days, I had, like most boys of my time, experimented with a clay pipe and some dark shag, I did not smoke. My father personally was extremely fond of cigars, but had he caught me smoking one, he would, I believe, have knocked me down.

In connection with those Grand Cafe gatherings I one day had a little adventure. It had been arranged that I should meet my father there, and turning into the Boulevards from the Madeleine I went slowly past what was then called the Rue Basse du Rempart. I was thinking of something or other--I do not remember what, but in any case I was absorbed in thought, and inadvertently I dogged the footsteps of two black-coated gentlemen who were deep in conversation. I was almost unconscious of their presence, and in any case I did not hear a word of what they were saying. But all at once one of them turned round, and said to me angrily: "Veux-tu bien t'en aller, petit espion!" otherwise: "Be off, little spy!" I woke up as it were, looked at him, and to my amazement recognized Gambetta, whom I had seen several times already, when I was with my mentor Brossard at either the Cafe de Suede or the Cafe de Madrid. At the same time, however, his companion also turned round, and proved to be Jules Simon, who knew me through a son of his. This was fortunate, for he immediately exclaimed: "Why, no! It is young Vizetelly, a friend of my son's," adding, "Did you wish to speak to me?"

I replied in the negative, saying that I had not even recognized him from behind, and trying to explain that it was purely by chance that I had been following him and M. Gambetta. "You know me, then?" exclaimed the future dictator somewhat sharply; whereupon I mentioned that he had been pointed out to me more than once, notably when he was in the company of M. Delescluze. "Ah, oui, fort bien," he answered. "I am sorry if I spoke as I did. But"--and here he turned to Simon--"one never knows, one can never take too many precautions. The Spaniard would willingly send both of us to Mazas." By "the Spaniard," of course, he meant the Empress Eugenie, just as people meant Marie-Antoinette when they referred to "the Austrian" during the first Revolution. That ended the affair. They both shook hands with me, I raised my hat, and hurried on to the Grand Cafe, leaving them to their private conversation. This was the first time that I ever exchanged words with Gambetta. The incident must have occurred just after his return from Switzerland, whither he had repaired fully anticipating the triumph of the French arms, returning, however, directly he heard of the first disasters. Simon and he were naturally drawn together by their opposition to the Empire, but they were men of very different characters, and some six months later they were at daggers drawn.

Events moved rapidly during Palikao's ministry. Reviving a former proposition of Jules Favre's, Gambetta proposed to the Legislative Body the formation of a Committee of National Defence, and one was ultimately appointed; but the only member of the Opposition included in it was Thiers. In the middle of August there were some revolutionary disturbances at La Villette. Then, after the famous conference at Chalons, where Rouher, Prince Napoleon, and others discussed the situation with the Emperor and MacMahon, Trochu was appointed Military Governor of Paris, where he soon found himself at loggerheads with Palikao. Meantime, the French under Bazaine, to whom the Emperor was obliged to relinquish the supreme command--the Opposition deputies particularly insisting on Bazaine's appointment in his stead--were experiencing reverse after reverse. The battle of Courcelles or Pange, on August 14, was followed two days later by that of Vionville or Mars-la-Tour, and, after yet another two days, came the great struggle of Gravelotte, and Bazaine was thrown back on Metz.

At the Chalons conference it had been decided that the Emperor should return to Paris and that MacMahon's army also should retreat towards the capital. But Palikao telegraphed to Napoleon: "If you abandon Bazaine there will be Revolution in Paris, and you yourself will be attacked by all the enemy's forces. Paris will defend herself from all assault from outside. The fortifications are completed." It has been argued that the plan to save Bazaine might have succeeded had it been immediately carried into effect, and in accordance, too, with Palikao's ideas; but the original scheme was modified, delay ensued, and the French were outmarched by the Germans, who came up with them at Sedan. As for Palikao's statement that the Paris fortifications were completed at the time when he despatched his telegram, that was absolutely untrue. The armament of the outlying forts had scarcely begun, and not a single gun was in position on any one of the ninety-five bastions of the ramparts. On the other hand, Palikao was certainly doing all he could for the city. He had formed the aforementioned Committee of Defence, and under his auspices the fosse or ditch in front of the ramparts was carried across the sixty-nine roads leading into Paris, whilst drawbridges were installed on all these points, with armed lunettes in front of them. Again, redoubts were thrown up in advance of some of the outlying forts, or on spots where breaks occurred in the chain of defensive works.

At the same time, ships' guns were ordered up from Cherbourg, Brest, Lorient, and Toulon, together with naval gunners to serve them. Sailors, customhouse officers, and provincial gendarmes were also conveyed to Paris in considerable numbers. Gardes-mobiles, francs-tireurs, and even firemen likewise came from the provinces, whilst the work of provisioning the city proceeded briskly, the Chamber never hesitating to vote all the money asked of it. At the same time, whilst there were many new arrivals in Paris, there were also many departures from the city. The general fear of a siege spread rapidly. Every day thousands of well-to-do middle-class folk went off in order to place themselves out of harm's way; and at the same time thousands of foreigners were expelled on the ground that, in the event of a siege occurring, they would merely be "useless mouths." In contrast with that exodus was the great inrush of people from the suburbs of Paris. They poured into the city unceasingly, from villas, cottages, and farms, employing every variety of vehicle to convey their furniture and other household goods, their corn, flour, wine, and other produce. There was a block at virtually every city gate, so many were the folk eager for shelter within the protecting ramparts raised at the instigation of Thiers some thirty years previously.

In point of fact, although the Germans were not yet really marching on Paris--for Bazaine's army had to be bottled up, and MacMahon's disposed of, before there could be an effective advance on the French capital--it was imagined in the city and its outskirts that the enemy might arrive at any moment. The general alarm was intensified when, on the night of August 21, a large body of invalided men, who had fought at Weissenburg or Worth, made their way into Paris, looking battle and travel-stained, some with their heads bandaged, others with their arms in slings, and others limping along with the help of sticks. It is difficult to conceive by what aberration the authorities allowed the Parisians to obtain that woeful glimpse of the misfortunes of France. The men in question ought never to have been sent to Paris at all. They might well have been cared for elsewhere. As it happened, the sorry sight affected all who beheld it. Some were angered by it, others depressed, and others well-nigh terrified.

As a kind of set-off, however, to that gloomy spectacle, fresh rumours of French successes began to circulate. There was a report that Bazaine's army had annihilated the whole of Prince Frederick-Charles's cavalry, and, in particular, there was a most sensational account of how three German army-corps, including the famous white Cuirassiers to which Bismarck belonged, had been tumbled into the "Quarries of Jaumont" and there absolutely destroyed! I will not say that there is no locality named Jaumont, but I cannot find any such place mentioned in Joanne's elaborate dictionary of the communes of France, and possibly it was as mythical as was the alleged German disaster, the rumours of which momentarily revived the spirits of the deluded Parisians, who were particularly pleased to think that the hated Bismarck's regiment had been annihilated.

On or about August 30, a friend of my eldest brother Adrian, a medical man named Blewitt, arrived in Paris with the object of joining an Anglo-American ambulance which was being formed in connection with the Red Cross Society. Dr. Blewitt spoke a little French, but he was not well acquainted with the city, and I was deputed to assist him whilst he remained there. An interesting account of the doings of the ambulance in question was written some sixteen or seventeen years ago by Dr. Charles Edward Ryan, of Glenlara, Tipperary, who belonged to it. Its head men were Dr. Marion-Sims and Dr. Frank, others being Dr. Ryan, as already mentioned, and Drs. Blewitt, Webb, May, Nicholl, Hayden, Howett, Tilghmann, and last but not least, the future Sir William MacCormack. Dr. Blewitt had a variety of business to transact with the officials of the French Red Cross Society, and I was with him at his interviews with its venerable-looking President, the Count de Flavigny, and others. It is of interest to recall that at the outbreak of the war the society's only means was an income of L5 6*s.* 3*d.*, but that by August 28 its receipts had risen to nearly L112,000. By October it had expended more than L100,000 in organizing thirty-two field ambulances. Its total outlay during the war exceeded half a million sterling, and in its various field, town, and village ambulances no fewer than 110,000 men were succoured and nursed.

In Paris the society's headquarters were established at the Palace de l'Industrie in the Champs Elysees, and among the members of its principal committee were several ladies of high rank. I well remember seeing there that great leader of fashion, the Marquise de Galliffet, whose elaborate ball gowns I had more than once admired at Worth's, but who, now that misfortune had fallen upon France, was, like all her friends, very plainly garbed in black. At the Palais de l'Industrie I also found Mme. de MacMahon, short and plump, but full of dignity and energy, as became a daughter of the Castries. I remember a brief address which she delivered to the Anglo-American Ambulance on the day when it quitted Paris, and in which she thanked its members for their courage and devotion in coming forward, and expressed her confidence, and that of all her friends, in the kindly services which they would undoubtedly bestow upon every sufferer who came under their care.

I accompanied the ambulance on its march through Paris to the Eastern Hallway Station. When it was drawn up outside the Palais de l'Industrie, Count de

Flavigny in his turn made a short but feeling speech, and immediately afterwards the *cortege* started. At the head of it were three young ladies, the daughters of Dr. Marion-Sims, who carried respectively the flags of France, England, and the United States. Then came the chief surgeons, the assistant-surgeons, the dressers and male nurses, with some waggons of stores bringing up the rear. I walked, I remember, between Dr. Blewitt and Dr. May. On either side of the procession were members of the Red Cross Society, carrying sticks or poles tipped with collection bags, into which money speedily began to rain. We crossed the Place de la Concorde, turned up the Rue Royale, and then followed the main Boulevards as far, I think, as the Boulevard de Strasbourg. There were crowds of people on either hand, and our progress was necessarily slow, as it was desired to give the onlookers full time to deposit their offerings in the collection-bags. From the Cercle Imperial at the corner of the Champs Elysees, from the Jockey Club, the Turf Club, the Union, the Chemins-de- Fer, the Ganaches, and other clubs on or adjacent to the Boulevards, came servants, often in liveries, bearing with them both bank-notes and gold. Everybody seemed anxious to give something, and an official of the society afterwards told me that the collection had proved the largest it had ever made. There was also great enthusiasm all along the line of route, cries of "Vivent les Anglais! Vivent les Americains!" resounding upon every side.

The train by which the ambulance quitted Paris did not start until a very late hour in the evening. Prior to its departure most of us dined at a restaurant near the railway-station. No little champagne was consumed at this repast, and, unaccustomed as I was to the sparkling wine of the Marne, it got, I fear, slightly into my head. However, my services as interpreter were requisitioned more than once by some members of the ambulance in connection with certain inquiries which they wished to make of the railway officials; and I recollect that when some question arose of going in and out of the station, and reaching the platform again without let or hindrance--the departure of the train being long delayed--the *sous-chef de gare* made me a most courteous bow, and responded: "A vous, messieurs, tout est permis. There are no regulations for you!" At last the train started, proceeding on its way to Soissons, where it arrived at daybreak on August 29, the ambulance then hastening to join MacMahon, and reaching him just in time to be of good service at Sedan. I will only add here that my friend Dr. Blewitt was with Dr. Frank at Balan and

Bazeilles, where the slaughter was so terrible. The rest of the ambulance's dramatic story must be read in Dr. Ryan's deeply interesting pages.

Whilst the Parisians were being beguiled with stories of how the Prince of Saxe-Meiningen had written to his wife telling her that the German troops were suffering terribly from sore feet, the said troops were in point of fact lustily outmarching MacMahon's forces. On August 30, General de Failly was badly worsted at Beaumont, and on the following day MacMahon was forced to move on Sedan. The first reports which reached Paris indicated, as usual, very favourable results respecting the contest there. My friend Captain Bingham, however, obtained some correct information-- from, I believe, the British Embassy--and I have always understood that it was he who first made the terrible truth known to one of the deputies of the Opposition party, who hastened to convey it to Thiers. The battle of Sedan was fought on Thursday, September 1; but it was only on Saturday, September 3, that Palikao shadowed forth the disaster in the Chamber, stating that MacMahon had failed to effect a junction with Bazaine, and that, after alternate reverses and successes--that is, driving a part of the German army into the Meuse!--he had been obliged to retreat on Sedan and Mezieres, some portion of his forces, moreover, having been compelled to cross the Belgian frontier.

That tissue of inaccuracies, devised perhaps to palliate the effect of the German telegrams of victory which were now becoming known to the incredulous Parisians, was torn to shreds a few hours later when the Legislative Body assembled for a night-sitting. Palikao was then obliged to admit that the French army and the Emperor Napoleon had surrendered to the victorious German force. Jules Favre, who was the recognized leader of the Republican Opposition, thereupon brought forward a motion of dethronement, proposing that the executive authority should be vested in a parliamentary committee. In accordance with the practice of the Chamber, Farve's motion had to be referred to its *bureaux*, or ordinary committees, and thus no decision was arrived at that night, it being agreed that the Chamber should reassemble on the morrow at noon.

The deputies separated at a very late hour. My father and myself were among all the anxious people who had assembled on the Place de la Concorde to await the issue of the debate. Wild talk was heard on every side, imprecations were levelled at the Empire, and it was already suggested that the country had been sold to the foreigner. At last, as the crowd became extremely restless, the authorities, who had taken their precautions in consequence of the revolutionary spirit which was abroad, decided to disperse it. During the evening a considerable body of mounted Gardes de Paris had been stationed in or near the Palais de l'Industrie, and now, on instructions being conveyed to their commander, they suddenly cantered down the Champs Elysees and cleared the square, chasing people round and round the fountains and the seated statues of the cities of France, until they fled by way either of the quays, the Rue de Rivoti, or the Rue Royale. The vigour which the troops displayed did not seem of good augury for the adversaries of the Empire. Without a doubt Revolution was already in the air, but everything indicated that the authorities were quite prepared to contend with it, and in all probability successfully.

It was with difficulty that my father and myself contrived to avoid the troopers and reach the Avenue Gabriel, whence we made our way home. Meantime there had been disturbances in other parts of Paris. On the Boulevard Bonne Nouvelle a band of demonstrators had come into collision with the police, who had arrested several of them. Thus, as I have already mentioned, the authorities seemed to be as vigilant and as energetic as ever. But, without doubt, on that night of Saturday, September 3, the secret Republican associations were very active, sending the ***mot d'ordre*** from one to another part of the city, so that all might be ready for Revolution when the Legislative Body assembled on the morrow.

It was on this same last night of the Empire that George Augustus Sala met with the very unpleasant adventure to which I previously referred. During the evening he went as usual to the Grand Cafe, and meeting Blanchard Jerrold there, he endeavoured to induce him to go to supper at the Cafe du Helder. Sala being in an even more talkative mood than usual, and--now that he had heard of the disaster of Sedan--more than ever inclined to express his contempt of the French in regard to military matters, Jerrold declined the invitation, fearing, as he afterwards said to my father in my presence, that some unpleasantness might well ensue, as Sala, in spite of all remonstrances, would not cease "gassing." Apropos of that expression, it is somewhat amusing to recall that Sala at one time designed for himself an illuminated visiting-card, on which appeared his initials G. A. S. in letters of gold, the A being intersected by a gas-lamp diffusing many vivid rays of light, whilst underneath it was a scroll bearing the appropriate motto, "Dux est Lux."

But, to return to my story, Jerrold having refused the invitation; Sala repaired alone to the Cafe du Helder, an establishment which in those imperial times was particularly patronized by officers of the Paris garrison and officers from the provinces on leave. It was the height of folly for anybody to "run down" the French army in such a place, unless, indeed, he wished to have a number of duels on his hands. It is true that on the night of September 3, there may have been few, if any, military men at the Helder. Certain it is, however, that whilst Sala was supping in the principal room upstairs, he entered into conversation with other people, spoke incautiously, as he had been doing for a week past, and on departing from the establishment was summarily arrested and conveyed to the Poste de Police on the Boulevard Bonne Nouvelle. The cells there were already more or less crowded with roughs who had been arrested during the disturbance earlier in the evening, and when a police official thrust Sala into their midst, at the same time calling him a vile Prussian spy, the patriotism of the other prisoners was immediately aroused, though, for the most part, they were utter scamps who had only created a disturbance for the purpose of filling their pockets.

Sala was subjected not merely to much ill-treatment, but also to indignities which only Rabelais or Zola could have (in different ways) adequately described; and it was not until the morning that he was able to communicate with the manager of the Grand Hotel, where he had his quarters. The manager acquainted the British Embassy with his predicament, and it was, I think, Mr. Sheffield who repaired to the Prefecture de Police to obtain an order for Sala's liberation. The story told me at the time was that Lord Lyons's representative found matters already in great confusion at the Prefecture. There had been a stampede of officials, scarcely any being at their posts, in such wise that he made his way to the Prefect's sanctum unannounced. There he found M. Pietri engaged with a confidential acolyte in destroying a large number of compromising papers, emptying boxes and pigeon-holes in swift succession, and piling their contents on an already huge fire, which was stirred incessantly in order that it might burn more swiftly. Pietri only paused in his task in order to write an order for Sala's release, and I have always understood that this was the last official order that emanated from the famous Prefect of the Second Empire. It is true that he presented himself at the Tuileries before he fled to Belgium, but the Empress, as we know, was averse from any armed conflict with the population of Paris. As a matter of fact, the Prefecture had spent its last strength during the night of September 3. Disorganized as it was on the morning of the 4th, it could not have fought the Revolution. As will presently appear, those police who on the night of the 3rd were chosen to assist in guarding the approaches to the Palais Bourbon on the morrow, were quite unable to do so.

Disorder, indeed, prevailed in many places. My father had recently found himself in a dilemma in regard to the requirements of the *Illustrated London News*. In those days the universal snap-shotting hand-camera was unknown. Every scene that it was desired to depict in the paper had to be sketched, and in presence of all the defensive preparations which were being made, a question arose as to what might and what might not be sketched. General Trochu was Governor of Paris, and applications were made to him on the subject. A reply came requiring a reference from the British Embassy before any permission whatever was granted. In due course a letter was obtained from the Embassy, signed not, I think, by Lord Lyons himself, but by one of the secretaries--perhaps Sir Edward Malet, or Mr. Wodehouse, or even Mr. Sheffield. At all events, on the morning of September 4, my father, being anxious to settle the matter, commissioned me to take the Embassy letter to Trochu's quarters at the Louvre. Here I found great confusion. Nobody was paying the slightest attention to official work. The *bureaux* were half deserted. Officers came and went incessantly, or gathered in little groups in the passages and on the stairs, all of them looking extremely upset and talking anxiously and excitedly together. I could find nobody to attend to any business, and was at a loss what to do, when a door opened and a general officer in undress uniform appeared on the threshold of a large and finely appointed room.

I immediately recognized Trochu's extremely bald head and determined jaw, for since his nomination as Governor, Paris had been flooded with portraits of him. He had opened the door, I believe, to look for an officer, but on seeing me standing there with a letter in my hand he inquired what I wanted. I replied that I had brought a letter from the British Embassy, and he may perhaps have thought that I was an Embassy messenger. At all events, he took the letter from me, saying curtly: "C'est bien, je m'en occuperai, revenez cet apres-midi." With those words he stepped back into the room and carefully placed the letter on the top of several others which were neatly disposed on a side-table.

The incident was trivial in itself, yet it afforded a glimpse of Trochu's character. Here was the man who, in his earlier years, had organized the French Expedition to the Crimea in a manner far superior to that in which our own had been organized; a man of method, order, precision, fully qualified to prepare the defence of Paris, though not to lead her army in the field. Brief as was that interview of mine, I could not help noticing how perfectly calm and self-possessed he was, for his demeanour greatly contrasted with the anxious or excited bearing of his subordinates. Yet he had reached the supreme crisis of his life. The Empire was falling, a first offer of Power had been made to him on the previous evening; and a second offer, which he finally accepted, [See my book, "Republican France," p. 8.] was almost imminent. Yet on that morning of Revolution he appeared as cool as a cucumber.

I quitted the Louvre, going towards the Rue Royale, it having been arranged with my father that we should take ***dejeuner*** at a well-known restaurant there. It was called "His Lordship's Larder," and was pre-eminently an English house, though the landlord bore the German name of Weber. He and his family were unhappily suffocated in the cellars of their establishment during one of the conflagrations which marked the Bloody Week of the Commune. At the time when I met my father, that is about noon, there was nothing particularly ominous in the appearance of the streets along which I myself passed. It was a fine bright Sunday, and, as was usual on such a day, there were plenty of people abroad. Recently enrolled National Guards certainly predominated among the men, but the latter included many in civilian attire, and there was no lack of women and children. As for agitation, I saw no sign of it.

As I was afterwards told, however, by Delmas, the landlord of the Cafe Gretry, [Note] matters were very different that morning on the Boulevards, and particularly on the Boulevard Montmartre. By ten o'clock, indeed, great crowds had assembled there, and the excitement grew apace. The same words were on all lips: "Sedan--the whole French army taken--the wretched Emperor's sword surrendered--unworthy to reign--dethrone him!" Just as, in another crisis of French history, men had climbed on to the chairs and tables in the garden of the Palais Royal to denounce Monsieur and Madame Veto and urge the Parisians to march upon Versailles, so now others climbed on the chairs outside the Boulevard cafes to denounce the Empire, and urge a march upon the Palais Bourbon, where the Legislative Body was about to meet. And amidst the general clamour one cry persistently prevailed. It was: "Decheance! Decheance!--Dethronement! Dethronement!"

[Note: This was a little cafe on the Boulevard des Italiens, and was noted for its quietude during the afternoon, though in the evening it was, by reason of its proximity to the "Petite Bourse" (held on the side-walk in front of it), invaded by noisy speculators. Captain Bingham, my father, and myself long frequented the Cafe Gretry, often writing our "Paris letters" there. Subsequent to the war, Bingham and I removed to the Cafe Cardinal, where, however, the everlasting rattle of dominoes proved very disturbing. In the end, on that account, and in order to be nearer to a club to which we both belonged, we emigrated to the Cafe Napolitain. One reason for writing one's copy at a cafe instead of at one's club was that, at the former, one could at any moment receive messengers bringing late news; in addition to which, afternoon newspapers were instantly available.]

At every moment the numbers of the crowd increased. New-comers continually arrived from the eastern districts by way of the Boulevards, and from the north by way of the Faubourg Montmartre and the Rue Drouot, whilst from the south--the Quartier Latin and its neighbourhood--contingents made their way across the Pont St. Michel and the Pont Notre Dame, and thence, past the Halles, along the Boulevard de Sebastopol and the Rue Montmartre. Why the Quartier Latin element did not advance direct on the Palais Bourbon from its own side of the river I cannot exactly say; but it was, I believe, thought desirable to join hands, in the first instance, with the Revolutionary elements of northern Paris. All this took place whilst my father and myself were partaking of our meal. When we quitted the "Larder," a little before one o'clock, all the small parties of National Guards and civilians whom we had observed strolling about at an earlier hour, had congregated on the Place de la Concorde, attracted thither by the news of the special Sunday sitting, at which the Legislative Body would undoubtedly take momentous decisions.

It should be added that nearly all the National Guards who assembled on the Place de la Concorde before one o'clock were absolutely unarmed. At that hour, however, a large force of them, equivalent to a couple of battalions or thereabouts, came marching down the Rue Royale from the Boulevards, and these men (who were preceded by a solitary drummer) carried, some of them, chassepots and others *fusils-a-tabatiere,* having moreover, in most instances, their bayonets fixed.

They belonged to the north of Paris, though I cannot say precisely to what particular districts, nor do I know exactly by whose orders they had been assembled and instructed to march on the Palais Bourbon, as they speedily did. But it is certain that all the fermentation of the morning and all that occurred afterwards was the outcome of the night-work of the secret Republican Committees.

As the guards marched on, loud cries of "Decheance! Decheance!" arose among them, and were at once taken up by the spectators. Perfect unanimity, indeed, appeared to prevail on the question of dethroning the Emperor. Even the soldiers who were scattered here and there--a few Linesmen, a few Zouaves, a few Turcos, some of them invalided from MacMahon's forces--eagerly joined in the universal cry, and began to follow the guards on to the Place de la Concorde. Never, I believe, had that square been more crowded--not even in the days when it was known as the Place Louis Quinze, and when hundreds of people were crushed to death there whilst witnessing a display of fireworks in connection with the espousals of the future Louis XVI and Marie Antoinette, not even when it had become the Place de la Revolution and was thronged by all who wished to witness the successive executions of the last King and Queen of the old French monarchy. From the end of the Rue Royale to the bridge conducting across the Seine to the Palais Bourbon, from the gate of the Tuileries garden to the horses of Marly at the entrance of the Champs Elysees, around the obelisk of Luxor, and the fountains which were playing as usual in the bright sunshine which fell from the blue sky, along all the balustrades connecting the seated statues of the cities of France, here, there, and everywhere, indeed, you saw human heads. And the clamour was universal. The great square had again become one of Revolution, and yet it remained one of Concord also, for there was absolute agreement among the hundred thousand or hundred and fifty thousand people who had chosen it as their meeting-place, an agreement attested by that universal and never-ceasing cry of "Dethronement!"

As the armed National Guards debouched from the Rue Royale, their solitary drummer plied his sticks. But the roll of the drum was scarcely heard in the general uproar, and so dense was the crowd that the men could advance but very slowly. For a while it took some minutes to make only a few steps. Meantime the ranks of the men were broken here and there, other people got among them, and at last my father and myself were caught in the stream and carried with it, still somewhat slowly, in the direction of the Pont de la Concorde. I read recently that the bridge was defended by mounted men of the Garde de Paris (the forerunner of the Garde Republicaine of to-day); a French writer, in recalling the scene, referring to "the men's helmets glistening in the sunshine." But that is pure imagination. The bridge was defended by a cordon of police ranged in front of a large body of Gendarmerie mobile, wearing the familiar dark blue white-braided **kepis** and the dark blue tunics with white aiguillettes. At first, as I have already said, we advanced but slowly towards that defending force; but, all at once, we were swept onward by other men who had come from the Boulevards, in our wake. A minute later an abrupt halt ensued, whereupon it was only with great difficulty that we were able to resist the pressure from behind.

    I at last contrived to raise myself on tiptoes. Our first ranks had effected a breach in those of the sergents-de-ville, but before us were the mounted gendarmes, whose officer suddenly gave a command and drew his sword. For an instant I saw him plainly: his face was intensely pale. But a sudden rattle succeeded his command, for his men responded to it by drawing their sabres, which flashed ominously. A minute, perhaps two minutes, elapsed, the pressure in our rear still and ever increasing. I do not know what happened exactly at the head of our column: the uproar was greater than ever, and it seemed as if, in another moment, we should be charged, ridden over, cut down, or dispersed. I believe, however, that in presence of that great concourse of people, in presence too of the universal reprobation of the Empire which had brought defeat, invasion, humiliation upon France, the officer commanding the gendarmes shrank from carrying out his orders. There must have been a brief parley with the leaders of our column. In any case, the ranks of the gendarmes suddenly opened, many of them taking to the footways of the bridge, over which our column swept at the double-quick, raising exultant shouts of "Vive la Republique!" It was almost a race as to who should be the first to reach the Palais Bourbon. Those in the rear were ever impelling the foremost onward, and there was no time to look about one. But in a rapid vision, as it were, I saw the gendarmes reining in their horses on either side of us; and, here and there, medals gleamed on their dark tunics, and it seemed to me as if more than one face wore an angry expression. These men had fought under the imperial eagles, they had been decorated for their valour in the Crimean, Italian, and Cochin-China wars. Veterans all, and faithful servants of the Empire, they saw the *regime* for which they had fought, collapsing. Had their commanding officer ordered it, they might well have charged us; but, obedient to discipline, they had opened their ranks, and now the Will of the People was sweeping past them.

None of our column had a particularly threatening mien; the general demeanour was rather suggestive of joyful expectancy. But, the bridge once crossed, there was a fresh pause at the gates shutting off the steps of the Palais Bourbon. Here infantry were assembled, with their chassepots in readiness. Another very brief but exciting interval ensued. Then the Linesmen were withdrawn, the gates swung open, and everybody rushed up the steps. I was carried hither and thither, and at last from the portico into the building, where I contrived to halt beside one of the statues in the "Salle des Pas Perdus." I looked for my father, but could not see him, and remained wedged in my corner for quite a considerable time. Finally, however, another rush of invaders dislodged me, and I was swept with many others into the Chamber itself. All was uproar and confusion there. Very few deputies were present. The public galleries, the seats of the members, the hemicycle in front of the tribune, were crowded with National Guards. Some were standing on the stenographers' table and on the ushers' chairs below the tribune. There were others on the tribune stairs. And at the tribune itself, with his hat on his head, stood Gambetta, hoarsely shouting, amidst the general din, that Louis Napoleon Bonaparte and his dynasty had for ever ceased to reign. Then, again and again, arose the cry of "Vive la Republique!" In the twinkling of an eye, however, Gambetta was lost to view--he and other Republican deputies betaking themselves, as I afterwards learnt, to the palace steps, where the dethronement of the Bonapartes was again proclaimed. The invaders of the chamber swarmed after them, and I was watching their departure when I suddenly saw my father quietly leaning back in one of the ministerial seats--perhaps that which, in the past, had been occupied by Billault, Rouher, Ollivier, and other powerful and prominent men of the fallen *regime*.

At the outset of the proceedings that day Palikao had proposed the formation of a Council of Government and National Defence which was to include five members of the Legislative Body. The ministers were to be appointed by this Council, and he was to be Lieutenant-General of France. It so happened that the more fervent Imperialists had previously offered him a dictatorship, but he had declined it. Jules Favre met the General's proposal by claiming priority for the motion which he had submitted at the midnight sitting, whilst Thiers tried to bring about a compromise by suggesting such a Committee as Palikao had indicated, but placing the choice of its members entirely in the hands of the Legislative Body, omitting all reference to Palikao's Lieutenancy, and, further, setting forth that a Constituent Assembly should be convoked as soon as circumstances might permit. The three proposals--Thiers', Favre's, and Palikao's--were submitted to the *bureaux*, and whilst these *bureaux* were deliberating in various rooms the first invasion of the Chamber took place in spite of the efforts of Jules Ferry, who had promised Palikao that the proceedings of the Legislature should not be disturbed. When the sitting was resumed the "invaders," who, at that moment, mainly occupied the galleries, would listen neither to President Schneider nor to their favourite Gambetta, though both appealed to them for silence and order. Jules Favre alone secured a few moments' quietude, during which he begged that there might be no violence. Palikao was present, but did not speak. [Later in the day, after urging Trochu to accept the presidency of the new Government, as otherwise "all might be lost," Palikao quitted Paris for Belgium. He stayed at Namur during the remainder of the war, and afterwards lived in retirement at Versailles, where he died in January, 1878.] Amidst the general confusion came the second invasion of the Chamber, when I was swept off my feet and carried on to the floor of the house. That second invasion precipitated events. Even Gambetta wished the dethronement of the dynasty to be signified by a formal vote, but the "invaders" would brook no delay.

Both of us, my father and I, were tired and thirsty after our unexpected experiences. Accordingly we did not follow the crowd back to the steps overlooking the Place de la Concorde, but, like a good many other people, we went off by way of the Place de Bourgogne. No damage had been done in the Chamber itself, but as we quitted the building we noticed several inscriptions scrawled upon the walls. In some instances the words were merely "Vive la Republique!" and "Mort aux Prussiens!" At other times, however, they were too disgusting to be set down here. In or near the Rue de Bourgogne we found a fairly quiet wine-shop, where we rested and refreshed ourselves with *cannettes* of so-called Biere de Strasbourg. We did not go at that moment to the Hotel-de-Ville, whither a large part of the crowd betook itself by way of the quays, and where the Republic was again proclaimed; but returned to the Place de la Concorde, where some thousands of people still remained. Everybody was looking very animated and very pleased. Everybody imagined that, the Empire being overthrown, France would soon drive back the German invader. All fears for the future seemed, indeed, to have departed. Universal confidence prevailed, and everybody congratulated everybody else. There was, in any case, one good cause for congratulation: the Revolution had been absolutely bloodless--the first and only phenomenon of the kind in all French history.

Whilst we were strolling about the Place de la Concorde I noticed that the chief gate of the Tuileries garden had been forced open and damaged. The gilded eagles which had decorated it had been struck off and pounded to pieces, this, it appeared, having been chiefly the work of an enterprising Turco. A few days later Victorien Sardou wrote an interesting account of how he and others obtained admittance, first to the reserved garden, and then to the palace itself. On glancing towards it I observed that the flag which had still waved over the principal pavilion that morning, had now disappeared. It had been lowered after the departure of the Empress. Of the last hours which she spent in the palace, before she quitted it with Prince Metternich and Count Nigra to seek a momentary refuge at the residence of her dentist, Dr. Evans, I have given a detailed account, based on reliable narratives and documents, in my "Court of the Tuileries."

Quitting, at last, the Place de la Concorde, we strolled slowly homeward. Some tradespeople in the Rue Royale and the Faubourg St. Honore, former purveyors to the Emperor or the Empress, were already hastily removing the imperial arms from above their shops. That same afternoon and during the ensuing Monday and Tuesday every escutcheon, every initial N, every crown, every eagle, every inscription that recalled the Empire, was removed or obliterated in one or another manner. George Augustus Sala, whose recent adventure confined him to his room at the Grand Hotel, spent most of his time in watching the men who removed the eagles, crowns, and Ns from the then unfinished Opera-house. Even the streets which recalled the imperial *regime* were hastily renamed. The Avenue de l'Imperatrice at once became the Avenue du Bois de Boulogne; and the Rue du Dix-Decembre (so called in memory of Napoleon's assumption of the imperial dignity) was rechristened Rue du Quatre Septembre--this being the "happy thought" of a Zouave, who, mounted on a ladder, set the new name above the old one, whilst the plate bearing the latter was struck off with a hammer by a young workman.

As we went home on the afternoon of that memorable Fourth, we noticed that all the cafes and wine-shops were doing a brisk trade. Neither then nor during the evening, however, did I perceive much actual drunkenness. It was rather a universal jollity, as though some great victory had been gained. Truth to tell, the increase of drunkenness in Paris was an effect of the German Siege of the city, when drink was so plentiful and food so scarce.

My father and I had reached the corner of our street when we witnessed an incident which I have related in detail in the first pages of my book, "Republican France." It was the arrival of Gambetta at the Ministry of the Interior, by way of the Avenue de Marigny, with an escort of red-shirted Francs-tireurs de la Presse. The future Dictator had seven companions with him, all huddled inside or on the roof of a four-wheel cab, which was drawn by two Breton nags. I can still picture him alighting from the vehicle and, in the name of the Republic, ordering a chubby little Linesman, who was mounting guard at the gate of the Ministry, to have the said gate opened; and I can see the sleek and elderly *concierge*, who had bowed to many an Imperial Minister, complying with the said injunction, and respectfully doffing his tasselled smoking-cap and bending double whilst he admitted his new master. Then the gate is closed, and from behind the finely-wrought ornamental iron-work Gambetta briefly addresses the little throng which has recognized him, saying that the Empire is dead, but that France is wounded, and that her very wounds will inflame her with fresh courage; promising, too, that the whole nation shall be armed; and asking one and all to place confidence in the new Government, even as the latter will place confidence in the people.

In the evening I strolled with my father to the Place de l'Hotel de Ville, where many people were congregated, A fairly large body of National Guards was posted in front of the building, most of whose windows were lighted up. The members of the New Government of National Defence were deliberating there. Trochu had become its President, and Jules Favre its Vice-President and Minister for Foreign Affairs. Henri Rochefort, released that afternoon by his admirers from the prison of Sainte Pelagie, was included in the administration, this being in the main composed of the deputies for Paris. Only one of the latter, the cautious Thiers, refused to join it. He presided, however, that same evening over a gathering of some two hundred members of the moribund Legislative Body, which then made a forlorn attempt to retain some measure of authority, by coming to some agreement with the new Government. But Jules Favre and Jules Simon, who attended the meeting on the latter's behalf, would not entertain the suggestion. It was politely signified to the deputies that their support in Paris was not required, and that if they desired to serve their country in any way, they had better betake themselves to their former constituencies in the provinces. So far as the Legislative Body and the Senate, [Note] also, were concerned, everything ended in a delightful bit of comedy. Not only were the doors of their respective meeting halls looked, but they were "secured" with strips of tape and seals of red wax. The awe with which red sealing-wax inspires Frenchmen is distinctly a trait of the national character. Had there been, however, a real Bonaparte in Paris at that time, he would probably have cut off the aforesaid seals with his sword.

[Note: The Senate, over which Rouher presided, dispensed quietly on hearing of the invasion of the Chamber. The proposal that it should adjourn till more fortunate times emanated from Rouher himself. A few cries of "Vive l'Empereur!" were raised as the assembly dispersed. Almost immediately afterwards, however, most of the Senators, including Rouher, who knew that he was very obnoxious to the Parisians, quitted the city and even France.]

On the morning of September 5, the ***Charivari***--otherwise the daily Parisian ***Punch***--came out with a cartoon designed to sum up the whole period covered by the imperial rule. It depicted France bound hand and foot and placed between the mouths of two cannons, one inscribed "Paris, 1851," and the other "Sedan, 1870"--those names and dates representing the Alpha and Omega of the Second Empire.

IV
FROM REVOLUTION TO SIEGE

The Government of National Defence--The Army of Paris--The Return of Victor Hugo--The German advance on Paris--The National Guard reviewed--Hospitable Preparations for the Germans--They draw nearer still--Departure of Lord Lyons--Our Last Day of Liberty--On the Fortifications--The Bois de Boulogne and our Live Stock--Mass before the Statue of Strasbourg--Devout Breton Mobiles--Evening on the Boulevards and in the Clubs--Trochu and Ducrot--The Fight and Panic of Chatillon--The Siege begins.

As I shall have occasion in these pages to mention a good many members of the self-constituted Government which succeeded the Empire, it may be as well for me to set down here their names and the offices they held. I have already mentioned that Trochu was President, and Jules Favre Vice-President, of the new administration. The former also retained his office as Governor of Paris, and at the same time became Generalissimo. Favre, for his part, took the Ministry for Foreign Affairs. With him and Trochu were Gambetta, Minister of the Interior; Jules Simon, Minister of Public Instruction; Adolphe Cremieux, Minister of Justice; Ernest Picard, Minister of Finance; Jules Ferry, Secretary-General to the Government, and later Mayor of Paris; and Henri Rochefort, President of the Committee of Barricades. Four of their colleagues, Emmanuel Arago, Garnier-Pages, Eugene Pelletan, and Glais-Bizoin, did not take charge of any particular administrative departments, the remainder of these being allotted to men whose co-operation was secured. For instance, old General Le Flo became Minister of War--under Trochu, however, and not over him. Vice-Admiral Fourichon was appointed Minister of Marine; Magnin, an iron-master, became Minister of Commerce and Agriculture; Frederic Dorian, another iron-master, took the department of Public Works; Count Emile de Keratry acted as Prefect of Police, and Etienne Arago, in the earlier days, as Mayor of Paris.

The new Government was fully installed by Tuesday, September 6. It had already issued several more or less stirring proclamations, which were followed by a despatch which Jules Favre addressed to the French diplomatic representatives abroad. As a set-off to the arrival of a number of dejected travel-stained fugitives from MacMahon's army, whose appearance was by no means of a nature to exhilarate the Parisians, the defence was reinforced by a large number of Gardes Mobiles, who poured into the city, particularly from Brittany, Trochu's native province, and by a considerable force of regulars, infantry, cavalry, and artillery, commanded by the veteran General Vinoy (then seventy years of age), who had originally been despatched to assist MacMahon, but, having failed to reach him before the disaster of Sedan, retreated in good order on the capital. At the time when the Siege actually commenced there were in Paris about 90,000 regulars (including all arms and categories), 110,000 Mobile Guards, and a naval contingent of 13,500 men, that is a force of 213,000, in addition to the National Guards, who were about 280,000 in number. Thus, altogether, nearly half a million armed men were assembled in Paris for the purpose of defending it. As all authorities afterwards admitted, this was a very great blunder, as fully 100,000 regulars and mobiles might have been spared to advantage for service in the provinces. Of course the National Guards themselves could not be sent away from the city, though they were often an encumbrance rather than a help, and could not possibly have carried on the work of defence had they been left to their own resources.

Besides troops, so long as the railway trains continued running, additional military stores and supplies of food, flour, rice, biscuits, preserved meats, rolled day by day into Paris. At the same time, several illustrious exiles returned to the capital. Louis Blanc and Edgar Quinet arrived there, after years of absence, in the most unostentatious fashion, though they soon succumbed to the prevailing mania of inditing manifestoes and exhortations for the benefit of their fellow-countrymen. Victor Hugo's return was more theatrical. In those famous "Chatiments" in which he had so severely flagellated the Third Napoleon (after, in earlier years, exalting the First to the dignity of a demi-god), he had vowed to keep out of France and to protest against the Empire so long as it lasted, penning, in this connection, the famous line:

"Et s'il n'en reste qu'un, je serai celui-la!"

But now the Empire had fallen, and so Hugo returned in triumph to Paris. When he alighted from the train which brought him, he said to those who had assembled to give him a fitting greeting, that he had come to do his duty in the hour of danger, that duty being to save Paris, which meant more than saving France, for it implied saving the world itself--Paris being the capital of civilization, the centre of mankind. Naturally enough, those fine sentiments were fervently applauded by the great poet's admirers, and when he had installed himself with his companions in an open carriage, two or three thousand people escorted him processionally along the Boulevards. It was night-time, and the cafes were crowded and the footways covered with promenaders as the *cortege* went by, the escort singing now the "Marseillaise" and now the "Chant du Depart," whilst on every side shouts of "Vive Victor Hugo!" rang out as enthusiastically as if the appointed "Saviour of Paris" were indeed actually passing. More than once I saw the illustrious poet stand up, uncover, and wave his hat in response to the acclamations, and I then particularly noticed the loftiness of his forehead, and the splendid crop of white hair with which it was crowned. Hugo, at that time sixty-eight years old, still looked vigorous, but it was beyond the power of any such man as himself to save the city from what was impending. All he could do was to indite perfervid manifestoes, and subsequently, in "L'Annee terrible," commemorate the doings and sufferings of the time. For the rest, he certainly enrolled himself as a National Guard, and I more than once caught sight of him wearing *kepi* and *vareuse*. I am not sure, however, whether he ever did a "sentry-go."

It must have been on the day following Victor Hugo's arrival that I momentarily quitted Paris for reasons in which my youthful but precocious heart was deeply concerned. I was absent for four days or so, and on returning to the capital I was accompanied by my stepmother, who, knowing that my father intended to remain in the city during the impending siege, wished to be with him for a while before the investment began. I recollect that she even desired to remain with us, though that was impossible, as she had young children, whom she had left at Saint Servan; and, besides, as I one day jocularly remarked to her, she would, by staying in Paris, have added to the "useless mouths," whose numbers the Republican, like the Imperial, Government was, with very indifferent success, striving to diminish. However, she only quitted us at the last extremity, departing on the evening of September 17, by the Western line, which, on the morrow, the enemy out at Conflans, some fourteen miles from Paris.

Day by day the Parisians had received news of the gradual approach of the German forces. On the 8th they heard that the Crown Prince of Prussia's army was advancing from Montmirail to Coulommiers--whereupon the city became very restless; whilst on the 9th there came word that the black and white pennons of the ubiquitous Uhlans had been seen at La Ferte-sous-Jouarre. That same day Thiers quitted Paris on a mission which he had undertaken for the new Government, that of pleading the cause of France at the Courts of London, St. Petersburg, Vienna, and Rome. Then, on the 11th, there were tidings that Laon had capitulated, though not without its defenders blowing up a powder-magazine and thereby injuring some German officers of exalted rank--for which reason the deed was enthusiastically commended by the Parisian Press, though it would seem to have been a somewhat treacherous one, contrary to the ordinary usages of war. On the 12th some German scouts reached Meaux, and a larger force leisurely occupied Melun. The French, on their part, were busy after a fashion. They offered no armed resistance to the German advance, but they tried to impede it in sundry ways. With the idea of depriving the enemy of "cover," various attempts were made to fire some of the woods in the vicinity of Paris, whilst in order to cheat him of supplies, stacks and standing crops were here and there destroyed. Then, too, several railway and other bridges were blown up, including the railway bridge at Creil, so that direct communication with Boulogne and Calais ceased on September 12.

The 13th was a great day for the National Guards, who were then reviewed by General Trochu. With my father and my young stepmother, I went to see the sight, which was in many respects an interesting one. A hundred and thirty-six battalions, or approximately 180,000 men, of the so-called "citizen soldiery" were under arms; their lines extending, first, along the Boulevards from the Bastille to the Madeleine, then down the Rue Royale, across the Place de la Concorde and up the Champs Elysees as far as the Rond Point. In addition, 100,000 men of the Garde

Mobile were assembled along the quays of the Seine and up the Champs Elysees from the Rond Point to the Arc de Triomphe. I have never since set eyes on so large a force of armed men. They were of all sorts. Some of the Mobiles, notably the Breton ones, who afterwards gave a good account of themselves, looked really soldierly; but the National Guards were a strangely mixed lot. They all wore *kepis*, but quite half of them as yet had no uniforms, and were attired in blouses and trousers of various hues. Only here and there could one see a man of military bearing; most of them struck happy-go-lucky attitudes, and were quite unable to keep step in marching. A particular feature of the display was the number of flowers and sprigs of evergreen with which the men had decorated the muzzles of the *fusils-a-tabatiere* which they mostly carried. Here and there, moreover, one and another fellow displayed on his bayonet-point some coloured caricature of the ex-Emperor or the ex-Empress. What things they were, those innumerable caricatures of the months which followed the Revolution! Now and again there appeared one which was really clever, which embodied a smart, a witty idea; but how many of them were simply the outcome of a depraved, a lewd, a bestial imagination! The most offensive caricatures of Marie-Antoinette were as nothing beside those levelled at that unfortunate woman, the Empress Eugenie.

Our last days of liberty were now slipping by. Some of the poorest folk of the environs of Paris were at last coming into the city, bringing their chattels with them. Strange ideas, however, had taken hold of some of the more simple-minded suburban bourgeois. Departing hastily into the provinces, so as to place their skins out of harm's reach, they had not troubled to store their household goods in the city; but had left them in their coquettish villas and pavilions, the doors of which were barely looked. The German soldiers would very likely occupy the houses, but assuredly they would do no harm to them. "Perhaps, however, it might be as well to propitiate the foreign soldiers. Let us leave something for them," said worthy Monsieur Durand to Madame Durand, his wife; "they will be hungry when they get here, and if they find something ready for them they will be grateful and do no damage." So, although the honest Durands carefully barred--at times even walled-up--their cellars of choice wines, they arranged that plenty of bottles, at times even a cask, of *vin ordinaire* should be within easy access; and ham, cheese, sardines, *saucissons de Lyon*, and *pates de foie gras* were deposited in the pantry cupboards, which were considerately left unlocked in order that the good, mild-mannered, honest Germans (who, according to a proclamation issued by "Unser Fritz" at an earlier stage of the hostilities, "made war on the Emperor Napoleon and not on the French nation") might regale themselves without let or hindrance. Moreover, the nights were "drawing in," the evenings becoming chilly; so why not lay the fires, and place matches and candles in convenient places for the benefit of the unbidden guests who would so soon arrive? All those things being done, M. and Mme. Durand departed to seek the quietude of Fouilly-les-Oies, never dreaming that on their return to Montfermeil, Palaiseau, or Sartrouville, they would find their *salon* converted into a pigstye, their furniture smashed, and their clocks and chimney-ornaments abstracted. Of course the M. Durand of to-day knows what happened to his respected parents; he knows what to think of the good, honest, considerate German soldiery; and, if he can help it, he will not in any similar case leave so much as a wooden spoon to be carried off to the Fatherland, and added as yet another trophy to the hundred thousand French clocks and the million French nick-nacks which are still preserved there as mementoes of the "grosse Zeit."

On September 15, we heard of some petty skirmishes between Uhlans and Francs-tireurs in the vicinity of Montereau and Melun; on the morrow the enemy captured a train at Senlis, and fired on another near Chantilly, fortunately without wounding any of the passengers; whilst on the same day his presence was signalled at Villeneuve-Saint-Georges, only ten miles south of Paris. That evening, moreover, he attempted to ford the Seine at Juvisy. On the 16th some of his forces appeared between Creteil and Neuilly-sur-Marne, on the eastern side of the city, and only some five miles from the fort of Vincennes. Then we again heard of him on the south--of his presence at Brunoy, Ablon, and Athis, and of the pontoons by which he was crossing the Seine at Villeneuve and Choisy-le-Roi.

Thus the advance steadily continued, quite unchecked by force of arms, save for just a few trifling skirmishes initiated by sundry Francs-tireurs. Not a road, not a barricade, was defended by the authorities; not once was the passage of a river contested. Here and there the Germans found obstructions: poplars had been felled and laid across a highway, bridges and railway tunnels had occasionally been blown up; but all such impediments to their advance were speedily overcome by the enemy, who marched on quietly, feeling alternately puzzled and astonished at never being confronted by any French forces. As the invaders drew nearer to Paris they found an abundance of vegetables and fruit at their disposal, but most of the peasantry had fled, taking their live stock with them, and, as a German officer told me in after years, eggs, cheese, butter, and milk could seldom be procured.

On the 17th the French began to recover from the stupor which seemed to have fallen on them. Old General Vinoy crossed the Marne at Charenton with some of his forces, and a rather sharp skirmish ensued in front of the village of Mesly. That same day Lord Lyons, the British Ambassador, took his departure from Paris, proceeding by devious ways to Tours, whither, a couple of days previously, three delegates of the National Defence--two septuagenarians and one sexagenarian, Cremieux, Glais-Bizoin, and Fourichon--had repaired in order to take over the general government of France. Lord Lyons had previously told Jules Favre that he intended to remain in the capital, but I believe that his decision was modified by instructions from London. With him went most of the Embassy staff, British interests in Paris remaining in the hands of the second secretary, Mr. Wodehouse, and the vice-consul. The consul himself had very prudently quitted Paris, in order "to drink the waters," some time previously. Colonel Claremont, the military attache, still remained with us, but by degrees, as the siege went on, the Embassy staff dwindled down to the concierge and two--or was it four?--sheep browsing on the lawn. Mr. Wodehouse went off (my father and myself being among those who accompanied him, as I shall relate in a future chapter) towards the middle of November; and before the bombardment began Colonel Claremont likewise executed a strategical retreat. Nevertheless--or should I say for that very reason?--he was subsequently made a general officer.

A day or two before Lord Lyons left he drew up a notice warning British subjects that if they should remain in Paris it would be at their own risk and peril. The British colony was not then so large as it is now, nevertheless it was a considerable one. A good many members of it undoubtedly departed on their own initiative. Few, if any, saw Lord Lyons's notice, for it was purely and simply conveyed to them through the medium of **Galignani's Messenger**, which, though it was patronized by tourists staying at the hotels, was seldom seen by genuine British residents, most of whom read London newspapers.

The morrow of Lord Lyons's departure, Sunday, September 18, was our last day of liberty. The weather was splendid, the temperature as warm as that of June. All Paris was out of doors. We were not without women-folk and children. Not only were there the wives and offspring of the working-classes; but the better halves of many tradespeople and bourgeois had remained in the city, together with a good many ladies of higher social rank. Thus, in spite of all the departures, "papa, mamma, and baby" were still to be met in many directions on that last day preceding the investment. There were gay crowds everywhere, on the Boulevards, on the squares, along the quays, and along the roads skirting the ramparts. These last were the "great attraction," and thousands of people strolled about watching the work which was in progress. Stone casements were being roofed with earth, platforms were being prepared for guns, gabions were being set in position at the embrasures, sandbags were being carried to the parapets, stakes were being pointed for the many *pieges-a-loups*, and smooth earthworks were being planted with an infinity of spikes. Some guns were already in position, others, big naval guns from Brest or Cherbourg, were still lying on the turf. Meanwhile, at the various city gates, the very last vehicles laden with furniture and forage were arriving from the suburbs. And up and down went all the promenaders, chatting, laughing, examining this and that work of defence or engine of destruction in such a good-humoured, light-hearted way that the whole *chemin-de-ronde* seemed to be a vast fair, held solely for the amusement of the most volatile people that the world has ever known.

Access to the Bois de Boulogne was forbidden. Acres of timber had already been felled there, and from the open spaces the mild September breeze occasionally wafted the lowing of cattle, the bleating of sheep, and the grunting of pigs. Our live stock consisted of 30,000 oxen, 175,000 sheep, 8,800 pigs, and 6,000 milch-cows. Little did we think how soon those animals (apart from the milch-cows) would be consumed! Few of us were aware that, according to Maxime Ducamp's great work on Paris, we had hitherto consumed, on an average, every day of the year, 935 oxen, 4680 sheep, 570 pigs, and 600 calves, to say nothing of 46,000 head of poultry, game, etc., 50 tons of fish, and 670,000 eggs.

Turning from the Bois de Boulogne, which had become our principal ranch and sheep-walk, one found companies of National Guards learning the "goose-step" in the Champs Elysees and the Cours-la-Reine. Regulars were appropriately encamped both in the Avenue de la Grande Armee and on the Champ de Mars. Field-guns and caissons filled the Tuileries garden, whilst in the grounds of the Luxembourg Palace one again found cattle and sheep; yet other members of the bovine and ovine species being installed, singularly enough, almost cheek by jowl with the hungry wild beasts of the Jardin des Plantes, whose mouths fairly watered at the sight of their natural prey. If you followed the quays of the Seine you there found sightseers gazing at the little gunboats and floating batteries on the water; and if you climbed to Montmartre you there came upon people watching "The Neptune," the captive balloon which Nadar, the aeronaut and photographer, had already provided for purposes of military observation. I shall have occasion to speak of him and his balloons again.

Among all that I myself saw on that memorable Sunday, I was perhaps most struck by the solemn celebration of Mass in front of the statue of Strasbourg on the Place de la Concorde. The capital of Alsace had been besieged since the middle of August, but was still offering a firm resistance to the enemy. Its chief defenders, General Uhrich and Edmond Valentin, were the most popular heroes of the hour. The latter had been appointed Prefect of the city by the Government of National Defence, and, resolving to reach his post in spite of the siege which was being actively prosecuted, had disguised himself and passed successfully through the German lines, escaping the shots which were fired at him. In Paris the statue of Strasbourg had become a place of pilgrimage, a sacred shrine, as it were, adorned with banners and with wreaths innumerable. Yet I certainly had not expected to see an altar set up and Mass celebrated in front of it, as if it had been, indeed, a statue of the Blessed Virgin.

At this stage of affairs there was no general hostility to the Church in Paris. The *bourgeoisie*--I speak of its masculine element--was as sceptical then as it is now, but it knew that General Trochu, in whom it placed its trust, was a practising and fervent Catholic, and that in taking the Presidency of the Government he had made it one of his conditions that religion should be respected. Such animosity as was shown against the priesthood emanated from some of the public clubs where the future Communards perorated. It was only as time went on, and the defence grew more and more hopeless, that Trochu himself was denounced as a *cagot* and a *souteneur de soutanes*; and not until the Commune did the Extremists give full rein to their hatred of the Church and its ministers.

In connection with religion, there was another sight which impressed me on that same Sunday. I was on the point of leaving the Place de la Concorde when a large body of Mobiles debouched either from the Rue Royale or the Rue de Rivoli, and I noticed, with some astonishment, that not only were they accompanied by their chaplains, but that they bore aloft several processional religious banners. They were Bretons, and had been to Mass, I ascertained, at the church of Notre Dame des Victoires--the favourite church of the Empress Eugenie, who often attended early Mass there--and were now returning to their quarters in the arches of the railway viaduct of the Point-du-Jour. Many people uncovered as they thus went by processionally, carrying on high their banners of the Virgin, she who is invoked by the Catholic soldier as "Auzilium Christianorum." For a moment my thoughts strayed back to Brittany, where, during my holidays the previous year, I had witnessed the "Pardon" of Guingamp,

In the evening I went to the Boulevards with my father, and we afterwards dropped into one or two of the public clubs. The Boulevard promenaders had a good deal to talk about. General Ambert, who under the Empire had been mayor of our arrondissement, had fallen out with his men, through speaking contemptuously of the Republic, and after being summarily arrested by some of them, had been deprived of his command. Further, the ***Official Journal*** had published a circular addressed by Bismarck to the German diplomatists abroad, in which he stated formally that if France desired peace she would have to give "material guarantees." That idea, however, was vigorously pooh-poohed by the Boulevardiers, particularly as rumours of sudden French successes, originating nobody knew how, were once more in the air. Scandal, however, secured the attention of many of the people seated in the cafes, for the ***Rappel***--Victor Hugo's organ--had that day printed a letter addressed to Napoleon III by his mistress Marguerite Bellenger, who admitted in it that she had deceived her imperial lover with respect to the paternity of her child.

However, we went, my father and I, from the Boulevards to the Folies-Bergere, which had been turned for the time into a public club, and there we listened awhile to Citizen Lermina, who, taking Thiers's mission and Bismarck's despatch as his text, protested against France concluding any peace or even any armistice so long as the Germans had not withdrawn across the frontier. There was still no little talk of that description. The old agitator Auguste Blanqui--long confined in one of the cages of Mont Saint-Michel, but now once more in Paris--never wearied of opposing peace in the discourses that he delivered at his own particular club, which, like the newspaper he inspired, was called "La Patrie en Danger." In other directions, for instance at the Club du Maine, the Extremists were already attacking the new Government for its delay in distributing cartridges to the National Guards, being, no doubt, already impatient to seize authority themselves.

Whilst other people were promenading or perorating, Trochu, in his room at the Louvre, was receiving telegram after telegram informing him that the Germans were now fast closing round the city. He himself, it appears, had no idea of preventing it; but at the urgent suggestion of his old friend and comrade General Ducrot, he had consented that an effort should be made to delay, at any rate, a complete investment. In an earlier chapter I had occasion to mention Ducrot in connexion with the warnings which Napoleon III received respecting the military preparations of Prussia. At this time, 1870, the general was fifty-three years old, and therefore still in his prime. As commander of a part of MacMahon's forces he had distinguished himself at the battle of Woerth, and when the Marshal was wounded at Sedan, it was he who, by right of seniority, at first assumed command of the army, being afterwards compelled, however, to relinquish the poet to Wimpfen, in accordance with an order from Palikao which Wimpfen produced. Included at the capitulation, among the prisoners taken by the Germans, Ducrot subsequently escaped--the Germans contending that he had broken his parole in doing so, though this does not appear to have been the case. Immediately afterwards he repaired to Paris to place himself at Trochu's disposal. At Woerth he had suggested certain tactics which might have benefited the French army; at Sedan he had wished to make a supreme effort to cut through the German lines; and now in Paris he proposed to Trochu a plan which if successful might, he thought, retard the investment and momentarily cut the German forces in halves.

In attempting to carry out this scheme (September 19) Ducrot took with him most of Vinoy's corps, that is four divisions of infantry, some cavalry, and no little artillery, having indeed, according to his own account, seventy-two guns with him. The action was fought on the plateau of Chatillon (south of Paris), where the French had been constructing a redoubt, which was still, however, in a very unfinished state. At daybreak that morning all the districts of Paris lying on the left bank of the Seine were roused by the loud booming of guns. The noise was at times almost deafening, and it is certain that the French fired a vast number of projectiles, though, assuredly, the number--25,000--given in a copy of the official report which I have before me must be a clerical error. In any case, the Germans replied with an even more terrific fire than that of the French, and, as had previously happened at Sedan and elsewhere, the French ordnance proved to be no match for that emanating from Krupp's renowned workshops. The French defeat was, however, precipitated by a sudden panic which arose among a provisional regiment of Zouaves, who suddenly turned tail and fled. Panic is often, if not always, contagious, and so it proved to be on this occasion. Though some of the Gardes Mobiles, notably the Bretons of Ile-et-Vilaine, fought well, thanks to the support of the artillery (which is so essential in the case of untried troops), other men weakened, and imitated the example of the Zouaves. Duorot soon realized that it was useless to prolong the encounter, and after spiking the guns set up in the Chatillon redoubt, he retired under the protection of the Forts of Vanves and Montrouge.

My father and I had hastened to the southern side of Paris as soon as the cannonade apprised us that an engagement was going on. Pitiful was the spectacle presented by the disbanded soldiers as they rushed down the Chaussee du Maine. Many had flung away their weapons. Some went on dejectedly; others burst into wine-shops, demanded drink with threats, and presently emerged swearing, cursing and shouting, "Nous sommes trahis!" Riderless horses went by, instinctively following the men, and here and there one saw a bewildered and indignant officer, whose orders were scouted with jeers. The whole scene was of evil augury for the defence of Paris.

At a later hour, when we reached the Boulevards, we found the wildest rumours in circulation there. Nobody knew exactly what had happened, but there was talk of 20,000 French troops having been annihilated by five times that number of Germans. At last a proclamation emanating from Gambetta was posted up and eagerly perused. It supplied no details of the fighting, but urged the Parisians to give way neither to excitement nor to despondency, and reminded them that a court-martial had been instituted to deal with cowards and deserters. Thereupon the excitement seemed to subside, and people went to dinner. An hour afterwards the Boulevards were as gay as ever, thronged once more with promenaders, among whom were many officers of the Garde Mobile and the usual regiment of painted women. Cynicism and frivolity were once more the order of the day. But in the midst of it there came an unexpected incident. Some of the National Guards of the district were not unnaturally disgusted by the spectacle which the Boulevards presented only a few hours after misfortune had fallen on the French arms. Forming, therefore, into a body, they marched along, loudly calling upon the cafes to close. Particularly were they indignant when, on reaching Brebant's Restaurant at the corner of the Faubourg Montmartre, they heard somebody playing a lively Offenbachian air on a piano there. A party of heedless **viveurs** and **demoiselles** of the half-world were enjoying themselves together as in the palmy imperial days. But the piano was soon silenced, the cafes and restaurants were compelled to close, and the Boulevardian world went home in a slightly chastened mood. The Siege of Paris had begun.

V
BESIEGED

The Surrender of Versailles--Captain Johnson, Queen's Messenger--No more Paris Fashions!--Prussians versus Germans--Bismarck's Hard Terms for Peace--Attempts to pass through the German Lines--Chartreuse Verte as an Explosive!--Tommy Webb's Party and the Germans--Couriers and Early Balloons--Our Arrangements with Nadar--Gambetta's Departure and Balloon Journey--The Amusing Verses of Albert Millaud--Siege Jokes and Satire--The Spy and Signal Craze--Amazons to the Rescue!

It was at one o'clock on the afternoon of September 19 that the telegraph wires between Paris and Versailles, the last which linked us to the outside world, were suddenly cut by the enemy; the town so closely associated with the Grand Monarque and his magnificence having then surrendered to a very small force of Germans, although it had a couple of thousand men--Mobile and National Guards--to defend it. The capitulation which was arranged between the mayor and the enemy was flagrantly violated by the latter almost as soon as it had been concluded, tins being only one of many such instances which occurred during the war. Versailles was required to provide the invader with a number of oxen, to be slaughtered for food, numerous casks of wine, the purpose of which was obvious, and a large supply of forage valued at L12,000. After all, however, that was a mere trifle in comparison with what the present Kaiser's forces would probably demand on landing at Hull or Grimsby or Harwich, should they some day do so. By the terms of the surrender of Versailles, however, the local National Guards were to have remained armed and entrusted with the internal police of the town, and, moreover, there were to have been no further requisitions. But Bismarck and Moltke pooh-poohed all such stipulations, and the Versaillese had to submit to many indignities.

In Paris that day the National Defence Government was busy in various ways, first in imposing fines, according to an ascending scale, on all absentees who ought to have remained in the city and taken their share of military duty; and, secondly, in decreeing that nobody with any money lodged in the Savings Bank should be entitled to draw out more than fifty francs, otherwise two pounds, leaving the entire balance of his or her deposit at the Government's disposal. This measure provoked no little dissatisfaction. It was also on September 19, the first day of the siege, that the last diplomatic courier entered Paris. I well remember the incident. Whilst I was walking along the Faubourg Saint Honore I suddenly perceived an open *caleche*, drawn by a pair of horses, bestriding one of which was a postillion arrayed in the traditional costume--hair a la Catogan, jacket with scarlet facings, gold-banded hat, huge boots, and all the other appurtenances which one saw during long years on the stage in Adolphe Adam's sprightly but "impossible" opera-comique "Le Postillon de Longjumeau." For an instant, indeed, I felt inclined to hum the famous refrain, "Oh, oh, oh, oh, qu'il etait beau"--but many National Guards and others regarded the equipage with great suspicion, particularly as it was occupied by on individual in semi-military attire. Quite a number of people decided in their own minds that this personage must be a Prussian spy, and therefore desired to stop his carriage and march him off to prison. As a matter of fact, however, he was a British officer, Captain Johnson, discharging the duties of a Queen's Messenger; and as he repeatedly flourished a cane in a very menacing manner, and the door-porter of the British Embassy--a German, I believe--energetically came to his assistance, he escaped actual molestation, and drove in triumph into the courtyard of the ambassadorial mansion.

At this time a great shock was awaiting the Parisians. During the same week the Vicomtesse de Renneville issued an announcement stating that in presence of the events which were occurring she was constrained to suspend the publication of her renowned journal of fashions, **La Gazette Rose**. This was a tragic blow both for the Parisians themselves and for all the world beyond them. There would be no more Paris fashions! To what despair would not millions of women be reduced? How would they dress, even supposing that they should contrive to dress at all? The thought was appalling; and as one and another great *couturier* closed his doors, Paris began to realize that her prestige was indeed in jeopardy.

A day or two after the investment the city became very restless on account of Thiers's mission to foreign Courts and Jules Favre's visit to the German headquarters, it being reported by the extremists that the Government did not intend to be a Government of National Defence but one of Capitulation. In reply to those rumours the authorities issued the famous proclamation in which they said;

"The Government's policy is that formulated in these terms: Not an Inch of our Territory.   Not a Stone of our Fortresses.   The Government will maintain it to the end."

On the morrow, September 21, Gambetta personally reminded us that it was the seventy-eighth anniversary of the foundation of the first French Republic, and, after recalling to the Parisians what their fathers had then accomplished, he exhorted them to follow that illustrious example, and to "secure victory by confronting death." That same evening the clubs decided that a great demonstration should be made on the morrow by way of insisting that no treaty should be discussed until the Germans had been driven out of France, that no territory, fort, vessel, or treasure should be surrendered, that all elections should be adjourned, and that a *levee en masse* should be decreed. Jules Favre responded that he and his colleagues personified Defence and not Surrender, and Rochefort--poor Rochefort!--solemnly promised that the barricades of Paris should be begun that very night. That undertaking mightily pleased the agitators, though the use of the said barricades was not apparent; and the demonstrators dispersed with the usual shouts of "Vive la Republique! Mort aux Prussiens!"

In connexion with that last cry it was a curious circumstance that from the beginning to the end of the war the French persistently ignored the presence of Saxons, Wuertembergers, Hessians, Badeners, and so forth in the invading armies. Moreover, on only one or two occasions (such as the Bazeilles episode of the battle of Sedan) did they evince any particular animosity against the Bavarians. I must have heard "Death to the Prussians!" shouted at least a thousand times; but most certainly I never once heard a single cry of "Death to the Germans!" Still in the same connexion, let me mention that it was in Paris, during the siege, that the eminent naturalist and biologist Quatrefages de Breau wrote that curious little book of his,

"La Race Prussienne," in which he contended that the Prussians were not Germans at all. There was at least some measure of truth in the views which he enunciated.

As I previously indicated, Jules Favre, the Foreign Minister of the National Defence, had gone to the German headquarters in order to discuss the position with Prince (then Count) Bismarck. He met him twice, first at the Comte de Rillac's Chateau de la Haute Maison, and secondly at Baron de Rothschild's Chateau de Ferrieres--the German staff usually installing itself in the lordly "pleasure-houses" of the French noble or financial aristocracy, and leaving them as dirty as possible, and, naturally, bereft of their timepieces. Baron Alphonse de Rothschild told me in later years that sixteen clocks were carried off from Ferrieres whilst King (afterwards the Emperor) William and Bismarck were staying there. I presume that they now decorate some of the salons of the schloss at Berlin, or possibly those of Varzin and Friedrichsruhe. Bismarck personally had an inordinate passion for clocks, as all who ever visited his quarters in the Wilhelmstrasse, when he was German Chancellor, will well remember.

But he was not content with the clocks of Ferrieres. He told Jules Favre that if France desired peace she must surrender the two departments of the Upper and the Lower Rhine, a part of the department of the Moselle, together with Metz, Chateau Salins, and Soissons; and he would only grant an armistice (to allow of the election of a French National Assembly to decide the question of War or Peace) on condition that the Germans should occupy Strasbourg, Toul, and Phalsburg, together with a fortress, such as Mont Valerien, commanding the city of Paris. Such conditions naturally stiffened the backs of the French, and for a time there was no more talk of negotiating.

During the earlier days of the Siege of Paris I came into contact with various English people who, having delayed their departure until it was too late, found themselves shut up in the city, and were particularly anxious to depart from it. The British Embassy gave them no help in the matter. Having issued its paltry notice in *Galignani's Messenger*, it considered that there was no occasion for it to do anything further. Moreover, Great Britain had not recognized the French Republic, so that the position of Mr. Wodehouse was a somewhat difficult one. However, a few "imprisoned" Englishmen endeavoured to escape from the city by devices of their own. Two of them who set out together, fully expecting to get through the

German lines and then reach a convenient railway station, followed the course of the Seine for several miles without being able to cross it, and in spite of their waving pocket-handkerchiefs (otherwise flags of truce) and their constant shouts of "English! Friends!" and so forth, were repeatedly fired at by both French and German outposts. At last they reached Rueil, where the villagers, on noticing how bad their French was, took them to be Prussian spies, and nearly lynched them. Fortunately, the local commissary of police believed their story, and they were sent back to Paris to face the horseflesh and the many other hardships which they had particularly desired to avoid.

I also remember the representative of a Birmingham small-arms factory telling me of his unsuccessful attempt to escape. He had lingered in Paris in the hope of concluding a contract with the new Republican Government. Not having sufficient money to charter a balloon, and the Embassy, as usual at that time, refusing any help (O shades of Palmerston!), he set out as on a walking-tour with a knapsack strapped to his shoulders and an umbrella in his hand. His hope was to cross the Seine by the bridge of Saint Cloud or that of Suresnes, but he failed in both attempts, and was repeatedly fired upon by vigilant French outposts. After losing his way in the Bois de Boulogne, awakening both the cattle and the sheep there in the course of his nightly ramble, he at last found one of the little huts erected to shelter the gardeners and wood-cutters, and remained there until daybreak, when he was able to take his bearings and proceed towards the Auteuil gate of the ramparts. As he did not wish to be fired upon again, he deemed it expedient to hoist his pocket handkerchief at the end of his umbrella as a sign of his pacific intentions, and finding the gate open and the drawbridge down, he attempted to enter the city, but was immediately challenged by the National Guards on duty. These vigilant patriots observed his muddy condition--the previous day had been a wet one--and suspiciously inquired where he had come from at that early hour. His answer being given in broken French and in a very embarrassed manner, he was at once regarded as a Prussian spy, and dragged off to the guard-room. There he was carefully searched, and everything in his pockets having been taken from him, including a small bottle which the sergeant on duty regarded with grave suspicion, he was told that his after-fate would be decided when the commanding officer of that particular *secteur* of the ramparts made his rounds.

When this officer arrived he closely questioned the prisoner, who tried to explain his circumstances, and protested that his innocence was shown by the British passport and other papers which had been taken from him. "Oh! papers prove nothing!" was the prompt retort. "Spies are always provided with papers. But, come, I have proof that you are an unmitigated villain!" So saying, the officer produced the small bottle which had been taken from the unfortunate traveller, and added: "You see this? You had it in your pocket. Now, don't attempt to deceive me, for I know very well what is the nature of the green liquid which it contains--it is a combustible fluid with which you wanted to set fire to our *chevaux-de-frise!*"

Denials and protests were in vain. The officer refused to listen to his prisoner until the latter at last offered to drink some of the terrible fluid in order to prove that it was not at all what it was supposed to be. With a little difficulty the tight-fitting cork was removed from the flask, and on the latter being handed to the prisoner he proceeded to imbibe some of its contents, the officer, meanwhile, retiring to a short distance, as if he imagined that the alleged "spy" would suddenly explode. Nothing of that kind happened, however. Indeed, the prisoner drank the terrible stuff with relish, smacked his lips, and even prepared to take a second draught, when the officer, feeling reassured, again drew near to him and expressed his willingness to sample the suspected fluid himself. He did so, and at once discovered that it was purely and simply some authentic Chartreuse verte! It did not take the pair of them long to exhaust this supply of the *liqueur* of St. Bruno, and as soon as this was done, the prisoner was set at liberty with profuse apologies.

Now and again some of those who attempted to leave the beleaguered city succeeded in their attempt. In one instance a party of four or five Englishmen ran the blockade in the traditional carriage and pair. They had been staying at the Grand Hotel, where another seven or eight visitors, including Labouchere, still remained, together with about the same number of servants to wait upon them; the famous caravanserai--then undoubtedly the largest in Paris--being otherwise quite untenanted. The carriage in which the party I have mentioned took their departure was driven by an old English jockey named Tommy Webb, who had been in France for nearly half a century, and had ridden the winners of some of the very first races started by the French Jockey Club. Misfortune had overtaken him, however, in his declining years, and he had become a mere Parisian "cabby." The party sallied forth from the courtyard of the Grand Hotel, taking with it several huge hampers of provisions and a quantity of other luggage; and all the participants in the attempt seemed to be quite confident of success. But a few hours later they returned in sore disappointment, having been stopped near Neuilly by the French outposts, as they were unprovided with any official *laisser-passer*. A document of that description having been obtained, however, from General Trochu on the morrow, a second attempt was made, and this time the party speedily passed through the French lines. But in trying to penetrate those of the enemy, some melodramatic adventures occurred. It became necessary, indeed, to dodge both the bullets of the Germans and those of the French Francs-tireurs, who paid not the slightest respect either to the Union Jack or to the large white flag which were displayed on either side of Tommy Webb's box-seat. At last, after a variety of mishaps, the party succeeded in parleying with a German cavalry officer, and after they had addressed a written appeal to the Crown Prince of Prussia (who was pleased to grant it), they were taken, blindfolded, to Versailles, where Blumenthal, the Crown Prince's Chief of Staff, asked them for information respecting the actual state of Paris, and then allowed them to proceed on their way.

Captain Johnson, the Queen's Messenger of whom I have already spoken, also contrived to quit Paris again; but the Germans placed him under strict surveillance, and Blumenthal told him that no more Queen's Messengers would be allowed to pass through the German lines. About this same time, however, the English man-servant of one of Trochu's aides-de-camp contrived, not only to reach Saint Germain-en-Laye, where his master's family was residing, but also to return to Paris with messages. This young fellow had cleverly disguised himself as a French peasant, and on the Prefect of Police hearing of his adventures, he sent out several detectives in similar disguises, with instructions to ascertain all they could about the enemy, and report the same to him. Meantime, the Paris Post Office was endeavouring to send out couriers. One of them, named Letoile, managed to get as far as Evreux, in Normandy, and to return to the beleaguered city with a couple of hundred letters. Success also repeatedly attended the efforts of two shrewd fellows named Geme and Brare, who made several journeys to Saint Germain, Triel, and even Orleans. On one occasion they brought as many as seven hundred letters with them on their return to Paris; but between twenty and thirty other couriers failed to get through the

German lines; whilst several others fell into the hands of the enemy, who at once confiscated the correspondence they carried, but did not otherwise molest them.

The difficulty in sending letters out of Paris and in obtaining news from relatives and friends in other parts of France led to all sorts of schemes. The founder and editor of that well-known journal *Le Figaro*, Hippolyte de Villemessant, as he called himself, though I believe that his real Christian name was Auguste, declared in his paper that he would willingly allow his veins to be opened in return for a few lines from his beloved and absent wife. Conjugal affection could scarcely have gone further. Villemessant, however, followed up his touching declaration by announcing that a thousand francs (L40) a week was to be earned by a capable man willing to act as letter-carrier between Paris and the provinces. All who felt qualified for the post were invited to present themselves at the office of *Le Figaro*, which in those days was appropriately located in the Rue Rossini, named, of course, after the illustrious composer who wrote such sprightly music round the theme of Beaumarchais' comedy. As a result of Villemessant's announcement, the street was blocked during the next forty-eight hours by men of all classes, who were all the more eager to earn the aforesaid L40 a week as nearly every kind of work was at a standstill, and the daily stipend of a National Guard amounted only to 1 *s.* 2-1/2 *d.*

It was difficult to choose from among so many candidates, but we were eventually assured that the right man had been found in the person of a retired poacher who knew so well how to circumvent both rural guards and forest guards, that during a career of twenty years or so he had never once been caught *in flagrante delicto*. Expert, moreover, in tracking game, he would also well know how to detect--and to avoid--the tracks of the Prussians. We were therefore invited to confide our correspondence to this sagacious individual, who would undertake to carry it through the German lines and to return with the answers in a week or ten days. The charge for each letter, which was to be of very small weight and dimensions, was fixed at five francs, and it was estimated that the ex-poacher would be able to carry about 200 letters on each journey.

Many people were anxious to try the scheme, but rival newspapers denounced it as being a means of acquainting the Prussians with everything which was occurring in Paris--Villemessant, who they declared had taken bribes from the fallen Empire, being probably one of Bismarck's paid agents. Thus the enterprise speedily collapsed without even being put to the proof. However, the public was successfully exploited by various individuals who attempted to improve on Villemessant's idea, undertaking to send letters out of Paris for a fixed charge, half of which was to be returned to the sender if his letter were not delivered. As none of the letters handed in on these conditions was even entrusted to a messenger, the ingenious authors of this scheme made a handsome profit, politely returning half of the money which they received, but retaining the balance without making the slightest effort to carry out their contract.

Dr. Rampont, a very clever man, who was now our postmaster-general, had already issued a circular bidding us to use the very thinnest paper and the smallest envelopes procurable. There being so many failures among the messengers whom he sent out of Paris with correspondence, the idea of a balloon postal service occurred to him. Although ninety years or so had elapsed since the days of the brothers Montgolfier, aeronautics had really made very little progress. There were no dirigible balloons at all. Dupuy de Lome's first experiments only dated from the siege days, and Renard's dirigible was not devised until the early eighties. We only had the ordinary type of balloon at our disposal; and at the outset of the investment there were certainly not more than half a dozen balloons within our lines. A great city like Paris, however, is not without resources. Everything needed for the construction of balloons could be found there. Gas also was procurable, and we had amongst us quite a number of men expert in the science of ballooning, such as it then was. There was Nadar, there was Tissandier, there were the Godard brothers, Yon, Dartois, and a good many others. Both the Godards and Nadar established balloon factories, which were generally located in our large disused railway stations, such as the Gare du Nord, the Gare d'Orleans, and the Gare Montparnasse; but I also remember visiting one which Nadar installed in the dancing hall called the Elysee Montmartre. Each of these factories provided work for a good many people, and I recollect being particularly struck by the number of women who were employed in balloon-making. Such work was very helpful to them, and Nadar used to say to me that it grieved him to have to turn away so many applicants for employment, for every day ten, twenty, and thirty women would come to implore him to "take them on." Nearly all their usual workrooms were closed; some were reduced to live on charity and only very small allowances, from fivepence to sevenpence a day, were made to the wives and families of National Guards.

But to return to the balloon postal-service which the Government organized, it was at once realized by my father and myself that it could be of little use to us so far as the work for the ***Illustrated London News*** was concerned, on account of the restrictions which were imposed in regard to the size and weight of each letter that might be posted. The weight, indeed, was fixed at no more than three grammes! Now, there were a number of artists working for the ***Illustrated*** in Paris, first and foremost among them being M. Jules Pelcoq, who must personally have supplied two-thirds of the sketches by which the British public was kept acquainted with the many incidents of Parisian siege-life. The weekly diary which I helped my father to compile could be drawn up in small handwriting on very thin, almost transparent paper, and despatched in the ordinary way. But how were we to circumvent the authorities in regard to our sketches, which were often of considerable size, and were always made on fairly substantial paper, the great majority of them being wash-drawings? Further, though I could prepare two or three drafts of our diary or our other "copy" for despatch by successive balloons--to provide for the contingency of one of the latter falling into the hands of the enemy--it seemed absurd that our artists should have to recopy every sketch they made. Fortunately, there was photography, the thought of which brought about a solution of the other difficulty in which we were placed.

I was sent to interview Nadar on the Place Saint Pierre at Montmartre, above which his captive balloon the "Neptune" was oscillating in the September breeze. He was much the same man as I had seen at the Crystal Palace a few years previously, tall, red-haired, and red-shirted. He had begun life as a caricaturist and humorous writer, but by way of buttering his bread had set up in business as a photographer, his establishment on the Boulevard de la Madeleine soon becoming very favourably known. There was still a little "portrait-taking" in Paris during those early siege days. Photographs of the celebrities or notorieties of the hour sold fairly well, and every now and again some National Guard with means was anxious to be photographed in his uniform. But, naturally enough, the business generally had declined. Thus, Nadar was only too pleased to entertain the proposal which I made to him on my father's behalf, this being that every sketch for the ***Illustrated*** should be taken to his establishment and there photographed, so that we might be able to send out copies in at least three successive balloons.

When I broached to Nadar the subject of the postal regulations in regard to the weight and size of letters, he genially replied: "Leave that to me. Your packets need not go through the ordinary post at all--at least, here in Paris. Have them stamped, however, bring them whenever a balloon is about to sail, and I will see that the aeronaut takes them in his pocket. Wherever he alights they will be posted, like the letters in the official bags."

That plan was carried out, and although several balloons were lost or fell within the German lines, only one small packet of sketches, which, on account of urgency, had not been photographed, remained subsequently unaccounted for. In all other instances either the original drawing or one of the photographic copies of it reached London safely.

The very first balloon to leave Paris (in the early days of October) was precisely Nadar's "Neptune," which had originally been intended for purposes of military observation. One day when I was with Nadar on the Place Saint Pierre, he took me up in it. I found the experience a novel but not a pleasing one, for all my life I have had a tendency to vertigo when ascending to any unusual height. I remember that it was a clear day, and that we had a fine bird's-eye view of Paris on the one hand and of the plain of Saint Denis on the other, but I confess that I felt out-of-my element, and was glad to set foot on ***terra firma*** once more.

From that day I was quite content to view the ascent of one and another balloon, without feeling any desire to get out of Paris by its aerial transport service. I must have witnessed the departure of practically all the balloons which left Paris until I myself quitted the city in November. The arrangements made with Nadar were perfected, and something very similar was contrived with the Godard brothers, the upshot being that we were always forewarned whenever it was proposed to send off a balloon. Sometimes we received by messenger, in the evening, an intimation that a balloon would start at daybreak on the morrow. Sometimes we were roused in the small hours of the morning, when everything intended for despatch had to be hastily got together and carried at once to the starting-place, such, for instance, as the Northern or the Orleans railway terminus, both being at a considerable distance from our flat in the Rue de Miromesnil. Those were by no means agreeable walks, especially when the cold weather had set in, as it did early that autumn; and every now and again at the end of the journey one found that it had been made in vain, for, the wind having shifted at the last moment, the departure of the balloon had been postponed. Of course, the only thing to be done was to trudge back home again. There was no omnibus service, all the horses having been requisitioned, and in the latter part of October there were not more than a couple of dozen cabs (drawn by decrepit animals) still plying for hire in all Paris. Thus Shanks's pony was the only means of locomotion.

In the earlier days my father accompanied me on a few of those expeditions, but he soon grew tired of them, particularly as his health became affected by the siege diet. We were together, however, when Gambetta took his departure on October 7, ascending from the Place Saint Pierre in a balloon constructed by Nadar. It had been arranged that he should leave for the provinces, in order to reinforce the three Government delegates who had been despatched thither prior to the investment. Jules Favre, the Foreign Minister, had been previously urged to join those delegates, but would not trust himself to a balloon, and it was thereupon proposed to Gambetta that he should do so. He willingly assented to the suggestion, particularly as he feared that the rest of the country was being overlooked, owing to the prevailing opinion that Paris would suffice to deliver both herself and all the rest of France from the presence of the enemy. Born in April, 1838, he was at this time in his thirty-third year, and full of vigour, as the sequel showed. The delegates whom he was going to join were, as I previously mentioned, very old men, well meaning, no doubt, but incapable of making the great effort which was made by Gambetta in conjunction with Charles de Freycinet, who was just in his prime, being the young Dictator's senior by some ten years.

I can still picture Gambetta's departure, and particularly his appearance on the occasion--his fur cap and his fur coat, which made him look somewhat like a Polish Jew. He had with him his secretary, the devoted Spuller. I cannot recall the name of the aeronaut who was in charge of the balloon, but, if my memory serves me rightly, it was precisely to him that Nadar handed the packet of sketches which failed to reach the ***Illustrated London News***. They must have been lost in the confusion of the aerial voyage, which was marked by several dramatic incidents. Some accounts say that Gambetta evinced no little anxiety during the preparations for the ascent, but to me he appeared to be in a remarkably good humour, as if, indeed, in pleasurable anticipation of what he was about to experience. When, in response to the call of "Lachez tout!" the seamen released the last cables which had hitherto prevented the balloon from rising, and the crowd burst into shouts of "Vive la Republique!" and "Vive Gambetta!" the "youthful statesman," as he was then called, leant over the side of the car and waved his cap in response to the plaudits. [Another balloon, the "George Sand," ascended at the same time, having in its car various officials who were to negotiate the purchase of fire-arms in the United States.]

The journey was eventful, for the Germans repeatedly fired at the balloon. A first attempt at descent had to be abandoned when the car was at an altitude of no more than 200 feet, for at that moment some German soldiers were seen almost immediately beneath it. They fired, and before the balloon could rise again a bullet grazed Gambetta's head. At four o'clock in the afternoon, however, the descent was renewed near Roye in the Somme, when the balloon was caught in an oak-tree, Gambetta at one moment hanging on to the ropes of the car, with his head downward. Some countryfolk came up in great anger, taking the party to be Prussians; but, on learning the truth, they rendered all possible assistance, and Gambetta and his companions repaired to the house of the mayor of the neighbouring village of Tricot. Alluding in after days to his experiences on this journey, the great man said that the earth, as seen by him from the car of the balloon, looked like a huge carpet woven chance-wise with different coloured wools. It did not impress him at all, he added, as it was really nothing but "une vilaine chinoiserie." It was from Rouen, where he arrived on the following day, that he issued the famous proclamation in which he called on France to make a compact with victory or death. On October 9, he joined the other delegates at Tours and took over the post of Minister of War as well as that of Minister of the Interior.

His departure from the capital was celebrated by that clever versifier of the period, Albert Millaud, who contributed to *Le Figaro* an amusing effusion, the first verse of which was to this effect:

> "Gambetta, pale and gloomy,
>   Much wished to go to Tours,
>   But two hundred thousand Prussians
>   In his project made him pause.

> To aid the youthful statesman
> Came the aeronaut Nadar,
> Who sent up the 'Armand Barbes'
> With Gambetta in its car."

Further on came the following lines, supposed to be spoken by Gambetta himself whilst he was gazing at the German lines beneath him--
> "See how the plain is glistening
> With their helmets in a mass!
> Impalement would be dreadful
> On those spikes of polished brass!"

Millaud, who was a Jew, the son, I think--or, at all events, a near relation--of the famous founder of *Le Petit Journal*, the advent of which constituted a great landmark in the history of the French Press--set himself, during several years of his career, to prove the truth of the axiom that in France "tout finit par des chansons." During those anxious siege days he was for ever striving to sound a gay note, something which, for a moment, at all events, might drive dull care away. Here is an English version of some verses which he wrote on Nadar:

> What a strange fellow is Nadar,
>   Photographer and aeronaut!
> He is as clever as Godard.
>   What a strange fellow is Nadar,
> Although, between ourselves, as far
>   As art's concerned he knoweth naught.
> What a strange fellow is Nadar,
>   Photographer and aeronaut!
>
> To guide the course of a balloon
>   His mind conceived the wondrous screw.
> Some day he hopes unto the moon
>   To guide the course of a balloon.

Of 'airy navies' admiral soon,
  We'll see him 'grappling in the blue'--
To guide the course of a balloon
  His mind conceived the wondrous screw.

Up in the kingdom of the air
  He now the foremost rank may claim.
If poor Gambetta when up there,
  Up in the kingdom of the air,
Does not find good cause to stare,
  Why, Nadar will not be to blame.
Up in the kingdom of the air
  He now the foremost rank may claim.

At Ferrieres, above the park,
  Behold him darting through the sky,
Soaring to heaven like a lark.
  At Ferrieres above the park;
Whilst William whispers to Bismarck--
  'Silence, see Nadar there on high!'
At Ferrieres above the park
  Behold him darting through the sky.

Oh, thou more hairy than King Clodion,
  Bearer on high of this report,
Thou yellower than a pure Cambodian,
  And far more daring than King Clodion,
We'll cast thy statue in collodion
  And mount it on a gas retort.
Oh, thou more hairy than King Clodion,
  Bearer on high of this report!

Perhaps it may not be thought too pedantic on my part if I explain that the

King Clodion referred to in Millaud's last verse was the legendary "Clodion the Hairy," a supposed fifth-century leader of the Franks, reputed to be a forerunner of the founder of the, Merovingian dynasty. Nadar's hair, however, was not long like that of **les rois chevelue**, for it was simply a huge curly and somewhat reddish mop. As for his complexion, Millaud's phrase, "yellow as a pure Cambodian," was a happy thought.

These allusions to Millaud's sprightly verse remind me that throughout the siege of Paris the so-called **mot pour rire** was never once lost sight of. At all times and in respect to everything there was a superabundance of jests--jests on the Germans, the National and the Mobile Guard, the fallen dynasty, and the new Republic, the fruitless sorties, the wretched rations, the failing gas, and many other people and things. One of the enemy's generals was said to have remarked one day: "I don't know how to satisfy my men. They complain of hunger, and yet I lead them every morning to the slaughterhouse." At another time a French colonel, of conservative ideas, was said to have replaced the inscription "Liberty, Equality, Fraternity," which he found painted on the walls of his barracks, by the words, "Infantry, Cavalry, Artillery," declaring that the latter were far more likely to free the country of the presence of the hated enemy. As for the "treason" mania, which was very prevalent at this time, it was related that a soldier remarked one day to a comrade: "I am sure that the captain is a traitor!" "Indeed! How's that?" was the prompt rejoinder. "Well," said the suspicious private, "have you not noticed that every time he orders us to march forward we invariably encounter the enemy?"

When Trochu issued a decree incorporating all National Guards, under forty-five years of age, in the marching battalions for duty outside the city, one of these Guards, on being asked how old he was, replied, "six-and-forty." "How is that?" he was asked. "A few weeks ago, you told everybody that you were only thirty-six." "Quite true," rejoined the other, "but what with rampart-duty, demonstrating at the Hotel-de-Ville, short rations, and the cold weather, I feel quite ten years older than I formerly did." When horseflesh became more or less our daily provender, many Parisian **bourgeois** found their health failing. "What is the matter, my dearest?" Madame du Bois du Pont inquired of her husband, when he had collapsed one evening after dinner. "Oh! it is nothing, **mon amie**" he replied; "I dare say I shall soon feel well again, but I used to think myself a better horseman!"

Directly our supply of gas began to fail, the wags insinuated that Henri Rochefort was jubilant, and if you inquired the reason thereof, you were told that owing to the scarcity of gas everybody would be obliged to buy hundreds of "***Lanternes***." We had, of course, plenty of sensations in those days, but if you wished to cap every one of them you merely had to walk into a cafe and ask the waiter for--a railway time-table.

Once before I referred to the caricatures of the period, notably to those libelling the Emperor Napoleon III and the Empress Eugenie, the latter being currently personified as Messalina--or even as something worse, and this, of course, without the faintest shadow of justification. But the caricaturists were not merely concerned with the fallen dynasty. One of the principal cartoonists of the ***Charivari*** at that moment was "Cham," otherwise the Vicomte Amedee de Noe, an old friend of my family's. It was he, by the way, who before the war insisted on my going to a fencing-school, saying: "Look here, if you mean to live in France and be a journalist, you must know how to hold a sword. Come with me to Ruze's. I taught your uncle Frank and his friend Gustave Dore how to fence many years ago, and now I am going to have you taught." Well, in one of his cartoons issued during the siege, Cham (disgusted, like most Frenchmen, at the seeming indifference of Great Britain to the plight in which France found herself) summed up the situation, as he conceived it, by depicting the British Lion licking the boots of Bismarck, who was disguised as Davy Crockett. When my father remonstrated with Cham on the subject, reminding him of his own connexion with England, the indignant caricaturist replied: "Don't speak of it. I have renounced England and all her works." He, like other Frenchmen of the time, contended that we had placed ourselves under great obligations to France at the period of the Crimean War.

Among the best caricatures of the siege-days was one by Daumier, which showed Death appearing to Bismarck in his sleep, and murmuring softly, "Thanks, many thanks." Another idea of the period found expression in a cartoon representing a large mouse-trap, labelled "France," into which a company of mice dressed up as German soldiers were eagerly marching, their officer meanwhile pointing to a cheese fixed inside the trap, and inscribed with the name of Paris. Below the design ran the legend: "Ah! if we could only catch them all in it!" Many, indeed most, of the caricatures of the time did not appear in the so-called humorous journals, but were issued separately at a penny apiece, and were usually coloured by the stencilling process. In one of them, I remember, Bismarck was seen wearing seven-league boots and making ineffectual attempts to step from Versailles to Paris. Another depicted the King of Prussia as Butcher William, knife in hand and attired in the orthodox slaughter-house costume; whilst in yet another design the same monarch was shown urging poor Death, who had fallen exhausted in the snow, with his scythe lying broken beside him, to continue on the march until the last of the French nation should be exterminated. Of caricatures representing cooks in connexion with cats there was no end, the ***lapin de gouttiere*** being in great demand for the dinner-table; and, after Gambetta had left us, there were designs showing the armies of succour (which were to be raised in the provinces) endeavouring to pass ribs of beef, fat geese, legs of mutton, and strings of sausages over several rows of German helmets, gathered round a bastion labelled Paris, whence a famished National Guard, eager for the proffered provisions, was trying to spring, but could not do so owing to the restraining arm of General Trochu.

Before the investment began Paris was already afflicted with a spy mania. Sala's adventure, which I recounted in an earlier chapter, was in a way connected with this delusion, which originated with the cry "We are betrayed!" immediately after the first French reverses. The instances of so-called "spyophobia" were innumerable, and often curious and amusing. There was a slight abatement of the mania when, shortly before the siege, 188,000 Germans were expelled from Paris, leaving behind them only some 700 old folk, invalids, and children, who were unable to obey the Government's decree. But the disease soon revived, and we heard of rag-pickers having their baskets ransacked by zealous National Guards, who imagined that these receptacles might contain secret despatches or contraband ammunition. On another occasion ***Le Figaro*** wickedly suggested that all the blind beggars in Paris were spies, with the result that several poor infirm old creatures were abominably ill-treated. Again, a fugitive sheet called ***Les Nouvelles*** denounced all the English residents as spies. Labouchere was one of those pounced upon by a Parisian mob in consequence of that idiotic denunciation, but as he had the presence of mind to invite those who assailed him to go with him to the nearest police-station, he was speedily released. On two occasions my father and myself were arrested and carried to guard-houses, and in the course of those experiences we discovered that the beautifully engraved but essentially ridiculous British passport, which recited all the honours and dignities of the Secretary of State or the Ambassador delivering it, but gave not the slightest information respecting the person to whom it had been delivered (apart, that is, from his or her name), was of infinitely less value in the eyes of a French officer than a receipt for rent or a Parisian tradesman's bill. [That was forty-three years ago. The British passport, however, remains to-day as unsatisfactory as it was then.]

But let me pass to other instances. One day an unfortunate individual, working in the Paris sewers, was espied by a zealous National Guard, who at once gave the alarm, declaring that there was a German spy in the aforesaid sewers, and that he was depositing bombs there with the intention of blowing up the city. Three hundred Guards at once volunteered their services, stalked the poor workman, and blew him to pieces the next time he popped his head out of a sewer-trap. The mistake was afterwards deplored, but people argued (wrote Mr. Thomas Gibson Bowles, who sent the story to The Morning Post) that it was far better that a hundred innocent Frenchmen should suffer than that a single Prussian should escape. Cham, to whom I previously alluded, old Marshal Vaillant, Mr. O'Sullivan, an American diplomatist, and Alexis Godillot, the French army contractor, were among the many well-known people arrested as spies at one or another moment. A certain Mme: de Beaulieu, who had joined a regiment of Mobiles as a *cantiniere*, was denounced as a spy "because her hands were so white." Another lady, who had installed an ambulance in her house, was carried off to prison on an equally frivolous pretext; and I remember yet another case in which a lady patron of the Societe de Secours aux Blesses was ill-treated. Matters would, however, probably be far worse at the present time, for Paris, with all her apaches and anarchists, now includes in her population even more scum than was the case three-and-forty years ago.

There were, however, a few authentic instances of spying, one case being that of a young fellow whom Etienne Arago, the Mayor of Paris, engaged as a secretary, on the recommendation of Henri Rochefort, but who turned out to be of German extraction, and availed himself of his official position to draw up reports which were forwarded by balloon post to an agent of the German Government in London. I have forgotten the culprit's name, but it will be found, with particulars of his case, in the Paris journals of the siege days. There was, moreover, the Hardt affair, which resulted in the prisoner, a former lieutenant in the Prussian army, being convicted of espionage and shot in the courtyard of the Ecole Militaire.

Co-existent with "spyophobia" there was another craze, that of suspecting any light seen at night-time in an attic or fifth-floor window to be a signal intended for the enemy. Many ludicrous incidents occurred in connexion with this panic. One night an elderly **bourgeois**, who had recently married a charming young woman, was suddenly dragged from his bed by a party of indignant National Guards, and consigned to the watch-house until daybreak. This had been brought about by his wife's maid placing a couple of lighted candles in her window as a signal to the wife's lover that, "master being at home," he was not to come up to the flat that night. On another occasion a poor old lady, who was patriotically depriving herself of sleep in order to make lint for the ambulances, was pounced upon and nearly strangled for exhibiting green and red signals from her window. It turned out, however, that the signals in question were merely the reflections of a harmless though charmingly variegated parrot which was the zealous old dame's sole and faithful companion.

No matter what might be the quarter of Paris in which a presumed signal was observed, the house whence it emanated was at once invaded by National Guards, and perfectly innocent people were often carried off and subjected to ill-treatment. To such proportions did the craze attain that some papers even proposed that the Government should forbid any kind of light whatever, after dark, in any room situated above the second floor, unless the windows of that room were "hermetically sealed"! Most victims of the mania submitted to the mob's invasion of their homes without raising any particular protest; but a volunteer artilleryman, who wrote to the authorities complaining that his rooms had been ransacked in his absence and his aged mother frightened out of her wits, on the pretext that some fusees had been fired from his windows, declared that if there should be any repetition of such an intrusion whilst he was at home he would receive the invaders bayonet and revolver in hand. From that moment similar protests poured into the Hotel-de-Ville, and Trochu ended by issuing a proclamation in which he said: "Under the most frivolous pretexts, numerous houses have been entered, and peaceful citizens have been maltreated. The flags of friendly nations have been powerless to protect the houses where they were displayed. I have ordered an inquiry on the subject, and I now command that all persons guilty of these abusive practices shall be arrested. A special service has been organized in order to prevent the enemy from keeping up any communication with any of its partisans in the city; and I remind everybody that excepting in such instances as are foreseen by the law every citizen's residence is inviolable."

We nowadays hear a great deal about the claims of women, but although the followers of Mrs. Pankhurst have carried on "a sort of a war" for a considerable time past, I have not yet noticed any disposition on their part to "join the colours." Men currently assert that women cannot serve as soldiers. There are, however, many historical instances of women distinguishing themselves in warfare, and modern conditions are even more favourable than former ones for the employment of women as soldiers. There is splendid material to be derived from the golf-girl, the hockey-girl, the factory- and the laundry-girl--all of them active, and in innumerable instances far stronger than many of the narrow-chested, cigarette-smoking "boys" whom we now see in our regiments. Briefly, a day may well come when we shall see many of our so-called superfluous women taking to the "career of arms." However, the attempts made to establish a corps of women-soldiers in Paris, during the German siege, were more amusing than serious. Early in October some hundreds of women demonstrated outside the Hotel-de-Ville, demanding that all the male nurses attached to the ambulances should be replaced by women. The authorities promised to grant that application, and the women next claimed the right to share the dangers of the field with their husbands and their brothers. This question was repeatedly discussed at the public clubs, notably at one in the Rue Pierre Levee, where Louise Michel, the schoolmistress who subsequently participated in the Commune and was transported to New Caledonia, officiated as high-priestess; and at another located at the Triat Gymnasium in the Avenue Montaigne, where as a rule no men were allowed to be present, that is, excepting a certain Citizen Jules Allix, an eccentric elderly survivor of the Republic of '48, at which period he had devised a system of telepathy effected by means of "sympathetic snails."

One Sunday afternoon in October the lady members of this club, being in urgent need of funds, decided to admit men among their audience at the small charge of twopence per head, and on hearing this, my father and myself strolled round to witness the proceedings. They were remarkably lively. Allix, while reading a report respecting the club's progress, began to libel some of the Paris convents, whereupon a National Guard in the audience flatly called him a liar. A terrific hubbub arose, all the women gesticulating and protesting, whilst their ***presidente*** energetically rang her bell, and the interrupter strode towards the platform. He proved to be none other than the Duc de Fitz-James, a lineal descendant of our last Stuart King by Marlborough's sister, Arabella Churchill. He tried to speak, but the many loud screams prevented him from doing so. Some of the women threatened him with violence, whilst a few others thanked him for defending the Church. At last, however, he leapt on the platform, and in doing so overturned both a long table covered with green baize, and the members of the committee who were seated behind it. Jules Allix thereupon sprang at the Duke's throat, they struggled and fell together from the platform, and rolled in the dust below it. It was long before order was restored, but this was finally effected by a good-looking young woman who, addressing the male portion of the audience, exclaimed: "Citizens! if you say another word we will fling what you have paid for admission in your faces, and order you out of doors!"

Business then began, the discussion turning chiefly upon two points, the first being that all women should be armed and do duty on the ramparts, and the second that the women should defend their honour from the attacks of the Germans by means of prussic acid. Allix remarked that it would be very appropriate to employ prussic acid in killing Prussians, and explained to us that this might be effected by means of little indiarubber thimbles which the women would place on their fingers, each thimble being tipped with a small pointed tube containing some of the acid in question. If an amorous Prussian should venture too close to a fair Parisienne, the latter would merely have to hold out her hand and prick him. In another instant he would fall dead! "No matter how many of the enemy may assail her," added Allix, enthusiastically, "she will simply have to prick them one by one, and we shall see her standing still pure and holy in the midst of a circle of corpses!" At these words many of the women in the audience were moved to tears, but the men laughed hilariously.

Such disorderly scenes occurred at this women's club, that the landlord of the Triat Gymnasium at last took possession of the premises again, and the ejected members vainly endeavoured to find accommodation elsewhere. Nevertheless, another scheme for organizing an armed force of women was started, and one day, on observing on the walls of Paris a green placard which announced the formation of a "Legion of Amazons of the Seine," I repaired to the Rue Turbigo, where this Legion's enlistment office had been opened. After making my way up a staircase crowded with recruits, who were mostly muscular women from five-and-twenty to forty years of age, the older ones sometimes being unduly stout, and not one of them, in my youthful opinion, at all good-looking, I managed to squeeze my way into the private office of the projector of the Legion, or, as he called himself, its "Provisional Chef de Bataillon." He was a wiry little man, with a grey moustache and a military bearing, and answered to the name of Felix Belly. A year or two previously he had unjustly incurred a great deal of ridicule in Paris, owing to his attempts to float a Panama Canal scheme. Only five years after the war, however, the same idea was taken up by Ferdinand de Lesseps, and French folk, who had laughed it to scorn in Belly's time, proved only too ready to fling their hard-earned savings into the bottomless gulf of Lesseps' enterprise.

I remember having a long chat with Belly, who was most enthusiastic respecting his proposed Amazons. They were to defend the ramparts and barricades of Paris, said he, being armed with light guns carrying some 200 yards; and their costume, a model of which was shown me, was to consist of black trousers with orange-coloured stripes down the outer seams, black blouses with capes, and black kepis, also with orange trimmings. Further, each woman was to carry a cartridge-box attached to a shoulder-belt. It was hoped that the first battalion would muster quite 1200 women, divided into eight companies of 150 each. There was to be a special medical service, and although the chief doctor would be a man, it was hoped to secure several assistant doctors of the female sex. Little M. Belly dwelt particularly on the fact that only women of unexceptionable moral character would be allowed to join the force, all recruits having to supply certificates from the Commissaries of Police of their districts, as well as the consent of their nearest connexions, such as their fathers or their husbands. "Now, listen to this," added M. Belly, enthusiastically, as he went to a piano which I was surprised to find, standing in a recruiting office; and seating himself at the instrument, he played for my especial benefit the stirring strains of a new, specially-commissioned battle-song, which, said he, "we intend to call the Marseillaise of the Paris Amazons!"

Unfortunately for M. Belly, all his fine projects and preparations collapsed a few days afterwards, owing to the intervention of the police, who raided the premises in the Rue Turbigo, and carried off all the papers they found there. They justified these summary proceedings on the ground that General Trochu had forbidden the formation of any more free corps, and that M. Belly had unduly taken fees from his recruits. I believe, however, that the latter statement was incorrect. At all events, no further proceedings were instituted. But the raid sufficed to kill M. Belly's cherished scheme, which naturally supplied the caricaturists of the time with more or less brilliant ideas. One cartoon represented the German army surrendering *en masse* to a mere battalion of the Beauties of Paris.

VI
MORE ABOUT THE SIEGE DAYS

Reconnaissances and Sorties--Casimir-Perier at Bagneux--Some of the Paris Clubs--Demonstrations at the Hotel-de-Ville--The Cannon Craze--The Fall of Metz foreshadowed--Le Bourget taken by the French--The Government's Policy of Concealment--The Germans recapture Le Bourget--Thiers, the Armistice, and Bazaine's Capitulation--The Rising of October 31--The Peril and the Rescue of the Government--Armistice and Peace Conditions--The Great Question of Rations--Personal Experiences respecting Food--My father, in failing Health, decides to leave Paris.

After the engagement of Chatillon, fought on September 19, various reconnaissances were carried out by the army of Paris. In the first of these General Vinoy secured possession of the plateau of Villejuif, east of Chatillon, on the south side of the city. Next, the Germans had to retire from Pierre-fitte, a village in advance of Saint Denis on the northern side. There were subsequent reconnaissances in the direction of Neuilly-sur-Marne and the Plateau d'Avron, east of Paris; and on Michaelmas Day an engagement was fought at L'Hay and Chevilly, on the south. But the archangel did not on this occasion favour the French, who were repulsed, one of their commanders, the veteran brigadier Guilhem, being killed. A fight at Chatillon on October 12 was followed on the morrow by a more serious action at Bagneux, on the verge of the Chatillon plateau. During this engagement the Mobiles from the Burgundian Cote d'Or made a desperate attack on a German barricade bristling with guns, reinforced by infantry, and also protected by a number of sharp-shooters installed in the adjacent village-houses, whose window-shutters and walls had been loop-holed. During the encounter, the commander of the Mobiles, the Comte de Dampierre, a well-known member of the French Jockey Club, fell mortally wounded whilst urging on his men, but was succoured by a captain of the Mobiles of the Aube, who afterwards assumed the chief command, and, by a rapid flanking movement, was able to carry the barricade. This captain was Jean Casimir-Perier, who, in later years, became President of the Republic. He was rewarded for his gallantry with the Cross of the Legion of Honour. Nevertheless, the French success was only momentary.

That same night the sky westward of Paris was illumined by a great ruddy glare. The famous Chateau of Saint Cloud, associated with many memories of the old *regime* and both the Empires, was seen to be on fire. The cause of the conflagration has never been precisely ascertained. Present-day French reference-books still declare that the destruction of the chateau was the wilful act of the Germans, who undoubtedly occupied Saint Cloud; but German authorities invariably maintain that the fire was caused by a shell from the French fortress of Mont Valerien. Many of the sumptuous contents of the Chateau of Saint Cloud--the fatal spot where that same war had been decided on--were consumed by the flames, while the remainder were appropriated by the Germans as plunder. Many very valuable paintings of the period of Louis XIV were undoubtedly destroyed.

By this time the word "reconnaissance," as applied to the engagements fought in the environs of the city, had become odious to the Parisians, who began to clamour for a real "sortie." Trochu, it may be said, had at this period no idea of being able to break out of Paris. In fact, he had no desire to do so. His object in all the earlier military operations of the siege was simply to enlarge the circle of investment, in the hope of thereby placing the Germans in a difficulty, of which he might subsequently take advantage. An attack which General Ducrot made, with a few thousand men, on the German position near La Malmaison, west of Paris, was the first action which was officially described as a "sortie." It took place on October 21, but the success which at first attended Ducrot's efforts was turned into a repulse by the arrival of German reinforcements, the affair ending with a loss of some four hundred killed and wounded on the French side, apart from that of another hundred men who were taken prisoners by the enemy.

This kind of thing did not appeal to the many frequenters of the public clubs which were established in the different quarters of Paris. All theatrical performances had ceased there, and there was no more dancing. Even the concerts and readings given in aid of the funds for the wounded were few and far between. Thus, if a Parisian did not care to while away his evening in a cafe, his only resource was to betake himself to one of the clubs. Those held at the Folies-Bergere music-hall, the Valentino dancing-hall, the Porte St. Martin theatre, and the hall of the College de France, were mostly frequented by moderate Republicans, and attempts were often made there to discuss the situation in a sensible manner. But folly, even insanity, reigned at many of the other clubs, where men like Felix Pyat, Auguste Blanqui, Charles Delescluze, Gustave Flourens, and the three Ms--Megy, Mottu, and Milliere--raved and ranted. Go where you would, you found a club. There was that of La Reine Blanche at Montmartre and that of the Salle Favie at Belleville; there was the club de la Vengeance on the Boulevard Rochechouart, the Club des Montagnards on the Boulevard de Strasbourg, the Club des Etats-Unis d'Europe in the Rue Cadet, the Club du Preaux-Clercs in the Rue du Bac, the Club de la Cour des Miracles on the Ile Saint Louis, and twenty or thirty others of lesser note. At times the demagogues who perorated from the tribunes at these gatherings, brought forward proposals which seemed to have emanated from some madhouse, but which were nevertheless hailed with delirious applause by their infatuated audiences. Occasionally new engines of destruction were advocated--so-called "Satan-fusees," or pumps discharging flaming petroleum! Another speaker conceived the brilliant idea of keeping all the wild beasts in the Jardin des Plantes on short commons for some days, then removing them from Paris at the next sortie, and casting them adrift among the enemy. Yet another imbecile suggested that the water of the Seine and the Marne should be poisoned, regardless of, the fact that, in any such event, the Parisians would suffer quite as much as the enemy.

But the malcontents were not satisfied with ranting at the clubs. On October 2, Paris became very gloomy, for we then received from outside the news that both Toul and Strasbourg had surrendered. Three days later, Gustave Flourens gathered the National Guards of Belleville together and marched with them on the Hotel-de-Ville, where he called upon the Government to renounce the military tactics of the Empire which had set one Frenchman against three Germans, to decree a *levee en masse*, to make frequent sorties with the National Guards, to arm the latter with chassepots, and to establish at once a municipal "Commune of Paris." On the subject of sorties the Government promised to conform to the general desire, and to allow the National Guards to co-operate with the regular army as soon as they should know how to fight and escape being simply butchered. To other demands made by Flourens, evasive replies were returned, whereupon he indignantly resigned his command of the Belleville men, but resumed it at their urgent request.

The affair somewhat alarmed the Government, who issued a proclamation forbidding armed demonstrations, and, far from consenting to the establishment of any Commune, postponed the ordinary municipal elections which were soon to have taken place. To this the Reds retorted by making yet another demonstration, which my father and myself witnessed. Thousands of people, many of them being armed National Guards, assembled on the Place de l'Hotel de Ville, shouting: "La Commune! La Commune! Nous voulons la Commune!" But the authorities had received warning of their opponents' intentions, and the Hotel-de-Ville was entirely surrounded by National Guards belonging to loyal battalions, behind whom, moreover, was stationed a force of trusty Mobile Guards, whose bayonets were already fixed. Thus no attempt could be made to raid the Hotel-de-Ville with any chance of success. Further, several other contingents of loyal National Guards arrived on the square, and helped to check the demonstrators.

While gazing on the scene from an upper window of the Cafe de la Garde Nationale, at one corner of the square, I suddenly saw Trochu ride out of the Government building, as it then was, followed by a couple of aides-de-camp, His appearance was attended by a fresh uproar. The yells of "La Commune! La Commune!" rose more loudly than ever, but were now answered by determined shouts of "Vive la Republique! Vive Trochu! Vive le Gouvernement!" whilst the drums beat, the trumpets sounded, and all the Government forces presented arms. The general rode up and down the lines, returning the salute, amidst prolonged acclamations, and presently his colleagues, Jules Favre and the others--excepting, of course, Gambetta, who had already left Paris--also came out of the Hotel-de-Ville and received an enthusiastic greeting from their supporters. For the time, the Reds were absolutely defeated, and in order to prevent similar disturbances in future, Keratry, the Prefect of Police, wished to arrest Flourens, Blanqui, Milliere, and others, which suggestion was countenanced by Trochu, but opposed by Rochefort and Etienne Arago. A few days later, Rochefort patched up a brief outward reconciliation between the contending parties. Nevertheless, it was evident that Paris was already sharply divided, both on the question of its defence and on that of its internal government.

On October 23, some of the National Guards were at last allowed to join in a sortie. They were men from Montmartre, and the action, or rather skirmish, in which they participated took place at Villemomble, east of Paris, the guards behaving fairly well under fire, and having five of their number wounded. Patriotism was now taking another form in the city. There was a loud cry for cannons, more and more cannons. The Government replied that 227 mitrailleuses with over 800,000 cartridges, 50 mortars, 400 carriages for siege guns, several of the latter ordnance, and 300 seven-centimetre guns carrying 8600 yards, together with half a million shells of different sizes, had already been ordered, and in part delivered. Nevertheless, public subscriptions were started in order to provide another 1500 cannon, large sums being contributed to the fund by public bodies and business firms. Not only did the newspapers offer to collect small subscriptions, but stalls were set up for that purpose in different parts of Paris, as in the time of the first Revolution, and people there tendered their contributions, the women often offering jewelry in lieu of money. Trochu, however, deprecated the movement. There were already plenty of guns, said he; what he required was gunners to serve them.

On October 25 we heard of the fall of the little town of Chateaudun in Eure-et-Loir, after a gallant resistance offered by 1200 National Guards and Francs-tireurs against 6000 German infantry, a regiment of cavalry, and four field batteries. Von Wittich, the German general, punished that resistance by setting fire to Chateaudun and a couple of adjacent villages, and his men, moreover, massacred a number of non-combatant civilians. Nevertheless, the courage shown by the people of Chateaudun revived the hopes of the Parisians and strengthened their resolution to brave every hardship rather than surrender. Two days later, however, Felix Pyat's journal *Le Combat* published, within a mourning border, the following announcement: "It is a sure and certain fact that the Government of National Defence retains in its possession a State secret, which we denounce to an indignant country as high treason. Marshal Bazaine has sent a colonel to the camp of the King of Prussia to treat for the surrender of Metz and for Peace in the name of Napoleon III."

The news seemed incredible, and, indeed, at the first moment, very few people believed it. If it were true, however, Prince Frederick Charles's forces, released from the siege of Metz, would evidently be able to march against D'Aurelle de Paladines' army of the Loire just when it was hoped that the latter would overthrow the Bavarians under Von der Tann and hasten to the relief of Paris. But people argued that Bazaine was surely as good a patriot as Bourbaki, who, it was already known, had escaped from Metz and offered his sword to the National Defence in the provinces. A number of indignant citizens hastened to the office of *Le Combat* in order to seize Pyat and consign him to durance, but he was an adept in the art of escaping arrest, and contrived to get away by a back door. At the Hotel-de-Ville Rochefort, on being interviewed, described Pyat as a cur, and declared that there was no truth whatever in his story. Public confidence completely revived on the following morning, when the official journal formally declared that Metz had not capitulated; and, in the evening, Paris became quite jubilant at the news that General Carre de Bellemare, who commanded on the north side of the city, had wrested from the Germans the position of Le Bourget, lying to the east of Saint Denis.

Pyat, however, though he remained in hiding, clung to his story respecting Metz, stating in *Le Combat*, on October 29, that the news had been communicated to him by Gustave Flourens, who had derived it from Rochefort, by whom it was now impudently denied. It subsequently became known, moreover, that another member of the Government, Eugene Pelletan, had confided the same intelligence to Commander Longuet, of the National Guard. It appears that it had originally been derived from certain members of the Red Cross Society, who, when it became necessary to bury the dead and tend the wounded after an encounter in the environs of Paris, often came in contact with the Germans. The report was, of course, limited to the statement that Bazaine was negotiating a surrender, not that he had actually capitulated. The Government's denial of it can only be described as a quibble--of the kind to which at times even British Governments stoop when faced by inconvenient questions in the House of Commons--and, as we shall soon see, the gentlemen of the National Defence spent a *tres mauvais quart d'heure* as a result of the *suppressio veri* of which they were guilty. Similar "bad quarters of an hour" have fallen upon politicians in other countries, including our own, under somewhat similar circumstances.

On October 30, Thiers, after travelling all over Europe, pleading his country's cause at every great Court, arrived in Paris with a safe-conduct from Bismarck, in order to lay before the Government certain proposals for an armistice, which Russia, Great Britain, Austria, and Italy were prepared to support. And alas! he also brought with him the news that Metz had actually fallen--having capitulated, indeed, on October 27, the very day on which Pyat had issued his announcement. There was consternation at the Hotel-de-Ville when this became known, and the gentlemen of the Government deeply but vainly regretted the futile tactics to which they had so foolishly stooped. To make matters worse, we received in the evening intelligence that the Germans had driven Carre de Bellemare's men out of Le Bourget after some brief but desperate fighting. Trochu declared that he had no need of the Bourget position, that it had never entered into his scheme of defence, and that Bellemare had been unduly zealous in attacking and taking it from the Germans. If that were the case, however, why had not the Governor of Paris ordered Le Bourget to be evacuated immediately after its capture, without waiting for the Germans to re-take it at the bayonet's point? Under the circumstances, the Parisians were naturally exasperated. Tumultuous were the scenes on the Boulevards that evening, and vehement and threatening were the speeches at the clubs.

When the Parisians quitted their homes on the morning of Monday, the 31st, they found the city placarded with two official notices, one respecting the arrival of Thiers and the proposals for an armistice, and the second acknowledging the disaster of Metz. A hurricane of indignation at once swept through the city. Le Bourget lost! Metz taken! Proposals for an armistice with the detested Prussians entertained! Could Trochu's plan and Bazaine's plan be synonymous, then? The one word "Treachery!" was on every lip. When noon arrived the Place de l'Hotel-de-Ville was crowded with indignant people. Deputations, composed chiefly of officers of the National Guard, interviewed the Government, and were by no means satisfied with the replies which they received from Jules Ferry and others. Meantime, the crowd on the square was increasing in numbers. Several members of the Government attempted to prevail on it to disperse; but no heed was paid to them.

At last a free corps commanded by Tibaldi, an Italian conspirator of Imperial days, effected an entrance into the Hotel-de-Ville, followed by a good many of the mob. In the throne-room they were met by Jules Favre, whose attempts to address them failed, the shouts of "La Commune! La Commune!" speedily drowning his voice. Meantime, two shots were fired by somebody on the square, a window was broken, and the cry of the invaders became "To arms! to arms! Our brothers are being butchered!" In vain did Trochu and Rochefort endeavour to stem the tide of invasion. In vain, also, did the Government, assembled in the council-room, offer to submit itself to the suffrages of the citizens, to grant the election of municipal councillors, and to promise that no armistice should be signed without consulting the population. The mob pressed on through one room after another, smashing tables, desks, and windows on their way, and all at once the very apartment where the Government were deliberating was, in its turn, invaded, several officers of the National Guard, subsequently prominent at the time of the Commune, heading the intruders and demanding the election of a Commune and the appointment of a new administration under the presidency of Dorian, the popular Minister of Public Works.

Amidst the ensuing confusion, M. Ernest Picard, a very corpulent, jovial-looking advocate, who was at the head of the department of Finances, contrived to escape; but all his colleagues were surrounded, insulted by the invaders, and summoned to resign their posts. They refused to do so, and the wrangle was still at its height when Gustave Flourens and his Belleville sharpshooters reached the Place de l'Hotel-de-Ville. Flourens entered the building, which at this moment was occupied by some seven or eight thousand men, and proposed that the Commune should be elected by acclamation. This was agreed upon; Dorian's name--though, by the way, he was a wealthy ironmaster, and in no sense a Communard--being put at the head of the list. This included Flourens himself, Victor Hugo, Louis Blanc, Raspail, Mottu, Delescluze, Blanqui, Ledru-Rollin, Rochefort, Felix Pyat, Ranvier, and Avrial. Then Flourens, in his turn, entered the council-room, climbed on to the table, and summoned the captive members of the Government to resign; Again they refused to do so, and were therefore placed under arrest. Jules Ferry and Emmanuel Arago managed to escape, however, and some friendly National Guards succeeded in entering the building and carrying off General Trochu. Ernest Picard, meanwhile, had been very active in devising plans for the recapture of the Hotel-de-Ville and providing for the safety of various Government departments. Thus, when Flourens sent a lieutenant to the treasury demanding the immediate payment of L600,000(!) the request was refused, and the messenger placed under arrest. Nevertheless, the insurgents made themselves masters of several district town-halls.

But Jules Ferry was collecting the loyal National Guards together, and at half-past eleven o'clock that night they and some Mobiles marched on the Hotel-de-Ville. The military force which had been left there by the insurgents was not large. A parley ensued, and while it was still in progress, an entire battalion of Mobiles effected an entry by a subterranean passage leading from an adjacent barracks. Delescluze and Flourens then tried to arrange terms with Dorian, but Jules Ferry would accept no conditions. The imprisoned members of the Government were released, and the insurgent leaders compelled to retire. About this time Trochu and Ducrot arrived on the scene, and between three and four o'clock in the morning I saw them pass the Government forces in review on the square.

On the following day, all the alleged conventions between M. Dorian and the Red Republican leaders were disavowed. There was, however, a conflict of opinion as to whether those leaders should be arrested or not, some members of the Government admitting that they had promised Delescluze and others that they should not be prosecuted. In consequence of this dispute, several officials, including Edmond Adam, Keratry's successor as Prefect of Police, resigned their functions. A few days later, twenty-one of the insurgent leaders were arrested, Pyat being among them, though nothing was done in regard to Flourens and Blanqui, both of whom had figured prominently in the affair.

On November 3 we had a plebiscitum, the question put to the Parisians being: "Does the population of Paris, yes or no, maintain the powers of the Government of National Defence?" So far as the civilian element--which included the National Guards--was concerned, the ballot resulted as follows: Voting "Yes," 321,373 citizens; voting "No," 53,585 citizens. The vote of the army, inclusive of the Mobile Guard, was even more pronounced: "Yes," 236,623; "No," 9063, Thus the general result was 557,996 votes in favour of the Government, and 62,638 against it--the proportion being 9 to 1 for the entire male population of the invested circle. This naturally rendered the authorities jubilant.

But the affair of October 31 had deplorable consequences with regard to the armistice negotiations. This explosion of sedition alarmed the German authorities. They lost confidence in the power of the National Defence to carry out such terms as might be stipulated, and, finally, Bismarck refused to allow Paris to be revictualled during the period requisite for the election of a legislative assembly--which was to have decided the question of peace or war--unless one fort, and possibly more than one, were surrendered to him. Thiers and Favre could not accept such a condition, and thus the negotiations were broken off. Before Thiers quitted Bismarck, however, the latter significantly told him that the terms of peace at that juncture would be the cession of Alsace to Germany, and the payment of three milliards of francs as an indemnity; but that after the fall of Paris the terms would be the cession of both Alsace and Lorraine, and a payment of five milliards.

In the earlier days of the siege there was no rationing of provisions, though the price of meat was fixed by Government decree. At the end of September, however, the authorities decided to limit the supply to a maximum of 500 oxen and 4000 sheep per diem. It was decided also that the butchers' shops should only open on every fourth day, when four days' meat should be distributed at the official prices. During the earlier period the daily ration ranged from 80 to 100 grammes, that is, about 2-2/3 oz. to 3-1/3 oz. in weight, one-fifth part of it being bone in the case of beef, though, with respect to mutton, the butchers were forbidden to make up the weight with any bones which did not adhere to the meat. At the outset of the siege only twenty or thirty horses were slaughtered each day; but on September 30 the number had risen to 275. A week later there were nearly thirty shops in Paris where horseflesh was exclusively sold, and scarcely a day elapsed without an increase in their number. Eventually horseflesh became virtually the only meat procurable by all classes of the besieged, but in the earlier period it was patronized chiefly by the poorer folk, the prices fixed for it by authority being naturally lower than those edicted for beef and mutton.

With regard to the arrangements made by my father and myself respecting food, they were, in the earlier days of the siege, very simple. We were keeping no servant at our flat in the Rue de Miromesnil. The concierge of the house, and his wife, did all such work as we required. This concierge, whose name was Saby, had been a Zouave, and had acted as orderly to his captain in Algeria. He was personally expert in the art of preparing "couscoussou" and other Algerian dishes, and his wife was a thoroughly good cook *a la francaise*. Directly meat was rationed, Saby said to me: "The allowance is very small; you and Monsieur votre pere will be able to eat a good deal more than that. Now, some of the poorer folk cannot afford to pay for butchers' meat, they are contented with horseflesh, which is not yet rationed, and are willing to sell their ration cards. You can well afford to buy one or two of them, and in that manner secure extra allowances of beef or mutton."

That plan was adopted, and for a time everything went on satisfactorily. On a few occasions I joined the queue outside our butcher's in the Rue de Penthievre, and waited an hour or two to secure our share of meat, We were not over-crowded in that part of Paris. A great many members of the aristocracy and bourgeoisie, who usually dwelt there, had left the city with their families and servants prior to the investment; and thus the queues and the waits were not so long as in the poorer and more densely populated districts. Saby, however, often procured our meat himself or employed somebody else to do so, for women were heartily glad of the opportunity to earn half a franc or so by acting as deputy for other people.

We had secured a small supply of tinned provisions, and would have increased it if the prices had not gone up by leaps and bounds, in such wise that a tin of corned beef or something similar, which one saw priced in the morning at about 5 francs, was labelled 20 francs a few hours later. Dry beans and peas were still easily procurable, but fresh vegetables at once became both rare and costly. Potatoes failed us at an early date. On the other hand, jam and preserved fruit could be readily obtained at the grocer's at the corner of our street. The bread slowly deteriorated in quality, but was still very fair down to the date of my departure from Paris (November 8 [See the following chapter.]). Milk and butter, however, became rare--the former being reserved for the hospitals, the ambulances, the mothers of infants, and so forth--whilst one sighed in vain for a bit of Gruyere, Roquefort, Port-Salut, Brie, or indeed any other cheese.

Saby, who was a very shrewd fellow, had conceived a brilliant idea before the siege actually began. The Chateaubriands having quitted the house and removed their horses from the stables, he took possession of the latter, purchased some rabbits--several does and a couple of bucks--laid in a supply of food for them, and resolved to make his fortune by rabbit-breeding. He did not quite effect his purpose, but rabbits are so prolific that he was repaid many times over for the trouble which he took in rearing them. For some time he kept the affair quite secret. More than once I saw him going in and out of the stables, without guessing the reason; but one morning, having occasion to speak to him, I followed him and discovered the truth. He certainly bred several scores of rabbits during the course of the siege, merely ceasing to do so when he found it impossible to continue feeding the animals. On two or three occasions we paid him ten francs or so for a rabbit, and that was certainly "most-favoured-nation treatment;" for, at the same period, he was charging twenty and twenty-five francs to other people. Cooks, with whom he communicated, came to him from mansions both near and far. He sold quite a number of rabbits to Baron Alphonse de Rothschild's *chef* at the rate of L2 apiece, and others to Count Pillet-Will at about the same price, so that, so far as his pockets were concerned, he in no wise suffered by the siege of Paris.

We were blessed with an abundance of charcoal for cooking purposes, and of coals and wood for ordinary fires, having at our disposal not only the store in our own cellars, but that which the Chateaubriand family had left behind. The cold weather set in very soon, and firing was speedily in great demand. Our artist Jules Pelcoq, who lived in the Rue Lepic at Montmartre, found himself reduced to great straits in this respect, nothing being procurable at the dealers' excepting virtually green wood which had been felled a short time previously in the Bois de Boulogne and Bois de Vincennes. On a couple of occasions Pelcoq and I carried some coals in bags to his flat, and my father, being anxious for his comfort, wished to provide him with a larger supply. Saby was therefore requisitioned to procure a man who would undertake to convey some coals in a handcart to Montmartre. The man was found, and paid for his services in advance. But alas! the coals never reached poor Pelcoq. When we next saw the man who had been engaged, he told us that he had been intercepted on his way by some National Guards, who had asked him what his load was, and, on discovering that it consisted of coals, had promptly confiscated them and the barrow also, dragging the latter to some bivouac on the ramparts. I have always doubted that story, however, and incline to the opinion that our improvised porter had simply sold the coals and pocketed the proceeds.

One day, early in November, when our allowance of beef or mutton was growing small by degrees and beautifully less and infrequent--horseflesh becoming more and more *en evidence* at the butchers' shops, [Only 1-1/2 oz. of beef or mutton was now allowed per diem, but in lieu thereof you could obtain 1/4 lb. of horseflesh.] I had occasion to call on one of our artists, Blanchard, who lived in the Faubourg Saint Germain. When we had finished our business he said to me: "Ernest, it is my *fete* day. I am going to have a superb dinner. My brother-in-law, who is an official of the Eastern Railway Line, is giving it in my honour. Come with me; I invite you." We thereupon went to his brother-in-law's flat, where I was most cordially received, and before long we sat down at table in a warm and well-lighted dining-room, the company consisting of two ladies and three men, myself included.

The soup, I think, had been prepared from horseflesh with the addition of a little Liebig's extract of meat; but it was followed by a beautiful leg of mutton, with beans a la Bretonne and--potatoes! I had not tasted a potato for weeks past, for in vain had the ingenious Saby endeavoured to procure some. But the crowning triumph of the evening was the appearance of a huge piece of Gruyere cheese, which at that time was not to be seen in a single shop in Paris. Even Chevet, that renowned purveyor of dainties, had declared that he had none.

My surprise in presence of the cheese and the potatoes being evident, Blanchard's brother-in-law blandly informed me that he had stolen them. "There is no doubt," said he, "that many tradespeople hold secret stores of one thing and another, but wish prices to rise still higher than they are before they produce them. I did not, however, take those potatoes or that cheese from any shopkeeper's cellar. But, in the store-places of the railway company to which I belong, there are tons and tons of provisions, including both cheese and potatoes, for which the consignees never apply, preferring, as they do, to leave them there until famine prices are reached. Well, I have helped myself to just a few things, so as to give Blanchard a good dinner this evening. As for the leg of mutton, I bribed the butcher--not with money, he might have refused it--but with cheese and potatoes, and it was fair exchange." When I returned home that evening I carried in my pockets more than half a pound of Gruyere and two or three pounds of potatoes, which my father heartily welcomed. The truth about the provisions which were still stored at some of the railway depots was soon afterwards revealed to the authorities.

Although my father was then only fifty years of age and had plenty of nervous energy, his health was at least momentarily failing him. He had led an extremely strenuous life ever since his twentieth year, when my grandfather's death had cast great responsibilities on him. He had also suffered from illnesses which required that he should have an ample supply of nourishing food. So long as a fair amount of ordinary butcher's meat could be procured, he did not complain; but when it came to eating horseflesh two or three times a week he could not undertake it, although, only a year or two previously, he had attended a great ***banquet hippophagique*** given in Paris, and had then even written favourably of ***viande de cheval*** in an article he prepared on the subject. For my own part, being a mere lad, I had a lad's appetite and stomach, and I did not find horseflesh so much amiss, particularly as prepared with garlic and other savouries by Mme. Saby's expert hands. But, after a day or two, my father refused to touch it. For three days, I remember, he tried to live on bread, jam, and preserved fruit; but the sweetness of such a diet became nauseous to him--even as it became nauseous to our soldiers when the authorities bombarded them with jam in South Africa. It was very difficult to provide something to my father's taste; there was no poultry and there were no eggs. It was at this time that Saby sold us a few rabbits, but, again, ***toujours lapin*** was not satisfactory.

People were now beginning to partake of sundry strange things. Bats were certainly eaten before the siege ended, though by no means in such quantities as some have asserted. However, there were already places where dogs and cats, skinned and prepared for cooking, were openly displayed for sale. Labouchere related, also, that on going one day into a restaurant and seeing ***cochon de lait***, otherwise sucking-pig, mentioned in the menu, he summoned the waiter and cross-questioned him on the subject, as he greatly doubted whether there were any sucking-pigs in all Paris. "Is it sucking-pig?" he asked the waiter. "Yes, monsieur," the man replied. But Labby was not convinced. "Is it a little pig?" he inquired. "Yes, monsieur, quite a little one." "Is it a young pig?" pursued Labby, who was still dubious. The waiter hesitated, and at last replied, "Well, I cannot be sure, monsieur, if it is quite young." "But it must be young if it is little, as you say. Come, what is it, tell me?" "Monsieur, it is a guinea-pig!" Labby bounded from his chair, took his hat, and fled. He did not feel equal to guinea-pig, although he was very hungry.

Perhaps, however, Labouchere's best story of those days was that of the old couple who, all other resources failing them, were at last compelled to sacrifice their little pet dog. It came up to table nicely roasted, and they both looked at it for a moment with a sigh. Then Monsieur summoned up his courage and helped Madame to the tender viand. She heaved another sigh, but, making a virtue of necessity, began to eat, and whilst she was doing so she every now and then deposited a little bone on the edge of her plate. There was quite a collection of little bones there by the time she had finished, and as she leant back in her chair and contemplated them she suddenly exclaimed: "Poor little Toto! If he had only been alive what a fine treat he would have had!"

To return, however, to my father and myself, I must mention that there was a little English tavern and eating-house in the Rue de Miromesnil, kept by a man named Lark, with whom I had some acquaintance. We occasionally procured English ale from him, and one day, late in October, when I was passing his establishment, he said to me: "How is your father? He seems to be looking poorly. Aren't you going to leave with the others?" I inquired of Lark what he meant by his last question; whereupon he told me that if I went to the Embassy I should see a notice in the consular office respecting the departure of British subjects, arrangements having been made to enable all who desired to quit Paris to do so. I took the hint and read the notice, which ran as Lark had stated, with this addendum: "The Embassy *cannot*, however, charge itself with the expense of assisting British subjects to leave Paris." Forthwith I returned home and imparted the information I had obtained to my father.

Beyond setting up that notice in the Consul's office, the Embassy took no steps to acquaint British subjects generally with the opportunity which was offered them to escape bombardment and famine. It is true that it was in touch with the British Charitable Fund and that the latter made the matter known to sundry applicants for assistance. But the British colony still numbered 1000 people, hundreds of whom would have availed themselves of this opportunity had it only come to their knowledge. My father speedily made up his mind to quit the city, and during the next few days arrangements were made with our artists and others so that the interests of the ***Illustrated London News*** might in no degree suffer by his absence. Our system had long been perfected, and everything worked well after our departure. I may add here, because it will explain something which follows, that my father distributed all the money he could possibly spare among those whom he left behind, in such wise that on quitting Paris we had comparatively little, and--as the sequel showed--insufficient money with us. But it was thought that we should be able to secure whatever we might require on arriving at Versailles.

VII
FROM PARIS TO VERSAILLES

I leave Paris with my Father--Jules Favre, Wodehouse, and Washburne--Through Charenton to Creteil--At the Outposts--First Glimpses of the Germans--A Subscription to shoot the King of Prussia--The Road to Brie-Comte-Robert--Billets for the Night--Chats with German Soldiers--The Difficulty with the Poorer Refugees--Mr. Wodehouse and my Father--On the Way to Corbeil--A Franco-German Flirtation--Affairs at Corbeil--On the Road in the Rain--Longjumeau--A Snow-storm--The Peasant of Champlan-- Arrival at Versailles.

Since Lord Lyons's departure from Paris, the Embassy had remained in the charge of the second Secretary, Mr. Wodehouse, and the Vice-Consul. In response to the notice set up in the latter's office, and circulated also among a tithe of the community by the British Charitable Fund, it was arranged that sixty or seventy persons should accompany the Secretary and Vice-Consul out of the city, the military attachee, Colonel Claremont, alone remaining there. The provision which the Charitable Fund made for the poorer folk consisted of a donation of L4 to each person, together with some three pounds of biscuits and a few ounces of chocolate to munch on the way. No means of transport, however, were provided for these people, though it was known that we should have to proceed to Versailles--where the German headquarters were installed--by a very circuitous route, and that the railway lines were out.

We were to have left on November 2, at the same time as a number of Americans, Russians, and others, and it had been arranged that everybody should meet at an early hour that morning at the Charenton gate on the south-east side of Paris.

On arriving there, however, all the English who joined the gathering were ordered to turn back, as information had been received that permission to leave the city was refused them. This caused no little consternation among the party, but the order naturally had to be obeyed, and half angrily and half disconsolately many a disappointed Briton returned to his recent quarters. We afterwards learnt that Jules Favre, the Foreign Minister, had in the first instance absolutely refused to listen to the applications of Mr. Wodehouse, possibly because Great Britain had not recognized the French Republic; though if such were indeed the reason, it was difficult to understand why the Russians received very different treatment, as the Czar, like the Queen, had so far abstained from any official recognition of the National Defence. On the other hand, Favre may, perhaps, have shared the opinion of Bismarck, who about this time tersely expressed his opinion of ourselves in the words: "England no longer counts"--so low, to his thinking, had we fallen in the comity of nations under our Gladstone *cum* Granville administration.

Mr. Wodehouse, however, in his unpleasant predicament, sought the assistance of his colleague, Mr. Washburne, the United States Minister, and the latter, who possessed more influence in Paris than any other foreign representative, promptly put his foot down, declaring that he himself would leave the city if the British subjects were still refused permission to depart. Favre then ungraciously gave way; but no sooner had his assent been obtained than it was discovered that the British Foreign Office had neglected to apply to Bismarck for permission for the English leaving Paris to pass through the German lines. Thus delay ensued, and it was only on the morning of November 8 that the English departed at the same time as a number of Swiss citizens and Austrian subjects.

The Charenton gate was again the appointed meeting-place. On our way thither, between six and seven o'clock in the morning, we passed many a long queue waiting outside butchers' shops for pittances of meat, and outside certain municipal depots where after prolonged waiting a few thimblesful of milk were doled out to those who could prove that they had young children. Near the Porte de Charenton a considerable detachment of the National Guard was drawn up as if to impart a kind of solemnity to the approaching exodus of foreigners. A couple of young staff-officers were also in attendance, with a mounted trumpeter and another trooper carrying the usual white flag on a lance.

The better-circumstanced of our party were in vehicles purchased for the occasion, a few also being mounted on valuable horses, which it was desired to save from the fate which eventually overtook most of the animals that remained in Paris. Others were in hired cabs, which were not allowed, however, to proceed farther than the outposts; while a good many of the poorer members of the party were in specially engaged omnibuses, which also had to turn back before we were handed over to a German escort; the result being that their occupants were left to trudge a good many miles on foot before other means of transport were procured. In that respect the Swiss and the Austrians were far better cared-for than the English. Although the weather was bitterly cold, Mr. Wodehouse, my father, myself, a couple of Mr. Wodehouse's servants, and a young fellow who had been connected, I think, with a Paris banking-house, travelled in an open pair-horse break. The Vice-Consul and his wife, who were also accompanying us, occupied a small private omnibus.

Before passing out of Paris we were all mustered and our *laisser-passers* were examined. Those held by British subjects emanated invariably from the United States Embassy, being duly signed by Mr. Washburne, so that we quitted the city virtually as American citizens. At last the procession was formed, the English preceding the Swiss and the Austrians, whilst in the rear, strangely enough, came several ambulance vans flaunting the red cross of Geneva. Nobody could account for their presence with us, but as the Germans were accused of occasionally firing on flags of truce, they were sent, perhaps, so as to be of service in the event of any mishap occurring. All being ready, we crossed the massive drawbridge of the Porte de Charenton, and wound in and out of the covered way which an advanced redoubt protected. A small detachment of light cavalry then joined us, and we speedily crossed the devastated track known as the "military zone," where every tree had been felled at the moment of the investment. Immediately afterwards we found ourselves in the narrow winding streets of Charenton, which had been almost entirely deserted by their inhabitants, but were crowded with soldiers who stood at doors and windows, watching our curious caravan. The bridge across the Marne was mined, but still intact, and defended at the farther end by an entrenched and loopholed redoubt, faced by some very intricate and artistic chevaux-de-frise. Once across the river, we wound round to the left, through the village of Alfort, where all the villas and river-side restaurants had been turned into military posts; and on looking back we saw the huge Charenton madhouse surmounting a wooded height and flying a large black flag. At the outset of the siege it had been suggested that the more harmless inmates should be released rather than remain exposed to harm from chance German shells; but the director of the establishment declared that in many instances insanity intensified patriotic feeling, and that if his patients were set at liberty they would at least desire to become members of the Government. So they were suffered to remain in their exposed position.

We went on, skirting the estate of Charentonneau, where the park wall had been blown down and many of the trees felled. On our right was the fort of Charenton, armed with big black naval guns. All the garden walls on our line of route had been razed or loopholed. The road was at times barricaded with trees, or intersected by trenches, and it was not without difficulty that we surmounted those impediments. At Petit Creteil we were astonished to see a number of market-gardeners working as unconcernedly as in times of peace. It is true that the village was covered by the fire of the Charenton fort, and that the Germans would have incurred great risk in making a serious attack on it. Nevertheless, small parties of them occasionally crept down and exchanged shots with the Mobiles who were stationed there, having their headquarters at a deserted inn, on reaching which we made our first halt.

The hired vehicles were now sent back to Paris, and after a brief interval we went on again, passing through an aperture in a formidable-looking barricade. We then readied Creteil proper, and there the first serious traces of the havoc of war were offered to our view. The once pleasant village was lifeless. Every house had been broken into and plundered, every door and every window smashed. Smaller articles of furniture, and so forth, had been removed, larger ones reduced to fragments. An infernal spirit of destruction had swept through the place; and yet, mark this, we were still within the French lines.

Our progress along the main street being suddenly checked by another huge barricade, we wound round to the right, and at last reached a house where less than a score of Mobiles were gathered, protected from sudden assault by a flimsy barrier of planks, casks, stools, and broken chairs. This was the most advanced French outpost in the direction we were following. We passed it, crossing some open fields where a solitary man was calmly digging potatoes, risking his life at every turn of his spade, but knowing that every pound of the precious tuber that he might succeed in taking into Paris would there fetch perhaps as much as ten francs.

Again we halted, and the trumpeter and the trooper with the white flag rode on to the farther part of the somewhat scattered village. Suddenly the trumpet's call rang out through the sharp, frosty air, and then we again moved on, passing down another village street where several gaunt starving cats attempted to follow us, with desperate strides and piteous mews. Before long, we perceived, standing in the middle of the road before us, a couple of German soldiers in long great-coats and boots reaching to the shins. One of them was carrying a white flag. A brief conversation ensued with them, for they both spoke French, and one of them knew English also. Soon afterwards, from behind a stout barricade which we saw ahead, three or four of their officers arrived, and somewhat stiff and ceremonious salutes were exchanged between them and the French officers in charge of our party.

Our arrival had probably been anticipated. At all events, a big and very welcome fire of logs and branches was blazing near by, and whilst one or two officers on either side, together with Colonel Claremont and some officials of the British Charitable Fund, were attending to the safe-conducts of her then Majesty's subjects, the other French and German officers engaged in conversation round the fire I have mentioned. The latter were probably Saxons; at all events, they belonged to the forces of the Crown Prince, afterwards King, of Saxony, who commanded this part of the investing lines, and with whom the principal English war-correspondent was Archibald Forbes, freshly arrived from the siege of Metz. The recent fall of that stronghold and the conduct of Marshal Bazaine supplied the chief subject of the conversation carried on at the Creteil outposts between the officers of the contending nations. Now and then, too, came a reference to Sedan and the overthrow of the Bonapartist Empire. The entire conversation was in French--I doubt, indeed, if our French custodians could speak German--and the greatest courtesy prevailed; though the French steadily declined the Hamburg cigars which their adversaries offered them.

I listened awhile to the conversation, but when the safe-conduct for my father and myself had been examined, I crossed to the other side of the road in order to scan the expanse of fields lying in that direction. All at once I saw a German officer, mounted on a powerful-looking horse, galloping over the rough ground in our direction. He came straight towards me. He was a well-built, middle-aged man of some rank--possibly a colonel. Reining in his mount, he addressed me in French, asking several questions. When, however, I had told him who we were, he continued the conversation in English and inquired if I had brought any newspapers out of Paris. Now, we were all pledged not to give any information of value to the enemy, but I had in my pockets copies of two of the most violent prints then appearing in the city--that is to say, **La Patrie en Danger**, inspired by Blanqui, and **Le Combat**, edited by Felix Pyat. The first-named was all sound and fury, and the second contained a subscription list for a pecuniary reward and rifle of honour to be presented to the Frenchman who might fortunately succeed in killing the King of Prussia. As the German officer was so anxious to ascertain what the popular feeling in Paris might be, and whether it favoured further resistance, it occurred to me, in a spirit of devilment as it were, to present him with the aforesaid journals, for which he expressed his heartfelt thanks, and then galloped away.

As I never met him again, I cannot say how he took the invectives and the "murder-subscription." Perhaps it was not quite right of me to foist on him, as examples of genuine Parisian opinion, two such papers as those I gave him; but, then, all is fair not merely in love but in war also, and in regard to the contentions of France and Germany, my sympathies were entirely on the side of France.

We had not yet been transferred to the German escort which was waiting for us, when all at once we heard several shots fired from the bank of the Marne, whereupon a couple of German dragoons galloped off in that direction. The firing ceased as abruptly as it had begun, and then, everything being in readiness so far as we were concerned, Colonel Claremont, the Charitable Fund people, the French officers and cavalry, and the ambulance waggons retraced their way to Paris, whilst our caravan went on in the charge of a detachment of German dragoons. Not for long, however, for the instructions received respecting us were evidently imperfect. The reader will have noticed that we left Paris on its southeastern side, although our destination was Versailles, which lies south-west of the capital, being in that direction only some eleven miles distant. Further, on quitting Creteil, instead of taking a direct route to the city of Louis Quatorze, we made, as the reader will presently see, an immense *detour,* so that our journey to Versailles lasted three full days. This occurred because the Germans wished to prevent us from seeing anything of the nearer lines of investment and the preparations which had already begun for the bombardment of Paris.

On our departure from Creteil, however, our route was not yet positively fixed, so we presently halted, and an officer of our escort rode off to take further instructions, whilst we remained near a German outpost, where we could not help noticing how healthy-looking, stalwart, and well-clad the men were. Orders respecting our movements having arrived, we set out again at a walking pace, perhaps because so many of our party were on foot. Troops were posted near every side-road that we passed. Officers constantly cantered up, inquiring for news respecting the position of affairs in Paris, wishing to know, in particular, if the National Defence ministers were still prisoners of the populace, and whether there was now a Red Republic with Blanqui at its head. What astounded them most was to hear that, although Paris was taking more and more to horseflesh, it was, as yet, by no means starving, and that, so far as famine might be concerned, it would be able to continue resisting for some months longer. In point of fact, this was on November 8, and the city did not surrender until January 28. But the German officers would not believe what we said respecting the resources of the besieged; they repeated the same questions again and again, and still looked incredulous, as if, indeed, they thought that we were fooling them.

At Boissy-Saint Leger we halted whilst the British, Austrian, and Swiss representatives interviewed the general in command there. He was installed in a trim little, chateau, in front of which was the quaintest sentry-box I have ever seen, for it was fashioned of planks, logs, and all sorts of scraps of furniture, whilst beside it lay a doll's perambulator and a little boy's toy-cart. But we again set out, encountering near Gros-Bois a long line of heavily-laden German provision-wagons; and presently, without addressing a word to any of us, the officer of our escort gave a command, his troopers wheeled round and galloped away, leaving us to ourselves.

By this time evening was approaching, and the vehicles of our party drove on at a smart trot, leaving the unfortunate pedestrians a long way in the rear. Nobody seemed to know exactly where we were, but some passing peasants informed us that we were on the road to Basle, and that the nearest locality was Brie-Comte-Robert. The horses drawing the conveyances of the Swiss and Austrian representatives were superior to those harnessed to Mr. Wodehouse's break, so we were distanced on the road, and on reaching Brie found that all the accommodation of the two inns--I can scarcely call them hotels--had been allotted to the first arrivals. Mr. Wodehouse's party secured a lodging in a superior-looking private house, whilst my father, myself, and about thirty others repaired to the *mairie* for billets.

A striking scene met my eyes there. By this time night had fallen. In a room which was almost bare of furniture, the mayor was seated at a little table on which two candles were burning. On either side of him stood a German infantryman with rifle and fixed bayonet. Here and there, too, were several German hussars, together with ten or a dozen peasants of the locality. And the unfortunate mayor, in a state of semi-arrest, was striving to comply with the enemy's requisitions of food, forage, wine, horses, and vehicles, the peasants meanwhile protesting that they had already been despoiled of everything, and had nothing whatever left. "So you want me to be shot?" said the mayor to them, at last. "You know very well that the things must be found. Go and get them together. Do the best you can. We will see afterwards."

When--acting as usual as my father's interpreter--I asked the mayor for billets, he raised his arms to the ceiling. "I have no beds," said he. "Every bit of available bedding, excepting at the inns, has been requisitioned for the Prussian ambulances. I might find some straw, and there are outhouses and empty rooms. But there are so many of you, and I do not know how I can accommodate you all."

It was not, however, the duty of my father or myself to attend to the requirements of the whole party. That was the duty rather of the Embassy officials, so I again pressed the mayor to give me at least a couple of decent billets. He thought for a moment, then handed me a paper bearing a name and address, whereupon we, my father and myself, went off. But it was pitch-dark, and as we could not find the place indicated, we returned to the *mairie*, where, after no little trouble, a second paper was given me. By this time the poorer members of the party had been sent to sheds and so forth, where they found some straw to lie upon. The address on my second paper was that of a basket-maker, whose house was pointed out to us. We were very cordially received there, and taken to a room containing a bed provided with a ***sommier elastique***. But there was no mattress, no sheet, no blanket, no bolster, no pillow--everything of that kind having been requisitioned for the German ambulances; and I recollect that two or three hours later, when my father and myself retired to rest in that icy chamber, the window of which was badly broken, we were glad to lay our heads on a couple of hard baskets, having left our bags in Mr. Wodehouse's charge.

Before trying to sleep, however, we required food; for during the day we had consumed every particle of a cold rabbit and some siege-bread which we had brought out of Paris. The innkeepers proved to be extremely independent and irritable, and we could obtain very little from them. Fortunately, we discovered a butcher's, secured some meat from him, and prevailed on the wife of our host, the basket-maker, to cook it for us. We then went out again, and found some cafes and wine-shops which were crowded with German soldiery. Wine and black coffee were obtainable there, and whilst we refreshed ourselves, more than one German soldier, knowing either French or English, engaged us in conversation. My own German was at that time very limited, for I had not taken kindly to the study of the language, and had secured, moreover, but few opportunities to attempt to converse in it. However, I well remember some of the German soldiers declaring that they were heartily sick of the siege, and expressing a hope that the Parisians would speedily surrender, so that they, the Germans, might return to the Fatherland in ample time to get their Christmas trees ready. A good-looking and apparently very genial Uhlan also talked to me about the Parisian balloons, relating that, directly any ascent was observed, news of it was telegraphed along all the investing lines, that every man had orders to fire if the aerial craft came approximately within range, and that he and his comrades often tried to ride a balloon down.

After a wretched night, we washed at the pump in the basket-maker's yard, and breakfasted off bread and *cafe noir*. Milk, by the way, was as scarce at Brie as in Paris itself, the Germans, it was said, having carried off all the cows that had previously supplied France with the far-famed Brie cheese. We now discovered that, in order to reach Versailles, we should have to proceed in the first instance to Corbeil, some fifteen miles distant, when we should be within thirty miles of the German headquarters. That was pleasant news, indeed! We had already made a journey of over twenty miles, and now another of some five-and-forty miles lay before us. And yet, had we only been allowed to take the proper route, we should have reached Versailles after travelling merely eleven miles beyond Paris!

Under the circumstances, the position of the unfortunate pedestrians was a very unpleasant one, and my father undertook to speak on their behalf to Mr. Wodehouse, pointing out to him that it was unfair to let these unfortunate people trudge all the way to Versailles.

"But what am I to do?" Mr. Wodehouse replied. "I am afraid that no vehicles can be obtained here."

"The German authorities will perhaps help you in the matter," urged my father.

"I doubt it. But please remember that everybody was warned before leaving Paris that he would do so at his own risk and peril, and that the Embassy could not charge itself with the expense."

"That is exactly what surprised me," said my father. "I know that the Charitable Fund has done something, but I thought that the Embassy would have done more."

"I had no instructions," replied Mr. Wodehouse.

"But, surely, at such a time as this, a man initiates his own instructions."

"Perhaps so; but I had no money."

On hearing this, my father, for a moment, almost lost his temper. "Surely, Mr. Wodehouse," said he, "you need only have gone to Baron de Rothschild--he would have let you have whatever money you required." [I have reconstructed the above dialogue from my diary, which I posted up on reaching Versailles.]

Mr. Wodehouse looked worried. He was certainly a most amiable man, but he was not, I think, quite the man for the situation. Moreover, like my father, he was in very poor health at this time. Still, he realized that he must try to effect something, and eventually, with the assistance of the mayor and the German authorities, a few farm-carts were procured for the accommodation of the poorer British subjects. During the long interval which had elapsed, however, a good many men had gone off of their own accord, tired of waiting, and resolving to try their luck in one and another direction. Thus our procession was a somewhat smaller one when we at last quitted Brie-Comte-Robert for Corbeil.

We met many German soldiers on our way--at times large detachments of them--and we scarcely ever covered a mile of ground without being questioned respecting the state of affairs in Paris and the probable duration of its resistance, our replies invariably disappointing the questioners, so anxious were they to see the war come to an end. This was particularly the case with a young non-commissioned officer who jumped on the step of Mr. Wodehouse's break, and engaged us in conversation whilst we continued on our way. Before leaving us he remarked, I remember, that he would very much like to pay a visit to England; whereupon my father answered that he would be very much pleased to see him there, provided, however, that he would come by himself and not with half a million of armed comrades.

While the German soldiers were numerous, the peasants whom we met on the road were few and far between. On reaching the little village of Lieusaint, however, a number of people rushed to the doors of their houses and gazed at us in bewilderment, for during the past two months the only strangers they had seen had been German soldiers, and they could not understand the meaning of our civilian caravan of carriages and carts. At last we entered Corbeil, and followed the main street towards the old stone bridge by which we hoped to cross the Seine, but we speedily discovered that it had been blown up, and that we could only get to the other side of the river by a pontoon-bridge lower down. This having been effected, we drove to the principal hotel, intending to put up there for the night, as it had become evident that we should be unable to reach Versailles at a reasonable hour.

However, the entire hotel was in the possession of German officers, several of whom we found flirting with the landlady's good-looking daughter--who, as she wore a wedding ring, was, I presume, married. I well recollect that she made some reference to the ladies of Berlin, whereupon one of the lieutenants who were ogling her, gallantly replied that they were not half so charming as the ladies of Corbeil. The young woman appeared to appreciate the compliment, for, on the lieutenant rising to take leave of her, she graciously gave him her hand, and said to him with a smile: "Au plaisir de vous revoir, monsieur."

But matters were very different with the old lady, her mother, who, directly the coast was clear, began to inveigh against the Germans in good set terms, describing them, I remember, as semi-savages who destroyed whatever they did not steal. She was particularly irate with them for not allowing M. Darblay, the wealthy magnate of the grain and flour trade, and at the same time mayor of Corbeil, to retain a single carriage or a single horse for his own use. Yet he had already surrendered four carriages and eight horses to them, and only wished to keep a little gig and a cob.

We obtained a meal at the hotel, but found it impossible to secure a bed there, so we sallied forth into the town on an exploring expedition. On all sides we observed notices indicating the rate of exchange of French and German money, and the place seemed to be full of tobacconists' shops, which were invariably occupied by German Jews trading in Hamburg cigars. On inquiring at a cafe respecting accommodation, we were told that we should only obtain it with difficulty, as the town was full of troops, including more than a thousand sick and wounded, fifteen or twenty of whom died every day. At last we crossed the river again, and found quarters at an inferior hotel, the top-floor of which had been badly damaged by some falling blocks of stone at the time when the French blew up the town bridge. However, our beds were fairly comfortable, and we had a good night's rest.

Black coffee was again the only available beverage in the morning. No milk was to be had, nor was there even a scrap of sugar. In these respects Corbeil was even worse off than Paris. The weather had now changed, and rain was falling steadily. We plainly had a nasty day before us. Nevertheless, another set of carts was obtained for the poorer folk of our party, on mustering which one man was found to be missing. He had fallen ill, we were told, and could not continue the journey. Presently, moreover, the case was discovered to be one of smallpox, which disease had lately broken out in Paris. Leaving the sufferer to be treated at the already crowded local hospital, we set out, and, on emerging from the town, passed a drove of a couple of hundred oxen, and some three hundred sheep, in the charge of German soldiers. We had scarcely journeyed another mile when, near Essonnes, noted for its paper-mills, one of our carts broke down, which was scarcely surprising, the country being hilly, the roads heavy, and the horses spavined. Again, the rain was now pouring in torrents, to the very great discomfort of the occupants of the carts, as well as that of Mr. Wodehouse's party in the break. But there was no help for it, and so on we drove mile after mile, until we were at last absolutely soaked.

The rain had turned to sleet by the time we reached Longjumeau, famous for its handsome and amorous postilion. Two-thirds of the shops there were closed, and the inns were crowded with German soldiers, so we drove on in the direction of Palaiseau. But we had covered only about half the distance when a snow-storm overtook us, and we had to seek shelter at Champlan. A German officer there assisted in placing our vehicles under cover, but the few peasants whom we saw eyeing us inquisitively from the doors of their houses declared that the only thing they could let us have to eat was dry bread, there being no meat, no eggs, no butter, no cheese, in the whole village. Further, they averred that they had not even a pint of wine to place at our disposal. "The Germans have taken everything," they said; "we have 800 of them in and around the village, and there are not more than a dozen of us left here, all the rest having fled to Paris when the siege began."

The outlook seemed bad, but Mr. Wodehouse's valet, a shrewd and energetic man of thirty or thereabouts, named Frost, said to me, "I don't believe all this. I dare say that if some money is produced we shall be able to get something." Accordingly we jointly tackled a disconsolate-looking fellow, who, if I remember rightly, was either the village wheelwright or blacksmith; and, momentarily leaving the question of food on one side, we asked him if he had not at least a fire in his house at which we might warm ourselves. Our party included a lady, the Vice-Consul's wife, and although she was making the journey in a closed private omnibus, she was suffering from the cold. This was explained to the man whom we addressed, and when he had satisfied himself that we were not Germans in disguise, he told us that we might come into his house and warm ourselves until the storm abated. Some nine or ten of us, including the lady I have mentioned, availed ourselves of this permission, and the man led us upstairs to a first-floor room, where a big wood-fire was blazing. Before it sat his wife and his daughter, both of them good specimens of French rustic beauty. With great good-nature, they at once made room for us, and added more fuel to the fire.

Half the battle was won, and presently we were regaled with all that they could offer us in the way of food--that is, bread and baked pears, which proved very acceptable. Eventually, after looking out of the window in order to make quite sure that no Germans were loitering near the house, our host locked the door of the room, and turning towards a big pile of straw, fire-wood, and household utensils, proceeded to demolish it, until he disclosed to view a small cask--a half hogshead, I think--which, said he, in a whisper, contained wine. It was all that he had been able to secrete. On the arrival of the enemy in the district a party of officers had come to his house and ordered their men to remove the rest of his wine, together with nearly all his bedding, and every fowl and every pig that he possessed. "They have done the same all over the district," the man added, "and you should see some of the chateaux--they have been absolutely stripped of their contents."

His face brightened when we told him that Paris seemed resolved on no surrender, and that, according to official reports, she would have a sufficiency of bread to continue resisting until the ensuing month of February. In common with most of his countrymen, our host of Champlan held that, whatever else might happen, the honour of the nation would at least be saved if the Germans could only be kept out of Paris; and thus he was right glad to hear that the city's defence would be prolonged.

He was well remunerated for his hospitality, and on the weather slightly improving we resumed our journey to Versailles, following the main road by way of Palaiseau and Jouy-en-Josas, and urging the horses to their quickest pace whilst the light declined and the evening shadows gathered around us.

VIII
FROM VERSAILLES TO BRITTANY

War-correspondents at Versailles--Dr. Russell--Lord Adare--David Dunglas Home and his Extraordinary Career--His *Seances* at Versallies--An Amusing Interview with Colonel Beauchamp Walker--Parliament's Grant for British Refugees--Generals Duff and Hazen, U.S.A.--American Help--Glimpses of King William and Bismarck--Our Safe-Conducts--From Versailles to Saint Germain-en-Laye--Trouble at Mantes--The German Devil of Destructiveness-- From the German to the French Lines--A Train at Last--Through Normandy and Maine--Saint Servan and its English Colony--I resolve to go to the Front.

It was dark when we at last entered Versailles by the Avenue de Choisy. We saw some sentries, but they did not challenge us, and we went on until we struck the Avenue de Paris, where we passed the Prefecture, every one of whose windows was a blaze of light. King, later Emperor, William had his quarters there; Bismarck, however, residing at a house in the Rue de Provence belonging to the French General de Jesse. Winding round the Place d'Armes, we noticed that one wing of Louis XIV's famous palace had its windows lighted, being appropriated to hospital purposes, and that four batteries of artillery were drawn up on the square, perhaps as a hint to the Versaillese to be on their best behaviour. However, we drove on, and a few moments later we pulled up outside the famous Hotel des Reservoirs.

There was no possibility of obtaining accommodation there. From its ground-floor to its garrets the hotel was packed with German princes, dukes, dukelets, and their suites, together with a certain number of English, American, and other war-correspondents. Close by, however-- indeed, if I remember rightly, on the other side of the way--there was a cafe, whither my father and myself directed our steps. We found it crowded with officers and newspaper men, and through one or other of the latter we succeeded in obtaining comfortable lodgings in a private house. The *Illustrated London News* artist with the German staff was Landells, son of the engraver of that name, and we speedily discovered his whereabouts. He was sharing rooms with Hilary Skinner, the *Daily News* representative at Versailles; and they both gave us a cordial greeting.

The chief correspondent at the German headquarters was William Howard Russell of the *Times*, respecting whom--perhaps because he kept himself somewhat aloof from his colleagues--a variety of scarcely good-natured stories were related; mostly designed to show that he somewhat over-estimated his own importance. One yarn was to the effect that whenever the Doctor mounted his horse, it was customary for the Crown Prince of Prussia--afterwards the Emperor Frederick--to hold his stirrup leather for him. Personally, I can only say that, on my father calling with me on Russell, he received us very cordially indeed (he had previously met my father, and had well known my uncle Frank), and that when we quitted Versailles, as I shall presently relate, he placed his courier and his private omnibus at our disposal, in after years one of my cousins, the late Montague Vizetelly, accompanied Russell to South America. I still have some letters which the latter wrote me respecting Zola's novel "La Debacle," in which he took a great interest.

Another war-correspondent at Versailles was the present Earl of Dunraven, then not quite thirty years of age, and known by the courtesy title of Lord Adare. He had previously acted as the *Daily Telegraph's* representative with Napier's expedition against Theodore of Abyssinia, and was now staying at Versailles, on behalf, I think, of the same journal. His rooms at the Hotel des Reservoirs were shared by Daniel Dunglas Home, the medium, with whom my father and myself speedily became acquainted. Very tall and slim, with blue eyes and an abundance of yellowish hair, Home, at this time about thirty-seven years of age, came of the old stock of the Earls of Home, whose name figures so often in Scottish history. His father was an illegitimate son of the tenth earl, and his mother belonged to a family which claimed to possess the gift of "second sight." Home himself--according to his own account--began to see visions and receive mysterious warnings at the period of his mother's death, and as time elapsed his many visitations from the other world so greatly upset the aunt with whom he was living--a Mrs. McNeill Cook of Greeneville, Connecticut [He had been taken from Scotland to America when he was about nine years old.]--that she ended by turning him out-of-doors. Other people, however, took an unhealthy delight in seeing their furniture move about without human agency, and in receiving more or less ridiculous messages from spirit-land; and in folk of this description Home found some useful friends.

He came to London in the spring of 1855, and on giving a *seance* at Cox's Hotel, in Jermyn Street, he contrived to deceive Sir David Brewster (then seventy-four years old), but was less successful with another septuagenarian, Lord Brougham. Later, he captured the imaginative Sir Edward Bulwer (subsequently Lord Lytton), who as author of "Zanoni" was perhaps fated to believe in him, and he also impressed Mrs. Browning, but not Browning himself The latter, indeed, depicted Home as "Sludge, the Medium." Going to Italy for a time, the already notorious adventurer gave *seances* in a haunted villa near Florence, but on becoming converted to the Catholic faith in 1856 he was received in private audience by that handsome, urbane, but by no means satisfactory pontiff, Pio Nono, who, however, eight years later caused him to be summarily expelled from Rome as a sorcerer in league with the Devil.

Meantime, Home had ingratiated himself with a number of crowned heads--Napoleon III and the Empress Eugenie, in whose presence he gave *seances* at the Tuileries, Fontainebleau, and Biarritz; the King of Prussia, by whom he was received at Baden-Baden; and Queen Sophia of Holland, who gave him hospitality at the Hague. On marrying a Russian lady, the daughter of General Count de Kroll, he was favoured with presents by the Czar Alexander II, and after returning to England became one of the "attractions" of Milner-Gibson's drawing-room--Mrs. Gibson, a daughter of the Rev. Sir Thomas Gery Cullum, being one of the early English patronesses of so-called spiritualism, to a faith in which she was "converted" by Home, whom she first met whilst travelling on the Continent. I remember hearing no little talk about him in my younger days. Thackeray's friend, Robert Bell, wrote an article about him in ***The Cornhill***, which was the subject of considerable discussion. Bell, I think, was also mixed up in the affair of the "Davenport Brothers," one of whose performances I remember witnessing. They were afterwards effectively shown up in Paris by Vicomte Alfred de Caston. Home, for his part, was scarcely taken seriously by the Parisians, and when, at a *seance* given in presence of the Empress Eugenie, he blundered grossly and repeatedly about her father, the Count of Montijo, he received an intimation that his presence at Court could be dispensed with. He then consoled himself by going to Peterhof and exhibiting his powers to the Czar.

Certain Scotch and English scientists, such as Dr. Lockhart Robertson, Dr. Robert Chambers, and Dr. James Manby Gully--the apostle of hydropathy, who came to grief in the notorious Bravo case--warmly supported Home. So did Samuel Carter Hall and his wife, William Howitt, and Gerald Massey; and he ended by establishing a so-called "Spiritual Athenaeum" in Sloane Street. A wealthy widow of advanced years, a Mrs. Jane Lyon, became a subscriber to that institution, and, growing infatuated with Home, made him a present of some L30,000, and settled on him a similar amount to be paid at her death. But after a year or two she repented of her infatuation, and took legal proceedings to recover her money. She failed to substantiate some of her charges, but Vice-Chancellor Giffard, who heard the case, decided it in her favour, in his judgment describing Home as a needy and designing man. Home, I should add, was at this time a widower and at loggerheads with his late wife's relations in Russia, in respect to her property.

Among the arts ascribed to Home was that called levitation, in practising which he was raised in the air by an unseen and unknown force, and remained suspended there; this being, so to say, the first step towards human flying without the assistance of any biplane, monoplane, or other mechanical contrivance. The first occasion on which Home is said to have displayed this power was in the late fifties, when he was at a chateau near Bordeaux as the guest of the widow of Theodore Ducos, the nephew of Bonaparte's colleague in the Consulate. In the works put forward on Home's behalf--one of them, called "Incidents in my Life," was chiefly written, it appears, by his friend and solicitor, a Mr. W.M. Wilkinson--it is also asserted that his power of levitation was attested in later years by Lord Lindsay, subsequently Earl of Crawford and Balcarres, and by the present Earl of Dunraven. We are told, indeed, that on one occasion the last-named actually saw Home float out of a room by one window, and into it again by another one. I do not know whether Home also favoured Professor Crookes with any exhibition of this kind, but the latter certainly expressed an opinion that some of Home's feats were genuine.

When my father and I first met him at Versailles he was constantly in the company of Lord Adare. He claimed to be acting as the correspondent of a Californian journal, but his chief occupation appeared to be the giving of *seances* for the entertainment of all the German princes and princelets staying at the Hotel des Reservoirs. Most of these highnesses and mightinesses formed part of what the Germans themselves sarcastically called their "Ornamental Staff," and as Moltke seldom allowed them any real share in the military operations, they doubtless found in Home's performances some relief from the *taedium vitae* which overtook them during their long wait for the capitulation of Paris. Now that Metz had fallen, that was the chief question which occupied the minds of all the Germans assembled at Versailles, [Note] and Home was called upon to foretell when it would take place. On certain occasions, I believe, he evoked the spirits of Frederick the Great, Napoleon, Bluecher, and others, in order to obtain from them an accurate forecast. At another time he endeavoured to peer into the future by means of crystal-gazing, in which he required the help of a little child. "My experiments have not succeeded," he said one day, while we were sitting with him at the cafe near the Hotel des Reservoirs; "but that is not my fault. I need an absolutely pure-minded child, and can find none here, for this French race is corrupt from its very infancy." He was fasting at this time, taking apparently nothing but a little *eau sucree* for several days at a stretch. "The spirits will not move me unless I do this," he said. "To bring them to me, I have to contend against the material part of my nature."

[Note: The Germans regarded it as the more urgent at the time of my arrival at Versailles, as only a few data previously (November 9), the new French Army of the Loire under D'Aurelle de Paladines had defeated the Bavarians at Coulmiers, and thereby again secured possession of Orleans.]

A couple of years later, after another visit to St. Petersburg, where, it seems, he was again well received by the Czar and again married a lady of the Russian nobility, Home's health began to fail him, perhaps on account of the semi-starvation to which at intervals he subjected himself. I saw him occasionally during his last years, when, living at Auteuil, he was almost a neighbour of mine. He died there in 1886, being then about fifty-three years old. Personally, I never placed faith in him. I regarded him at the outset with great curiosity, but some time before the war

I had read a good deal about Cagliostro, Saint Germain, Mesmer, and other charlatans, also attending a lecture about them at the Salle des Conferences; and all that, combined with the exposure of the Davenport Brothers and other spiritualists and illusionists, helped to prejudice me against such a man as Home. At the same time, this so-called "wizard of the nineteenth century" was certainly a curious personality, possessed, I presume, of considerable suggestive powers, which at times enabled him to make others believe as he desired. We ought to have had Charcot's opinion of his case.

As it had taken my father and myself three days to reach Versailles from Paris, and we could not tell what other unpleasant experiences the future might hold in store for us, our pecuniary position gave rise to some concern. I mentioned previously that we quitted the capital with comparatively little money, and it now seemed as if our journey might become a long and somewhat costly affair, particularly as the German staff wished to send us off through Northern France and thence by way of Belgium. On consulting Landells, Skinner, and some other correspondents, it appeared that several days might elapse before we could obtain remittances from England. On the other hand, every correspondent clung to such money as he had in his possession, for living was very expensive at Versailles, and at any moment some emergency might arise necessitating an unexpected outlay. It was suggested, however, that we should apply to Colonel Beauchamp Walker, who was the official British representative with the German headquarters' staff, for, we were told, Parliament, in its generosity, had voted a sum of L4000 to assist any needy British subjects who might come out of Paris, and Colonel Walker had the handling of the money in question.

Naturally enough, my father began by demurring to this suggestion, saying that he could not apply *in forma pauperis* for charity. But it was pointed out that he need do no such thing. "Go to Walker," it was said, "explain your difficulty, and offer him a note of hand or a draft on the ***Illustrated***, and if desired half a dozen of us will back it." Some such plan having been decided on, we called upon Colonel Walker on the second or third day of our stay at Versailles.

His full name was Charles Pyndar Beauchamp Walker. Born in 1817, he had seen no little service. He had acted as an ***aide-de-camp*** to Lord Lucan in the Crimea, afterwards becoming Lieutenant-Colonel of the 2nd Dragoon Guards. He was in India during the final operations for the suppression of the Mutiny, and subsequently in China during the Franco-British expedition to that country. During the Austro-Prussian war of 1866 he was attached as British Commissioner to the forces of the Crown Prince of Prussia, and witnessed the battle of Koeniggratz. He served in the same capacity during the Franco-German War, when he was at Weissenburg, Woerth, and Sedan. In later years he became a major-general, a lieutenant-general, a K.C.B., and Colonel of the 2nd Dragoon Guards; and from 1878 until his retirement in 1884 he acted as Inspector General of military education. I have set out those facts because I have no desire to minimise Walker's services and abilities. But I cannot help smiling at a sentence which I found in the account of him given in the "Dictionary of National Biography." It refers to his duties during the Franco-German War, and runs as follows: "The irritation of the Germans against England, and the number of roving Englishmen, made his duty not an easy one, but he was well qualified for it by his tact and geniality, and his action met with the full approval of the Government."

The Government in question would have approved anything. But let that pass. We called on the colonel at about half-past eleven in the morning, and were shown into a large and comfortably furnished room, where decanters and cigars were prominently displayed on a central table. In ten minutes' time the colonel appeared, arrayed in a beautiful figured dressing-gown with a tasselled girdle. I knew that the British officer was fond of discarding his uniform, and I was well aware that French officers also did so when on furlough in Paris, but it gave my young mind quite a shock to see her Majesty's military representative with King William arrayed in a gaudy dressing-gown in the middle of the day. He seated himself, and querulously inquired of my father what his business was. It was told him very briefly. He frowned, hummed, hawed, threw himself back in his armchair, and curtly exclaimed, "I am not a money-lender!"

The fact that the ***Illustrated London News*** was the world's premier journal of its class went for nothing. The offers of the other correspondents of the English Press to back my father's signature were dismissed with disdain. When the colonel was reminded that he held a considerable amount of money voted by Parliament, he retorted: "That is for necessitous persons! But you ask me to ***lend*** you money!" "Quite so," my father replied; "I do not wish to be a charge on the Treasury. I simply want a loan, as I have a difficult and perhaps an expensive journey before me." "How much do you want?" snapped the colonel. "Well," said my father, "I should feel more comfortable if I had a thousand francs (L40) in my pocket." "Forty pounds!" cried Colonel Walker, as if lost in amazement. And getting up from his chair he went on, in the most theatrical manner possible: "Why, do you know, sir, that if I were to let you have forty pounds, I might find myself in the greatest possible difficulty. To-morrow--perhaps, even to-night--there might be hundreds of our suffering fellow-countrymen outside the gates of Versailles, and I unable to relieve them!" "But," said my father quietly, "you would still be holding L3960, Colonel Walker." The colonel glared, and my father, not caring to prolong such an interview, walked out of the room, followed by myself.

A good many of the poorer people who quitted Paris with us never repaired to Versailles at all, but left us at Corbeil or elsewhere to make their way across France as best they could. Another party, about one hundred strong, was, however, subsequently sent out of the capital with the assistance of Mr. Washburne, and in their case Colonel Walker had to expend some money. But every grant was a very niggardly one, and it would not surprise me to learn that the bulk of the money voted by Parliament was ultimately returned to the Treasury--which circumstance would probably account for the "full approval" which the Government bestowed on the colonel's conduct at this period. He died early in 1894, and soon afterwards some of his correspondence was published in a volume entitled "Days of a Soldier's Life." On reading a review of that work in one of the leading literary journals, I was struck by a passage in which Walker was described as a disappointed and embittered man, who always felt that his merits were not sufficiently recognized, although he was given a knighthood and retired with the honorary rank of general. I presume that his ambition was at least a viscounty, if not an earldom, and a field-marshal's *baton*.

On leaving the gentleman whose "tact and geniality" are commemorated in the "Dictionary of National Biography," we repaired--my father and I--to the cafe where most of the English newspaper men met. Several were there, and my father was at once assailed with inquiries respecting his interview with Colonel Walker. His account of it led to some laughter and a variety of comments, which would scarcely have improved the colonel's temper. I remember, however, that Captain, afterwards Colonel Sir, Henry Hozier, the author of "The Seven Weeks' War," smiled quietly, but otherwise kept his own counsel. At last my father was asked what he intended to do under the circumstances, and he replied that he meant to communicate with England as speedily as possible, and remain in the interval at Versailles, although he particularly wished to get away.

Now, it happened that among the customers at the cafe there were two American officers, one being Brigadier-General Duff, a brother of Andrew Halliday, the dramatic author and essayist, whose real patronymic was also Duff. My father knew Halliday through their mutual friends Henry Mayhew and the Broughs. The other American officer was Major-General William Babcook Hazen, whose name will be found occasionally mentioned in that popular record of President Garfield's career, "From Log Cabin to White House." During the Civil War in the United States he had commanded a division in Sherman's march to the sea. He also introduced the cold-wave signal system into the American army, and in 1870-71 he was following the operations of the Germans on behalf of his Government.

I do not remember whether General Duff (who, I have been told, is still alive) was also at Versailles in an official capacity, but in the course of conversation he heard of my father's interview with Colonel Walker, and spoke to General Hazen on the subject. Hazen did not hesitate, but came to my father, had a brief chat with him, unbuttoned his uniform, produced a case containing bank-notes, and asked my father how much he wanted, telling him not to pinch himself. The whole transaction was completed in a few minutes. My father was unwilling to take quite as much as he had asked of Colonel Walker, but General Hazen handed him some L20 or L30 in notes, one or two of which were afterwards changed, for a handsome consideration, by one of the German Jews who then infested Versailles and profited by the scarcity of gold. We were indebted, then, on two occasions to the representatives of the United States. The *laisser-passer* enabling us to leave Paris had been supplied by Mr. Washburne, and the means of continuing our journey in comfort were furnished by General Hazen. I raise my hat to the memory of both those gentlemen.

During the few days that we remained at Versailles, we caught glimpses of King William and Bismarck, both of whom we had previously seen in Paris in 1867, when they were the guests of Napoleon III. I find in my diary a memorandum, dictated perhaps by my father: "Bismarck much fatter and bloated." We saw him one day leaving the Prefecture, where the King had his quarters. He stood for a moment outside, chatting and laughing noisily with some other German personages, then strode away with a companion. He was only fifty-five years old, and was full of vigour at that time, even though he might have put on flesh during recent years, and therefore have renounced dancing--his last partner in the waltz having been Mme. Carette, the Empress Eugenie's reader, whom he led out at one of the '67 balls at the Tuileries. Very hale and hearty, too, looked the King whom Bismarck was about to turn into an Emperor. Yet the victor of Sedan was already seventy-three years old. I only saw him on horseback during my stay at Versailles. My recollections of him, Bismarck, and Moltke, belong more particularly to the year 1872, when I was in Berlin in connexion with the famous meeting of the three Emperors.

My father and myself had kept in touch with Mr. Wodehouse, from whom we learnt that we should have to apply to the German General commanding at Versailles with respect to any further safe-conducts. At first we were informed that there could be no departure from the plan of sending us out of France by way of Epernay, Reims, and Sedan, and this by no means coincided with the desires of most of the Englishmen who had come out of Paris, they wishing to proceed westward, and secure a passage across the Channel from Le Havre or Dieppe. My father and myself also wanted to go westward, but in order to make our way into Brittany, my stepmother and her children being at Saint Servan, near Saint Malo. At last the German authorities decided to give us the alternative routes of Mantes and Dreux, the first-named being the preferable one for those people who were bound for England. It was chosen also by my father, as the Dreux route would have led us into a region where hostilities were in progress, and where we might suddenly have found ourselves "held up."

The entire party of British refugees was now limited to fifteen or sixteen persons, some, tired of waiting, having taken themselves off by the Sedan route, whilst a few others--such as coachmen and grooms--on securing employment from German princes and generals, resolved to stay at Versailles. Mr. Wodehouse also remained there for a short time. Previously in poor health, he had further contracted a chill during our three days' drive in an open vehicle. As most of those who were going on to England at once now found themselves almost insolvent, it was arranged to pay their expenses through the German lines, and to give each of them a sum of fifty shillings, so that they might make their way Channelwards when they had reached an uninvaded part of France. Colonel Walker, of course, parted with as little money as possible.

At Versailles it was absolutely impossible to hire vehicles to take us as far as Mantes, but we were assured that conveyances might be procured at Saint Germain-en-Laye; and it was thus that Dr. Russell lent my father his little omnibus for the journey to the last-named town, at the same time sending his courier to assist in making further arrangements. I do not recollect that courier's nationality, but he spoke English, French, and German, and his services were extremely useful. We drove to Saint Germain by way of Rocquencourt, where we found a number of country-folk gathered by the roadside with little stalls, at which they sold wine and fruit to the German soldiers. This part of the environs of Paris seemed to have suffered less than the eastern and southern districts. So far, there had been only one sortie on this side--that made by Ducrot in the direction of La Malmaison. It had, however, momentarily alarmed the investing forces, and whilst we were at Versailles I learnt that, on the day in question, everything had been got ready for King William's removal to Saint Germain in the event of the French achieving a real success. But it proved to be a small affair, Ducrot's force being altogether incommensurate with the effort required of it.

At Saint Germain, Dr. Russell's courier assisted in obtaining conveyances for the whole of our party, and we were soon rolling away in the direction of Mantes-la-Jolie, famous as the town where William the Conqueror, whilst bent on pillage and destruction, received the injuries which caused his death. Here we had to report ourselves to the German Commander, who, to the general consternation, began by refusing its permission to proceed. He did so because most of the safe-conducts delivered to us at Versailles, had, in the first instance, only stated that we were to travel by way of Sedan; the words "or Mantes or Dreux" being afterwards added between the lines. That interlineation was irregular, said the General at Mantes; it might even be a forgery; at all events, he could not recognize it, so we must go back whence we had come, and quickly, too--indeed, he gave us just half an hour to quit the town! But it fortunately happened that in a few of the safe-conducts there was no interlineation whatever, the words "Sedan or Mantes or Dreux" being duly set down in the body of the document, and on this being pointed out, the General came to the conclusion that we were not trying to impose on him. He thereupon cancelled his previous order, and decided that, as dusk was already falling, we might remain at Mantes that night, and resume our journey on the morrow at 5.45 a.m., in the charge of a cavalry escort.

Having secured a couple of beds, and ordered some dinner at one of the inns, my father and I strolled about the town, which was full of Uhlans and Hussars. The old stone bridge across the Seine had been blown up by the French before their evacuation of the town, and a part of the railway line had also been destroyed by them. But the Germans were responsible for the awful appearance of the railway-station. Never since have I seen anything resembling it. A thousand panes of glass belonging to windows or roofing had been shivered to atoms. Every mirror in either waiting or refreshment-rooms had been pounded to pieces; every gilt frame broken into little bits. The clocks lay about in small fragments; account-books and printed forms had been torn to scraps; partitions, chairs, tables, benches, boxes, nests of drawers, had been hacked, split, broken, reduced to mere strips of wood. The large stoves were overturned and broken, and the marble refreshment counter--some thirty feet long, and previously one of the features of the station--now strewed the floor in particles, suggesting gravel. It was, indeed, an amazing sight, the more amazing as no such work of destruction could have been accomplished without extreme labour. When we returned to the inn for dinner, I asked some questions. "Who did it?" "The first German troops that came here," was the answer. "Why did they do it?--was it because your men had cut the telegraph wires and destroyed some of the permanent way?" "Oh no! They expected to find something to drink in the refreshment-room, and when they discovered that everything had been taken away, they set about breaking the fixtures!" Dear, nice, placid German soldiers, baulked, for a few minutes, of some of the wine of France!

In the morning we left Mantes by moonlight at the appointed hour, unaccompanied, however, by any escort. Either the Commandant had forgotten the matter, or his men had overslept themselves. In the outskirts, we were stopped by a sentry, who carried our pass to a guard-house, where a noncommissioned officer inspected it by the light of a lantern. Then on we went again for another furlong or so, when we were once more challenged, this time by the German advanced-post. As we resumed our journey, we perceived, in the rear, a small party of Hussars, who did not follow us, but wheeled suddenly to the left, bent, no doubt, on some reconnoitering expedition. We were now beyond the German lines, and the dawn was breaking. Yonder was the Seine, with several islands lying on its bosom, and some wooded heights rising beyond it. Drawing nearer to the river, we passed through the village of Rolleboise, which gives its name to the chief tunnel on the Western Line, and drove across the debatable ground where French Francstireurs were constantly on the prowl for venturesome Uhlans. At last we got to Bonnieres, a little place of some seven or eight hundred inhabitants, on the limits of Seine-et-Oise; and there we had to alight, for the vehicles, which had brought us from Saint Germain, could proceed no further.

Fortunately, we secured others, and went on towards the village of Jeufosse, where the nearest French outposts were established. We were displaying the white flag, but the first French sentries we met, young fellows of the Mobile Guard, refused for a little while to let us pass. Eventually they referred the matter to an officer, who, on discovering that we were English and had come from Paris, began to chat with us in a very friendly manner, asking all the usual questions about the state of affairs in the capital, and expressing the usual satisfaction that the city could still hold out. When we took leave, he cordially wished us ***bon voyage***, and on we hastened, still following the course of the Seine, to the little town of Vernon. Its inquisitive inhabitants at once surrounded us, eager to know who we were, whence we had come, and whither we were going. But we did not tarry many minutes, for we suddenly learnt that the railway communication with Rouen only began at Gaillon, several leagues further on, and that there was only one train a day. The question which immediately arose was--could we catch it?

On we went, then, once more, this time up, over, and down a succession of steep hills, until at last we reached Gaillon station, and found to our delight that the train would not start for another twenty minutes. All our companions took tickets for Rouen, whence they intended to proceed to Dieppe or Le Havre. But my father and I branched off before reaching the Norman capital, and, after, arriving at Elbeuf, travelled through the departments of the Eure and the Orne, passing Alencon on our way to Le Mans. On two or three occasions we had to change from one train to another. The travelling was extremely slow, and there were innumerable stoppages. The lines were constantly encumbered with vans laden with military supplies, and the stations were full of troops going in one and another direction. In the waiting-rooms one found crowds of officers lying on the couches, the chairs, and the tables, and striving to snatch a few hours' sleep; whilst all over the floors and the platforms soldiers had stretched themselves for the same purpose. Very seldom could any food be obtained, but I luckily secured a loaf, some cheese, and a bottle of wine at Alencon. It must have been about one o'clock in the morning when we at last reached Le Mans, and found that there would be no train going to Rennes for another four or five hours.

The big railway-station of Le Mans was full of reinforcements for the Army of the Loire. After strolling about for a few minutes, my father and I sat down on the platform with our backs against a wall, for not a bench or a stool was available. Every now and again some train prepared to start, men were hastily mustered, and then climbed into all sorts of carriages and vans. A belated general rushed along, accompanied by eager ***aides-de-camp***. Now and again a rifle slipped from the hand of some Mobile Guard who had been imbibing too freely, and fell with a clatter on the platform. Then stores were bundled into trucks, whistles sounded, engines puffed, and meanwhile, although men were constantly departing, the station seemed to be as crowded as ever. When at last I got up to stretch myself, I noticed, affixed to the wall against which I had been leaning, a proclamation of Gambetta's respecting D'Aurelle de Paladines' victory over Von der Tann at Orleans. In another part of the station were lithographed notices emanating from the Prefect of the department, and reciting a variety of recent Government decrees and items of war news, skirmishes, reconnaissances, and so forth. At last, however, our train came in. It was composed almost entirely of third-class carriages with wooden seats, and we had to be content with that accommodation.

Another long and wearisome journey then began. Again we travelled slowly, again there were innumerable stoppages, again we passed trains crowded with soldiers, or crammed full of military stores. At some place where we stopped there was a train conveying some scores of horses, mostly poor, miserable old creatures. I looked and wondered at the sight of them. "They have come from England," said a fellow-passenger; "every boat from Southampton to Saint Malo brings over quite a number." It was unpleasant to think that such sorry-looking beasts had been shipped by one's own countrymen. However, we reached Rennes at last, and were there able to get a good square meal, and also to send a telegram to my stepmother, notifying her of our early arrival. It was, however, at a late hour that we arrived at Saint Malo, whence we drove to La Petite Amelia at Saint Servan.

The latter town then contained a considerable colony of English people, among whom the military element predominated. Quite a number of half-pay or retired officers had come to live there with their families, finding Jersey overcrowded and desiring to practise economy. The colony also included several Irish landlords in reduced circumstances, who had quitted the restless isle to escape assassination at the hands of "Rory of the Hills" and folk of his stamp. In addition, there were several maiden ladies of divers ages, but all of slender means; one or two courtesy lords of high descent, but burdened with numerous offspring; together with a riding-master who wrote novels, and an elderly clergyman appointed by the Bishop of Gibraltar. I dare say there may have been a few black sheep in the colony; but the picture which Mrs. Annie Edwardes gave of it in her novel, "Susan Fielding," was exaggerated, though there was truth in the incidents which she introduced into another of her works, "Ought We to Visit Her?" On the whole, the Saint Servan colony was a very respectable one, even if it was not possessed of any great means. Going there during my holidays, I met many young fellows of my own age or thereabouts, and mostly belonging to military families. There were also several charming girls, both English and Irish. With the young fellows I boated, with the young ladies I played croquet.

Now, whilst my father and I had been shut up in Paris, we had frequently written to my stepmother by balloon-post, and on some of our letters being shown to the clergyman of the colony, he requested permission to read them to his congregation--which he frequently did, omitting, of course, the more private passages, but giving all the items of news and comments on the situation which the letters contained. As a matter of fact, this helped the reverend gentleman out of a difficulty. He was an excellent man, but, like many others of his cloth, he did not know how to preach. In fact, a year or two later, I myself wrote one or two sermons for him, working into them certain matters of interest to the colony. During the earlier part of the siege of Paris, however, the reading of my father's letters and my own from the pulpit at the close of the usual service saved the colony's pastor from the trouble of composing a bad sermon, or of picking out an indifferent one from some forgotten theological work. My father, on arriving at Saint Servan, secluded himself as far as possible, so as to rest awhile before proceeding to England; but I went about much as usual; and my letters read from the pulpit, and sundry other matters, having made me a kind of "public character," I was at once pounced upon in the streets, carried off to the club and to private houses, and there questioned and cross-questioned by a dozen or twenty Crimean and Indian veteran officers who were following the progress of the war with a passionate interest. A year or two previously, moreover, my stepmother had formed a close friendship with one of the chief French families of the town. The father, a retired officer of the French naval service, was to have commanded a local Marching Battalion, but he unfortunately sickened and died, leaving his wife with one daughter, a beautiful girl who was of about my own age. Now, this family had been joined by the wife's parents, an elderly couple, who, on the approach of the Germans to Paris, had quitted the suburb where they resided. I was often with these friends at Saint Servan, and on arriving there from Paris, our conversation naturally turned on the war. As the old gentleman's house in the environs of the capital was well within the French lines, he had not much reason to fear for its safety, and, moreover, he had taken the precaution to remove his valuables into the city. But he was sorely perturbed by all the conflicting news respecting the military operations in the provinces, the reported victories which turned out to be defeats, the adverse rumours concerning the condition of the French forces, the alleged scandal of the Camp of Conlie, where the more recent Breton levies were said to be dying off like rotten sheep, and many other matters besides. Every evening when I called on these friends the conversation was the same. The ladies, the grandmother, the daughter, and the granddaughter, sat there making garments for the soldiers or preparing lint for the wounded--those being the constant occupations of the women of Brittany during all the hours they could spare from their household duties--and meanwhile the old gentleman discussed with me both the true and the spurious news of the day. The result of those conversations was that, as soon as my father had betaken himself to England, I resolved to go to the front myself, ascertain as much of the truth as I could, and become, indeed, a war-correspondent on "my own." In forming that decision I was influenced, moreover, by one of those youthful dreams which life seldom, if ever, fulfils.

IX
THE WAR IN THE PROVINCES

First Efforts of the National Defence Delegates--La Motte-Rouge and his Dyed Hair--The German Advance South of Paris--Moltke and King William-- Bourges, the German Objective--Characteristics of Beauce, Perche, and Sologne--French Evacuation of Orleans--Gambetta arrives at Tours--His Coadjutor, Charles Louis de Saulces de Freycinet--Total Forces of the National Defence on Gambetta's Arrival--D'Aurelle de Paladines supersedes La Motte-Rouge--The Affair of Chateaudun--Cambriels--Garibaldi--Jessie White Mario--Edward Vizetelly--Catholic Hatred of Garibaldi--The Germans at Dijon--The projected Relief of Paris--Trochu's Errors and Ducrot's Schemes--The French Victory of Coulmiers--Change of Plan in Paris--My Newspaper Work--My Brother Adrian Vizetelly--The General Position.

When I reached Brittany, coming from Paris, early in the second fortnight of November, the Provincial Delegation of the Government of National Defence was able to meet the Germans with very considerable forces. But such had not been the case immediately after Sedan. As I pointed out previously--quite apart from the flower of the old Imperial Army, which was beleaguered around Metz--a force far too large for mere purposes of defence was confined within the lines with which the Germans invested Paris. In the provinces, the number of troops ready to take the field was very small indeed. Old Cremieux, the Minister of Justice, was sent out of Paris already on September 12, and took with him a certain General Lefort, who was to attend to matters of military organization in the provinces. But little or no confidence was placed in the resources there. The military members of the National Defence Government--General Trochu, its President, and General Le Flo, its Minister of War, had not the slightest idea that provincial France might be capable of a great effort. They relied chiefly on the imprisoned army of Paris, as is shown by all their despatches and subsequent apologies. However, Glais-Bizoin followed Cremieux to Tours, where it had been arranged that the Government Delegation should instal itself, and he was accompanied by Admiral Fourichon, the Minister of Marine. On reaching the Loire region, the new authorities found a few battalions of Mobile Guards, ill-armed and ill-equipped, a battalion of sharpshooters previously brought from Algeria, one or two batteries of artillery, and a cavalry division of four regiments commanded by General Reyau. This division had been gathered together in the final days of the Empire, and was to have been sent to Mezieres, to assist MacMahon in his effort to succour Bazaine; but on failing to get there, it had made just a few vain attempts to check the Germans in their advance on Paris, and had then fallen back to the south of the capital.

General Lefort's first task was to collect the necessary elements for an additional army corps--the 15th--and he summoned to his assistance the veteran General de la Motte-Rouge, previously a very capable officer, but now almost a septuagenarian, whose particular fad it was to dye his hair, and thereby endeavour to make himself look no more than fifty. No doubt, hi the seventeenth century, the famous Prince de Conde with the eagle glance took a score of wigs with him when he started on a campaign; but even such a practice as that is not suited to modern conditions of warfare, though be it admitted that it takes less time to change one's wig than to have one's hair dyed. The latter practice may, of course, help a man to cut a fine figure on parade, but it is of no utility in the field. In a controversy which arose after the publication of Zola's novel "La Debaole," there was a conflict of evidence as to whether the cheeks of Napoleon III were or were not rouged in order to conceal his ghastly pallor on the fatal day of Sedan. That may always remain a moot point; but it is, I think, certain that during the last two years of his rule his moustache and "imperial" were dyed.

But let me return to the National Defence. Paris, as I formerly mentioned, was invested on September 19. On the 22nd a Bavarian force occupied the village of Longjumeau, referred to in my account of my journey to Versailles. A couple of days later, the Fourth Division of German cavalry, commanded by Prince Albert (the elder) of Prussia, started southward through the departments of Eure-et-Loir and Loiret, going towards Artenay in the direction of Orleans. This division, which met at first with little opposition, belonged to a force which was detached from the main army of the Crown Prince of Prussia, and placed under the command of the Grand-Duke Frederick Francis of Mecklenburg-Schwerin. Near this "Armee-Abtheilung," as the Germans called it, was the first Bavarian army corps, which had fought at Bazeilles on the day of Sedan. It was commanded by General von und zu der Tann-Rathsamhausen, commonly called Von der Tann, *tout court*.

As Prince Albert of Prussia, on drawing near to Artenay, found a good many French soldiers, both regulars and irregulars, that is Francs-tireurs, located in the district, he deemed it best to retire on Toury and Pithiviers. But his appearance so far south had sufficed to alarm the French commander at Orleans, General de Polhes, who at once, ordered his men to evacuate the city and retire, partly on Blois, and partly on La Motte-Beuvron. This pusillanimity incensed the Delegates of the National Defence, and Polhes was momentarily superseded by General Reyau, and later (October 5) by La Motte-Rouge.

It is known, nowadays, that the Germans were at first perplexed as to the best course to pursue after they had completed the investment of Paris. Moltke had not anticipated a long siege of the French capital. He had imagined that the city would speedily surrender, and that the war would then come to an end. Fully acquainted with the tract of country lying between the Rhine and Paris, he had much less knowledge of other parts of France; and, moreover, although he had long known how many men could be placed in the field by the military organisation of the Empire, he undoubtedly underestimated the further resources of the French, and did not anticipate any vigorous provincial resistance. His sovereign, King William, formed a more correct estimate respecting the prolongation of the struggle, and, as was mentioned by me in my previous book--"Republican France"--he more than once rectified the mistakes which were made by the great German strategist.

The invader's objective with respect to central France was Bourges, the old capital of Berry, renowned for its ordnance and ammunition works, and, in the days when the troops of our Henry V overran France, the scene of Charles VII's retirement, before he was inspirited either by Agnes Sorel or by Joan of Arc. To enable an army coming from the direction of Paris to seize Bourges, it is in the first instance necessary--as a reference to any map of France will show--to secure possession of

Orleans, which is situated at the most northern point, the apex, so to say, of the course of the Loire, and is only about sixty-eight miles from Paris. At the same time it is advisable that any advance upon Orleans should be covered, westward, by a corresponding advance on Chartres, and thence on Chateaudun. This became the German plan, and whilst a force under General von Wittich marched on Chartres, Von der Tann's men approached Orleans through the Beauce region.

From the forest of Dourdan on the north to the Loire on the south, and from the Chartres region on the west to the Gatinais on the east, this great grain-growing plateau (the scene of Zola's famous novel "La Terre") is almost level. Although its soil is very fertile there are few watercourses in Beauce, none of them, moreover, being of a nature to impede the march of an army. The roads are lined with stunted elms, and here and there a small copse, a straggling farm, a little village, may be seen, together with many a row of stacks, the whole forming in late autumn and in winter--when hurricanes, rain, and snow-storms sweep across the great expanse-- as dreary a picture as the most melancholy-minded individual could desire. Whilst there is no natural obstacle to impede the advance of an invader, there is also no cover for purposes of defence. All the way from Chartres to Orleans the high-road is not once intersected by a river. Nearly all of the few streams which exist thereabouts run from south to north, and they supply no means of defence against an army coming from the direction of Paris. The region is one better suited for the employment of cavalry and artillery than for that of foot-soldiers.

The Chartres country is better watered than Beaude. Westward, in both of the districts of Perche, going either towards Mortagne or towards Nogent-le-Rotrou, the country is more hilly and more wooded; and hedges, ditches, and dingle paths abound there. In such districts infantry can well be employed for defensive purposes. Beyond the Loir--not the Loire-- S.S.W. of Chartres, is the Pays Dunois, that is the district of Chateaudun, a little town protected on the north and the west by the Loir and the Conie, and by the hills between which those rivers flow, but open to any attack on the east, from which direction, indeed, the Germans naturally approached it.

Beyond the Loire, to the south-east of Beauce and Orleans, lies the sheep-breeding region called Sologne, which the Germans would have had to cross had they prosecuted their intended march on Bourges. Here cavalry and artillery are of little use, the country abounding in streams, ponds, and marshes. Quite apart, however, from natural obstacles, no advance on Bourges could well be prosecuted so long as the French held Orleans; and even when that city had fallen into the hands of the Germans, the presence of large French forces on the west compelled the invaders to carry hostilities in that direction and abandon their projected march southward. Thus the campaign in which I became interested was carried on principally in the departments of Eure-et-Loir, Loiret, Loir-et-Cher, and Sarthe, to terminate, at last, in Mayenne.

Great indiscipline prevailed among the troops whom La Motte-Rouge had under his orders. An attack by Von der Tann to the north of Orleans on October 10, led to the retreat of a part of the French forces. On the following day, when the French had from 12,000 to 13,000 men engaged, they were badly defeated, some 1800 of their men being put *hors de combat*, and as many being taken prisoners. This reverse, which was due partly to some mistakes made by La Motte-Rouge, and partly to the inferior quality of his troops, led to the immediate evacuation of Orleans. Now, it was precisely at this moment that Gambetta appeared upon the scene. He had left Paris, it will be remembered, on October 7; on the 8th he was at Rouen, on the 9th he joined the other Government delegates at Tours, and on the 10th--the eve of La Motte-Rouge's defeat--he became Minister of War as well as Minister of the Interior.

Previously the portfolio for war had been held in the provinces by Admiral Fourichon, with General Lefort as his assistant; but Fourichon had resigned in connexion with a Communalist rising which had taken place at Lyons towards the end of September, when the Prefect, Challemel-Lacour, was momentarily made a prisoner by the insurgents, but was afterwards released by some loyal National Guards. [See my book, "The Anarchists: Their Faith and their Record," John Lane, 1911.] Complaining that General Mazure, commander of the garrison, had not done his duty on this occasion, Challemel-Lacour caused him to be arrested, and Fourichon, siding with the general, thereupon resigned the War Ministry, Cremieux taking it over until Gambetta's arrival. It may well be asked how one could expect the military affairs of France to prosper when they were subordinated to such wretched squabbles.

Among the men whom Gambetta found at Tours, was an engineer, who, after the Revolution of September 4, had been appointed Prefect of Tarn-et-Garonne, but who, coming into conflict with the extremists of Montauban, much as Challemel-Lacour had come into conflict with those of Lyons, had promptly resigned his functions. His name was Charles Louis de Saulces de Freycinet, and, though he was born at Foix near the Pyrenees, he belonged to an ancient family of Dauphine. At this period (October, 1870), Freycinet had nearly completed his forty-second year. After qualifying as an engineer at the Ecole Polytechnique, he had held various posts at Mont-de-Marsan, Chartres, and Bordeaux, before securing in 1864 the position of traffic-manager to the Chemin de Fer du Midi. Subsequently he was entrusted with various missions abroad, and in 1869 the Institute of France crowned a little work of his on the employment of women and children in English factories. Mining engineering was his speciality, but he was extremely versatile and resourceful, and immediately attracted the notice of Gambetta. Let it be said to the latter's credit that in that hour of crisis he cast all prejudices aside. He cared nothing for the antecedents of any man who was willing to cooperate in the defence of France; and thus, although Freycinet came of an ancient-aristocratic house, and had made his way under the Empire, which had created him first a chevalier and then an officer of the Legion of Honour, Gambetta at once selected him to act as his chef-de-cabinet, and delegate in military affairs.

At this moment the National Defence had in or ready for the field only 40,000 regular infantry, a like number of Mobile Guards, from 5000 to 6000 cavalry, and about 100 guns, some of antiquated models and with very few men to serve them. There were certainly a good many men at various regimental depots, together with Mobile Guards and National Guards in all the uninvaded provinces of France; but all these had to be drilled, equipped, and armed. That was the first part of the great task which lay before Gambetta and Freycinet. Within a month, however--leaving aside what was done in other parts of the country--France had on the Loire alone an army of 100,000 men, who for a moment, at all events, turned the tide of war. At the same time I would add that, before Gambetta's arrival on the scene, the National Defence Delegates had begun to concentrate some small bodies of troops both in Normandy and in Picardy and Artois, the latter forming the first nucleus of the Army of the North which Faidherbe afterwards commanded. Further, in the east of France there was a force under General Cambriels, whose object was to cut the

German communications in the Vosges.

Von der Tann, having defeated La Motte-Rouge, occupied Orleans, whilst the French withdrew across the Loire to La Motte-Beuvron and Gien, south and southeast of their former position. Gambetta had to take action immediately. He did so by removing La Motte-Rouge from his command, which he gave to D'Aurelle de Paladines. The latter, a general on the reserve list, with a distinguished record, was in his sixty-sixth year, having been born at Languedoc in 1804. He had abilities as an organiser, and was known to be a disciplinarian, but he was growing old, and looked confidence both in himself and in his men. At the moment of D'Aurelle's appointment, Von der Tann wished to advance on Bourges, in accordance with Moltke's instructions, and, in doing so, he proposed to evacuate Orleans; but this was forbidden by King William and the Crown Prince, and in the result the Bavarian general suffered a repulse at Salbris, which checked his advance southward. Still covering Bourges and Vierzon, D'Aurelle soon had 60,000 men under his orders, thanks to the efforts of Gambetta and Freyeinet. But the enemy were now making progress to the west of Orleans, in which direction the tragic affair of Chateaudun occurred on October 18. The German column operating on that side under General von Wittich, consisted of 6000 infantry, four batteries, and a cavalry regiment, which advanced on Chateaudun from the east, and, on being resisted by the villagers of Varize and Civry, shot them down without mercy, and set all their houses (about 130 in number) on fire. Nevertheless, that punishment did not deter the National Guards of Chateaudun, and the Francs-tireurs who had joined them, from offering the most strenuous opposition to the invaders, though the latter's numerical superiority alone was as seven to one. The fierce fight was followed by terrible scenes. Most of the Francs-tireurs, who had not fallen in the engagement, effected a retreat, and on discovering this, the infuriated Germans, to whom the mere name of Franc-tireur was as a red rag to a bull, did not scruple to shoot down a number of non-combatants, including women and children.

I remember the excitement which the news of the Chateaudun affair occasioned in besieged Paris; and when I left the capital a few weeks later I heard it constantly spoken of. In vain did the Germans strive to gloss over the truth. The proofs were too numerous and the reality was too dreadful. Two hundred and thirty-five of the devoted little town's houses were committed to the flames. For the first time in the whole course of the war women were deliberately assaulted, and a couple of German Princes disgraced their exalted station in a drunken and incendiary orgie.

Meantime, in the east of France, Cambriels had failed in his attempt to cut the German communications, and had been compelled to beat a retreat. It must be said for him that his troops were a very sorry lot, who could not be depended upon. Not only were they badly disciplined and addicted to drunkenness, but they took to marauding and pillage, and were in no degree a match for the men whom the German General von Werder led against them. Garibaldi, the Italian Liberator, had offered his sword to France, soon after the fall of the Second Empire. On October 8--that is, a day before Gambetta--he arrived at Tours, to arrange for a command, like that of Cambriels, in the east of France. The little Army of the Vosges, which was eventually constituted under his orders, was made up of very heterogeneous elements. Italians, Switzers, Poles, Hungarians, Englishmen, as well as Frenchmen, were to be found in its ranks. The general could not be called a very old man, being indeed only sixty-three years of age, but he had led an eventful and arduous life; and, as will be remembered, ever since the affair of Aspromonte in 1862, he had been lame, and had gradually become more and more infirm. He had with him, however, two of his sons, Menotti and Ricoiotti (the second a more competent soldier than the first), and several, able men, such as his compatriot Lobbia, and the Pole, Bosak-Hauke. His chief of staff, Bordone, previously a navy doctor, was, however, a very fussy individual who imagined himself to be a military genius. Among the Englishmen with Garibaldi were Robert Middleton and my brother Edward Vizetelly; and there was an Englishwoman, Jessie White Mario, daughter of White the boat-builder of Cowes, and widow of Mario, Garibaldi's companion in arms in the glorious Liberation days. My brother often told me that Mme. Mario was equally at home in an ambulance or in a charge, for she was an excellent nurse and an admirable horsewoman as well as a good shot. She is one of the women of whom I think when I hear or read that the members of the completing sex cannot fight. But that of course is merely the opinion of some medical and newspaper men.

Mme. Mario contributed a certain number of articles to the ***Daily News***. So did my brother--it was indeed as ***Daily News*** correspondent that he first joined Garibaldi's forces--but he speedily became an orderly to the general, and later a captain on the staff. He was at the battles of Dijon and Autun, and served under Lobbia in the relief of Langres. Some French historians of these later days have written so slightingly of the little Army of the Vosges, that I am sorry my brother did not leave any permanent record of his experiences. Garibaldi's task was no easy one. In the first instance, the National Defence hesitated to employ him; secondly, they wished to subordinate him to Cambriels, and he declined to take any such position; not that he objected to serve under any superior commander who would treat him fairly, but because he, Garibaldi, was a freethinker, and knew that he was bitterly detested by the fervently Catholic generals, such as Cambriels. As it happened, he secured an independent command. But in exercising it he had to co-operate with Cambriels in various ways, and in later years my brother told me how shamefully Cambriels acted more than once towards the Garibaldian force. It was indeed a repetition of what had occurred at the very outset of the war, when such intense jealousy had existed among certain marshals and generals that one had preferred to let another be defeated rather than march "at the sound of the guns" to his assistance.

I also remember my brother telling me that when Langres (which is in the Haute Marne, west of the Aube and the Cote d'Or) was relieved by Lobbia's column, the commander of the garrison refused at first to let the Garibaldians enter the town. He was prepared to surrender to the Germans, if necessary; but the thought that he, a devout Catholic, should owe any assistance to such a band of unbelieving brigands as the Garibaldian enemies of the Pope was absolutely odious to him. Fortunately, this kind of feeling did not show itself in western France. There was, at one moment, some little difficulty respecting the position of Cathelineau, the descendant of the famous Vendeen leader, but, on the whole, Catholics, Royalists, and Republicans loyally supported one another, fired by a common patriotism.

The failure of Cambriel's attempts to cut the German communications, and the relatively small importance of the Garibaldian force, inspired Gambetta with the idea of forming a large Army of the East which, with Langres, Belfort, and Besancon as its bases, would vigorously assume the offensive in that part of France. Moltke, however, had already sent General von Werder orders to pursue the retreating Cambriels. Various engagements, late in October, were followed by a German march on Dijon. There were at this time 12,000 or 13,000 Mobile Guards in the Cote d'Or, but no general in command of them. Authority was exercised by a civilian, Dr. Lavalle. The forces assembled at Dijon and Beaune amounted, inclusive of regulars and National Guards, to about 20,000 men, but they were very badly equipped and armed, and their officers were few in number and of very indifferent ability. Werder came down on Dijon in a somewhat hesitating way, like a man who is not sure of his ground or of the strength of the enemy in front of him. But the French were alarmed by his approach, and on October 30 Dijon was evacuated, and soon afterwards occupied by Werder with two brigades.

Three days previously Metz had surrendered, and France was reeling under the unexpected blow in spite of all the ardent proclamations with which Gambetta strove to impart hope and stimulate patriotism. Bazaine's capitulation naturally implied the release of the forces under Prince Frederick Charles, by which he had been invested, and their transfer to other parts of France for a more vigorous prosecution of the invasion. Werder, after occupying Dijon, was to have gone westward through the Nivernais in order to assist other forces in the designs on Bourges. But some days before Metz actually fell, Moltke sent him different instructions, setting forth that he was to take no further account of Bourges, but to hold Dijon, and concentrate at Vesoul, keeping a watch on Langres and Besancon. For a moment, however, 3600 French under an officer named Fauconnet suddenly recaptured Dijon, though there were more than 10,000 Badeners installed there under General von Beyer. Unfortunately Fauconnet was killed in the affair, a fresh evacuation of the Burgundian capital ensued, and the Germans then remained in possession of the city for more than a couple of months.

In the west the army of the Loire was being steadily increased and consolidated, thanks to the untiring efforts of Gambetta, Freycinet, and D'Aurelle, the last of whom certainly contributed largely to the organization of the force, though he was little inclined to quit his lines and assume the offensive. It was undoubtedly on this army that Gambetta based his principal hopes. The task assigned to it was greater than those allotted to any of the other armies which were gradually assuming shape--being, indeed, the relief of beleaguered Paris.

Trochu's own memoirs show that at the outset of the siege his one thought was to remain on the defensive. In this connexion it is held, nowadays, that he misjudged the German temperament, that remembering the vigorous attempts of the Allies on Sebastopol--he was, as we know, in the Crimea, at the time--he imagined that the Germans would make similarly vigorous attempts on Paris. He did not expect a long and so to say passive siege, a mere blockade during which the investing army would simply content itself with repulsing the efforts of the besieged to break through its lines. He knew that the Germans had behaved differently in the case of Strasbourg and some other eastern strongholds, and anticipated a similar line of action with respect to the French capital. But the Germans preferred to follow a waiting policy towards both Metz and Paris. It has been said that this was less the idea of Moltke than that of Bismarck, whose famous phrase about letting the Parisians stew in their own juice will be remembered. But one should also recollect that both Metz and Paris were defended by great forces, and that there was little likelihood of any *coup de main* succeeding; whilst, as for bombardment, though it might have some moral, it would probably have very little material effect. Metz was not really bombarded, and the attempt to bombard Paris was deferred for several months. When it at last took place a certain number of buildings were damaged, 100 persons were killed and 200 persons wounded--a material effect which can only be described as absolutely trivial in the case of so great and so populous a city.

Trochu's idea to remain merely on the defensive did not appeal to his coadjutor General Ducrot. The latter had wished to break through the German lines on the day of Sedan, and he now wished to break through them round Paris. Various schemes occurred to him. One was to make a sortie in the direction of Le Bourget and the plain of Saint Denis, but it seemed useless to attempt to break out on the north, as the Germans held Laon, Soissons, La Fere, and Amiens. There was also an idea of making an attempt on the south, in the direction of Villejuif, but everything seemed to indicate that the Germans were extremely strong on this side of the city and occupied no little of the surrounding country. The question of a sortie on the east, across the Marne, was also mooted and dismissed for various reasons; the idea finally adopted being to break out by way of the Gennevilliers peninsula formed by the course of the Seine on the north-west, and then (the heights of Cormeil having been secured) to cross the Oise, and afterwards march on Rouen, where it would be possible to victual the army. Moreover, instructions were to be sent into the provinces in order that both the forces on the Loire and those in the north might bear towards Normandy, and there join the army from Paris, in such wise that there would be a quarter of a million men between Dieppe, Rouen, and Caen. Trochu ended by agreeing to this scheme, and even entertained a hope that he might be able to revictual Paris by way of the Seine, for which purpose a flotilla of boats was prepared. Ducrot and he expected to be ready by November 15 or 20, but it is said that they were hampered in their preparations by the objections raised by Guiod and Chabaud-Latour, the former an engineer, and the latter an artillery general. Moreover, the course of events in the provinces suddenly caused a complete reversal of Ducrot's plans.

On November 9, D'Aurelle de Paladines defeated Von der Tann at Coulmiers, west of Orleans. The young French troops behaved extremely well, but the victory not being followed up with sufficient vigour by D'Aurelle, remained somewhat incomplete, though it constrained the Germans to evacuate Orleans. On the whole this was the first considerable success achieved by the French since the beginning of the war, and it did much to revive the spirits which had been drooping since the fall of Metz. Another of its results was to change Ducrot's plans respecting the Paris sortie. He and Trochu had hitherto taken little account of the provincial armies, and the success of Coulmiers came to them as a surprise and a revelation. There really was an army of the Loire, then, and it was advancing on Paris from Orleans. The Parisian forces must therefore break out on the south-east and join hands with this army of relief in or near the forest of Fontainebleau. Thus, all the preparations for a sortie by way of Gennevilliers were abandoned, and followed by others for an attempt in the direction of Champigny.

Such was roughly the position at the time when I reached Brittany and conceived the idea of joining the French forces on the Loire and forwarding some account of their operations to England. During my stay in Paris with my father I had assisted him in preparing several articles, and had written others on my own account. My eldest brother, Adrian Vizetelly, was at this time assistant-secretary at the Institution of Naval Architects. He had been a student at the Royal School of Naval Architecture with the Whites, Elgars, Yarrows, Turnbulls, and other famous shipbuilders, and on quitting it had taken the assistant-secretaryship in question as an occupation pending some suitable vacancy in the Government service or some large private yard. The famous naval constructor, E. J. Reed, had started in life in precisely the same post, and it was, indeed, at his personal suggestion that my brother took it. A year or two later he and his friend Dr. Francis Elgar, subsequently Director of Dockyards and one of the heads of the Fairfield Shipbuilding Company, were assisting Reed to run his review *Naval Science*. At the time of the Franco-German war, however, my brother, then in his twenty-sixth year, was writing on naval subjects for the *Daily News* and the *Pall Mall Gazette,* edited respectively by John Robinson and Frederick Greenwood. A few articles written by me during my siege days were sent direct to the latter by balloon-post, but I knew not what their fate might be. The *Pall Mall* might be unable to use them, and there was no possibility of their being returned to me in Paris. My father, whom I assisted in preparing a variety of articles, suggested that everything of this kind--that is, work not intended for the *Illustrated London News*--should be sent to my brother for him to deal with as opportunity offered. He placed a few articles with *The Times*--notably some rather long ones on the fortifications and armament of Paris, whilst others went to the *Daily News* and the *Pall Mall*.

When, after coming out of Paris, I arrived in Brittany, I heard that virtually everything sent from the capital by my father or myself had been used in one or another paper, and was not a little pleased to receive a draft on a Saint Malo banking-house for my share of the proceeds. This money enabled me to proceed, in the first instance, in the direction of Le Mans, which the Germans were already threatening. Before referring, however, to my own experiences I must say something further respecting the general position. The battle of Coulmiers (November 9) was followed by a period of inaction on the part of the Loire Army. Had D'Aurelle pursued Von der Tann he might have turned his barren victory to good account. But he had not much confidence in his troops, and the weather was bad--sleet and snow falling continually. Moreover, the French commander believed that the Bavarian retreat concealed a trap. At a conference held between him, Gambetta, Freyoinet, and the generals at the head of the various army corps, only one of the latter---Chanzy--favoured an immediate march on Paris. Borel, who was chief of D'Aurelle's staff, proposed to confine operations to an advance on Chartres, which would certainly have been a good position to occupy, for it would have brought the army nearer to the capital, giving it two railway lines, those of Le Mans and Granville, for revictualling purposes, and enabling it to retreat on Brittany in the event of any serious reverse. But no advance at all was made. The Germans were allowed all necessary time to increase their forces, the French remaining inactive within D'Aurelle's lines, and their *morale* steadily declining by reason of the hardships to which they were subjected. The general-in-chief refused to billet them in the villages--for fear, said he, of indiscipline--and compelled them to bivouack, under canvas, in the mud; seldom, moreover, allowing any fires to be kindled. For a score of days did this state of affairs continue, and the effect of it was seen at the battle of Beaune-la-Rolande.

The responsibility for the treatment of the troops rests on D'Aurelle's memory and that of some of his fellow-generals. Meantime, Gambetta and Freycinet were exerting themselves to improve the situation generally. They realized that the release of Prince Frederick Charles's forces from the investment of Metz necessitated the reinforcement of the Army of the Loire, and they took steps accordingly. Cambriels had now been replaced in eastern France by a certain General Michel, who lost his head and was superseded by his comrade Crouzat. The last-named had with him 30,000 men and 40 guns to contend against the 21,000 men and the 70 guns of Werder's army. In order to strengthen the Loire forces, however, half of Crouzat's men and he himself received orders to approach Orleans by way of Nevers and Gien, the remainder of his army being instructed to retire on Lyons, in order to quiet the agitation prevailing in that city, which regarded itself as defenceless and complained bitterly thereof, although there was no likelihood at all of a German attack for at least some time to come.

The new arrangements left Garibaldi chief commander in eastern France, though the forces directly under his orders did not at this time exceed 5000 men, and included, moreover, no fewer than sixty petty free-corps, who cared little for discipline. [There were women in several of these companies, one of the latter including no fewer than eighteen amazons.] A month or two previously the advent of from twenty to thirty thousand Italian volunteers had been confidently prophesied, but very few of these came forward. Nevertheless, Ricciotti Garibaldi (with whom was my brother Edward) defeated a German force in a sharp engagement at Chatillon-sur- Seine (November 19), and a week later the Garibaldians made a gallant attempt to recapture the city of Dijon. Five thousand men, however, were of no avail against an army corps; and thus, even if the Garibaldian attack had momentarily succeeded, it would have been impossible to hold Dijon against Werder's troops. The attempt having failed, the German commander resolved to crush the Army of the Vosges, which fled and scattered, swiftly pursued by a brigade under General von Keller. Great jealousy prevailed at this moment among the French generals in command of various corps which might have helped the Garibaldians. Bressolles, Crevisier, and Cremer were at loggerheads. On November 30 the last-named fought an indecisive action at Nuits, followed nearly three weeks later by another in which he claimed the victory.

Meantime, Crouzat's force, now known as the 20th Army Corps, had been moving on Nevers. To assist the Loire Army yet further, General Bourbaki had been summoned from the north-west of France. At the fall of the Empire the defence in that part of the country had been entrusted to Fririon, whom Espinet de la Villeboisnet succeeded. The resources at the disposal of both those generals were very limited, confined, indeed, to men of the regimental depots and some Mobile Guards. There was a deficiency both of officers and of weapons, and in the early skirmishes which took place with the enemy, the principal combatants were armed peasants, rural firemen, and the National Guards of various towns. It is true that for a while the German force consisted only of a battalion of infantry and some Saxon cavalry. Under Anatole de la Forge, Prefect of the Aisne, the open town of Saint Quentin offered a gallant resistance to the invader, but although this had some moral effect, its importance was not great. Bourbaki, who succeeded La Villeboisnet in command of the region, was as diffident respecting the value of his troops as was D'Aurelle on the Loire. He had previously commanded the very pick of the French army, that is the Imperial Guard, and the men now placed under his orders were by no means of the same class. Bourbaki was at this time only fifty-four years of age, and when, after being sent out of Metz on a mission to the Empress Eugenie at Hastings, he had offered his services to the National Defence, the latter had given him the best possible welcome. But he became one of the great military failures of the period.

After the fall of Metz the Germans despatched larger forces under Manteuffel into north-west France. Altogether there were 35,000 infantry and 4000 cavalry, with 174 guns, against a French force of 22,000 men who were distributed with 60 guns over a front of some thirty miles, their object being to protect both Amiens and Rouen. When Bourbaki was summoned to the Loire, he left Farre as chief commander in the north, with Faidherbe and Lecointe as his principal lieutenants. There was bad strategy on both sides, but La Fere capitulated to the Germans on November 26, and Amiens on the 29th.

Meantime, the position in beleaguered Paris was becoming very bad. Some ten thousand men, either of the regular or the auxiliary forces, were laid up in hospital, less on account of wounds than of disease. Charcoal--for cooking purposes according to the orthodox French system--was being strictly rationed, On November 20 only a certain number of milch cows and a few hundred oxen, reserved for hospital and ambulance patients, remained of all the bovine live stock collected together before the siege. At the end of November, 500 horses were being slaughtered every day. On the other hand, the bread allowance had been raised from 750 grammes to a kilogramme per diem, and a great deal of bread was given to the horses as food. Somewhat uncertain communications had been opened with the provinces by means of pigeon-post, the first pigeon to bring despatches into the city arriving there on November 15. The despatches, photographed on the smallest possible scale, were usually enclosed in quills fastened under one or another of the birds' wings. Each balloon that left the city now took with it a certain number of carrier-pigeons for this service. Owing, however, to the bitter cold which prevailed that winter, many of the birds perished on the return journey, and thus the despatches they carried did not reach Paris. Whenever any such communications arrived there, they had to be enlarged by means of a magic-lantern contrivance, in order that they might be deciphered. Meantime, the aeronauts leaving the city conveyed Government despatches as well as private correspondence, and in this wise Trochu was able to inform Gambetta that the army of Paris intended to make a great effort on November 29.

X
WITH THE "ARMY OF BRITTANY"

The German Advance Westward--Gambetta at Le Mans--The "Army of Brittany" and Count de Keratry--The Camp of Conlie--The Breton Marching Division-- Keratry resigns--The Champigny Sortie from Paris--The dilatory D'Aurelle-- The pitiable 20th Army Corps--Battles of Beaune-la-Rolande and Loigny-- Loss of Orleans--D'Aurelle superseded by Chanzy--Chanzy's Slow Retreat-- The 21st Corps summoned to the Front--I march with the Breton Division-- Marchenoir and Fretevel--Our Retreat--Our Rearguard Action at Droue-- Behaviour of the Inhabitants--We fight our Way from Fontenelle to Saint Agil--Guns and Quagmires--Our Return to Le Mans--I proceed to Bennes and Saint Malo.

After the Chateaudun affair the Germans secured possession of Chartres, whence they proceeded to raid the department of the Eure. Going by way of Nogent-le-Roi and Chateauneuf-en-Thimerais, they seized the old ecclesiastical town of Evreux on November 19, whereupon the French hastily retreated into the Orne. Some minor engagements followed, all to the advantage of the Germans, who on the 22nd attacked and occupied the ancient and strategically important town of Nogent-le-Rotrou--the lordship of which, just prior to the great Revolution, belonged to the family of the famous Count D'Orsay, the lover of Lady Blessington and the friend of Napoleon III. The occupation of Nogent brought the Germans to a favourable point on the direct railway-line between Paris and Le Mans, the capital of Maine. The region had been occupied by a somewhat skeleton French army corps--the 21st--commanded by a certain General Fiereck. On the loss of Nogent, Gambetta immediately replaced him by one of the many naval officers who were now with the French armies, that is Post-Captain (later Admiral) Constant Jaures, uncle of the famous Socialist leader of more recent times. Jaures at once decided to retreat on Le Mans, a distance of rather more than a hundred miles, and this was effected within two days, but under lamentable circumstances. Thousands of starving men deserted, and others were only kept with the columns by the employment of cavalry and the threat of turning the artillery upon them.

Directly Gambetta heard of the state of affairs, he hastened to Le Mans to provide for the defence of that extremely important point, where no fewer than five great railway lines converged, those of Paris, Alencon, Rennes, Angers, and Tours. The troops commanded by Jaures were in a very deplorable condition, and it was absolutely necessary to strengthen them. It so happened that a large body of men was assembled at Conlie, sixteen or seventeen miles away. They formed what was called the "Army of Brittany," and were commanded by Count Emile de Keratry, the son of a distinguished politician and literary man who escaped the guillotine during the Reign of Terror. The Count himself had sat in the Legislative Body of the Second Empire, but had begun life as a soldier, serving both in the Crimea and in Mexico, in which latter country he had acted as one of Bazaine's orderly officers. At the Revolution Keratry was appointed Prefect of Police, but on October 14 he left Paris by balloon, being entrusted by Trochu and Jules Favre with a mission to Prim, in the hope that he might secure Spanish support for France. Prim and his colleagues refused to intervene, however, and Keratry then hastened to Tours, where he placed himself at the disposal of Gambetta, with whom he was on terms of close friendship. It was arranged between them that Keratry should gather together all the available men who were left in Brittany, and train and organize them, for which purposes a camp was established at Conlie, north-west of Le Mans.

Conlie was the first place which I decided to visit on quitting Saint Servan. The most appalling rumours were current throughout Brittany respecting the new camp. It was said to be grossly mismanaged and to be a hotbed of disease. I visited it, collected a quantity of information, and prepared an article which was printed by the ***Daily News*** and attracted considerable attention, being quoted by several other London papers and taken in two instances as the text for leading articles. So far as the camp's defences and the arming of the men assembled within it were concerned, my strictures were fully justified, but certain official documents, subsequently published, indicate that I was in error on some points. The whole question having given rise to a good deal of controversy among writers on the Franco-German War--some of them regarding Conlie as a flagrant proof of Gambetta's mismanagement of military affairs--I will here set down what I believe to be strictly the truth respecting it.

The camp was established near the site of an old Roman one, located between Conlie and Domfront, the principal part occupying some rising ground in the centre of an extensive valley. It was intended to be a training camp rather than an entrenched and fortified one, though a redoubt was erected on the south, and some works were begun on the northern and the north-eastern sides. When the Grand Duke of Mecklenburg reached Conlie after the battle of Le Mans, he expressed his surprise that the French had not fortified so good a position more seriously, and defended it with vigour. Both the railway line and the high-road between Laval and Le Mans were near at hand, and only a few miles away there was the old town of Sille-le-Guillaume, one of the chief grain and cattle markets of the region. There was considerable forest-land in the vicinity, and wood was abundant. But there was no watercourse, and the wells of the various adjacent little farms yielded but a very inadequate supply of water for a camp in which at one moment some 40,000 men were assembled. Thus, at the outset, the camp lacked one great essential, and such was the case when I visited it in November. But I am bound to add that a source was soon afterwards found in the very centre of the camp, and tapped so successfully by means of a steam-pumping arrangement that it ended by yielding over 300,000 litres of water per diem. The critics of the camp have said that the spot was very damp and muddy, and therefore necessarily unhealthy, and there is truth in that assertion; but the same might be remarked of all the camps of the period, notably that of D'Aurelle de Paladines in front of Orleans. Moreover, when a week's snow was followed by a fortnight's thaw, matters could scarcely be different. [From first to last (November 12 to January 7) 1942 cases of illness were treated in the five ambulances of the camp. Among them were 264 cases of small-pox. There were a great many instances of bronchitis and kindred affections, but not many of dysentery. Among the small-pox cases 88 proved fatal.]

I find on referring to documents of the period that on November 23, the day before Gambetta visited the camp, as I shall presently relate, the total effective was

665 officers with 23,881 men. By December 5 (although a marching division of about 12,000 men had then left for the front) the effective had risen to 1241 officers with about 40,000 men. [The rationing of the men cost on an average about 7 *d.* per diem.] There were 40 guns for the defence of the camp, and some 50 field-pieces of various types, often, however, without carriages and almost invariably without teams. At no time, I find, were there more than 360 horses and fifty mules in the camp. There was also a great scarcity of ammunition for the guns. On November 23, the 24,000 men assembled in the camp had between them the following firearms and ammunition:--

Weapons	*Cartridges*	
Spencers (without bayonets)	5,000	912,080
Chassepots	2,080	100,000
Remingtons	2,000	218,000
Snyders	1,866	170,000
Muskets of various types ..	9,684	*Insufficient*
Revolvers	500	*Sufficient*
	21,130	

Such things as guns, gun-carriages, firearms, cartridges, bayonets, and so forth formed the subject of innumerable telegrams and letters exchanged between Keratry and the National Defence Delegation at Tours. The former was constantly receiving promises from Gambetta, which were seldom kept, supplies at first intended for him being at the last moment sent in other directions, according to the more pressing requirements of the hour. Moreover, a good many of the weapons which Keratry actually received were defective. In the early days of the camp, many of the men were given staves--broom-sticks in some instances--for use at drill.

When Gambetta arrived at Le Mans after Jaures had retreated thither, he learnt that action had become the more urgent as the Germans were steadily prosecuting their advance. By orders of the Grand Duke of Mecklenburg, to whose army these forces belonged, the French were followed to La Ferte-Bernard; and whilst one German column then went west towards Saint Cosme, another advanced southward to Vibraye, thus seriously threatening Le Mans. Such was the position on November 23. Fortunately, Freycinet was able to send Jaures reinforcements which brought his effective to about 35,000 men, and at the same time Gambetta urged Keratry to prepare a marching division of the men at Conlie. Early on the 24th, Gambetta (who, by the way, had travelled from Tours to Le Mans at full speed on a railway engine) visited the camp, and expressed his approval of all he saw there. I caught a glimpse of him, muffled in his fur coat, and looking, as well he might, intensely cold. His orders to Keratry were to proceed to Saint Calais, and thence to the forest of Vibraye, so as to cover Le Mans on the east. It took fourteen hours and twenty-one trains to convey the marching division to Yvre l'Eveque on the Huisne, just beyond Le Mans. The effective of the division was roughly 12,000 men, nearly all of them being Breton Mobilises. The artillery consisted of one battery of 12's, and one of 4's, with the necessary horses, two batteries of 4's dragged by naval volunteers, and several Gatling guns, which had only just been delivered. These Gatlings, which at that time were absolutely unknown in France, were not mounted, but packed in sections in sealed zinc cases, which were opened in the railway vans on the journey, the guns being there put together by a young naval officer and a couple of civilian engineers. A little later the artillery of the force was augmented.

After these troops had taken up position at Yvre, in order to prevent the enemy from crossing the Huisne, various conferences were held between Gambetta, Jaures, and Keratry. General Le Bouedec had been left in command at Conlie, and General Trinite had been selected to command the marching division of the Bretons. From the very outset, however, Keratry objected to the plans of Gambetta and Jaures, and, for the moment, the duties of the Bretons were limited to participating in a reconnaissance on a somewhat large scale--two columns of Jaures' forces, under Generals Colin and Rousseau, joining in this movement, which was directed chiefly on Bouloire, midway between Le Mans and Saint Calais on the east. When Bouloire was reached, however, the Germans who had momentarily occupied it had retired, and the French thereupon withdrew to their former positions near Le Mans.

Then came trouble. Gambetta placed Keratry under the orders of Jaures, and Keratry would not accept the position. Great jealousy prevailed between these two men; Keratry, who had served ten years in the French Army, claiming that he knew a good deal more about military matters than Jaures, who, as I previously mentioned, had hitherto been a naval officer. In the end Keratry threw up his command. Le Bouedec succeeded him at Conlie, and Frigate-Captain Gougeard (afterwards Minister of Marine in Gambetta's Great Ministry) took charge of the Bretons at Yvre, where he exerted himself to bring them to a higher state of efficiency.

I must now refer to some other matters. Trochu had informed Gambetta of his intention to make a sortie on the south-eastern side of Paris. The plans adopted were mainly those of Ducrot, who took chief command. A diversion made by Vinoy to the south of the city on November 29 gave the Germans an inkling of what was intended, and proved a fruitless venture which cost the French 1000 men. Another diversion attempted by General Susbielle on November 30 led to a similar result, with a loss of 1200 men. Ducrot, however, crossed the Marne, and very desperate fighting ensued at Champigny and neighbouring localities. But Ducrot's force (less than 100,000 men) was insufficient for his purpose. The weather, moreover, was extremely cold, the men had brought with them neither tents nor blankets, and had to bivouac without fires. According to Trochu's memoirs there was also an insufficiency of ammunition. Thus the Champigny sortie failed, and the French retired to their former lines. [From November 30 to December 3 the French lost 9482 men; and the Germans 5288 men.]

At the very moment when the Army of Paris was in full retreat, the second battle of Orleans was beginning. Gambetta and Freyoinet wished D'Aurelle to advance with the Loire Army in order to meet the Parisians, who, if victorious, were expected to march on Fontainebleau by way of Melun. In the latter days of November D'Aurelle was still covering Orleans on the north with the 15th and 16th army corps (Generals Martin des Pallieres and Chanzy). On his left was the 17th under Durrieu, who, a few days later, was succeeded by a dashing cavalry officer, General de Sonis. Near at hand, also, there was the 18th army corps, to command which Bourbaki had been summoned from northern France, his place being taken temporarily by young General Billot, who was appointed to be his chief of staff. The former Army of the East under Crouzat [This had now become the 20th Army Corps.] was on the southern side of the Loire, somewhere between Gien and Nevers, and it was in a very deplorable condition. Boots were wanted for 10,000 men, tents for a like number, and knapsacks for 20,000. In some battalions there were only sufficient knapsacks for a quarter of the men, the others carrying their clothes, provisions, and cartridges all higgledy-piggledy in canvas bags. I once heard an eyewitness relate that many of Crouzat's soldiers marched with their biscuits (four days' supply) strung together like chaplets, which hung from their necks or shoulders.

The Germans had heard of the removal of Crouzat's force to the Loire country, and by way of creating a diversion the Grand Duke of Mecklenburg was ordered to march on Beaugenoy, southwest of Orleans. Meantime, Gambetta and Freyoinet were vainly imploring D'Aurelle to advance. He made all sorts of excuses. At one moment he offered to consider their plans-- not to comply with them; at another he wished to wait for decisive news from Trochu and Ducrot. Finally, instead of the five army corps resolutely advancing in the direction of Paris, it was resolved just to open the way with the 18th (Billot), the 20th (Crouzat), and some detachments of the 15th (Martin des Pallieres). The result was the sharp battle and serious defeat of Beaune-la-Rolande (November 28), when the 18th corps behaved extremely well, whilst the 20th, to whose deplorable condition I have just referred, retreated after a little fighting; the men of the 15th on their side doing little or nothing at all. In this engagement the French, whose forces ought to have been more concentrated, lost 4000 men in killed and wounded, and 1800 who were taken prisoners; the German loss not exceeding 1000 men. Four days later (December 2) came the very serious repulse of Loigny-Poupry, in which the 15th, 16th, and 17th army corps were engaged. The French then lost from 6000 to 7000 men (2500 of them being taken prisoners), and though the German losses exceeded 4000, the engagement ended by quite demoralising D'Aurelle's army.

Under those conditions came the battle of Orleans on December 3 and 4--the Germans now being under the chief command of that able soldier, Prince Frederick Charles of Prussia, father of the Duchess of Connaught. On this occasion D'Aurelle ordered the corps engaged at Loigny to retreat on his entrenched camp. The 18th and 20th could not cooperate in this movement, however; and on the three others being driven back, D'Aurelle instructed Chanzy to retire on Beaugency and Marchenoir, but sent no orders to Bourbaki, who was now on the scene of action. Finally, the commander-in- chief decided to abandon his entrenched camp, the troops disbanded and scattered, and Orleans was evacuated, the flight being so precipitate that two of the five bridges across the Loire were left intact, at the enemy's disposal.

Moreover, the French Army was now dislocated, Bourbaki, with the 18th, and Des Pallieres, with the 15th corps, being on the south of the river, whilst the other three corps were on the northern side. The former retired in the direction of Bourges and Nevers, whilst Chanzy, who was now placed in chief command of the others, D'Aurelle being removed from his post, withdrew gradually towards the forest of Marchenoir. In that second battle of Orleans the French lost 20,000 men, but 18,000 of them were taken prisoners. On their side, the Germans (who captured 74 guns) lost fewer than 1800 men.

For three days (December 8 to 10) Chanzy contested the German advance at Villorceau, but on December 12 Blois had to be evacuated, and the army withdrew to the line of the Loir in the neighbourhood of Vendome. Meantime, at the very moment when the fate of Orleans was being sealed, orders reached Jaures at Le Mans to advance to the support of the Loire Army. I was lodging at an inn in the town, my means being too slender to enable me to patronize any of the big hotels on the Place des Halles, which, moreover, were crowded with officers, functionaries, and so forth. I had become acquainted with some of the officers of the Breton division under Gougeard, and on hearing that they were going to the front, I managed to obtain from Colonel Bernard, Gougeard's chief of staff, permission to accompany the column with one of the ambulance parties. Now and again during the advance I rode in one of the vans, but for the most part I marched with the men, this, moreover, being the preferable course, as the weather was extremely cold. Even had I possessed the means (and at most I had about L10 in my pocket), I could not have bought a horse at Le Mans. I was stoutly clad, having a very warm overcoat of grey Irish frieze, with good boots, and a pair of gaiters made for me by Nicholas, the Saint Malo bootmaker, younger brother (so he himself asserted) of Niccolini the tenor, sometime husband of Mme. Patti.

There were from 10,000 to 12,000 men in our force, which now ranked as the fourth division of the 21st army corps. Nearly all the men of both brigades were Breton Mobilises, adjoined to whom, however, perhaps for the purpose of steadying them, were three or four very small detachments of former regiments of the line. There was also a small contingent of the French Foreign Legion, which had been brought from Algeria. Starting from Yvre l'Eveque towards, noon on December 4, we marched to Ardenay, where we spent the night. The weather was fine and dry, but intensely cold. On the 5th we camped on some hills near the town of Saint Calais, moved only a mile or two farther on the 6th--there being a delay in the receipt of certain orders--then, at seven o'clock on the 7th, started in the direction of Vendome, marching for about twelve hours with only the briefest halts. We passed from the department of the Sarthe into that of Loir-et-Cher, going on until we reached a little place called Ville-aux-Cleros, where we spent the night under uncomfortable conditions, for it snowed. Early the following day we set out again, and, leaving Vendome a couple of miles or so away on our right, we passed Freteval and camped on the outskirts of the forest of Marchenoir.

The night proved bitterly cold, the temperature being some fourteen degrees (centigrade) below freezing-point. I slept huddled up in a van, but the men generally were under canvas, and there was very little straw for them to lie upon, in such wise that in the morning some of them actually found their garments frost-bound to the ground! Throughout the night of the 10th we heard guns booming in the distance. On the 11th, the 12th, and the 13th December we were continually marching, always going in the direction of the guns. We went from Ecoman to Moree, to Saint Hilaire-la-Gravelle, and thence to the Chateau de Rougemont near Freteval, a spot famous as the scene of a victory gained by our Richard Coeur-de-Lion over Philip Augustus. The more or less distant artillery fire was incessant both by day and by night; but we were only supporting other divisions of the corps, and did not find ourselves actually engaged. On the 15th, however, there was very sharp fighting both at Freteval and Moree, and on the morning of the 16th our Gatlings went forward to support the second division of our army corps, which was being hard pressed by the Germans.

All at once, however, orders for a general retreat arrived, Chanzy having at last decided to fall back on Le Mans. There was considerable confusion, but at last our men set out, taking a north-westerly direction. Fairly good order prevailed on the road, and the wiry little Bretons at least proved that their marching powers were unimpaired. We went on incessantly though slowly during the night, and did not make a real halt until about seven o'clock on the following morning, when, almost dead-beat, we reached a little town called Droue.

Jaures, I should mention, had received the order to retreat at about four o'clock on the afternoon of December 16, and had speedily selected three different routes for the withdrawal of the 21st army corps. Our division, however, was the last to quit its positions, it being about eight o'clock at night when we set out. Thus our march lasted nine hours. The country was a succession of sinuous valleys and stiff slopes, and banks often overlooked the roads, which were edged with oaks and bushes. There were several streams, a few woods, and a good many little copses. Farms often lay close together, and now and again attempts were made to buy food and drink of the peasantry, who, upon hearing our approach, came at times with lights to their thresholds. But they were a close-fisted breed, and demanded exorbitant prices. Half a franc was the lowest charge for a piece of bread. Considering how bad the men's boots were, the marching was very good, but a number of men deserted under cover of the night. Generally speaking, though there was a slight skirmish at Cloyes and an engagement at Droue, as I shall presently relate, the retreat was not greatly hampered by the enemy. In point of fact, as the revelations of more recent years have shown, Moltke was more anxious about the forces of Bourbaki than about those of Chanzy, and both Prince Frederick Charles and the Grand Duke of Mecklenburg had instructions to keep a strict watch on the movements of Bourbaki's corps. Nevertheless, some of the Grand Duke's troops--notably a body of cavalry--attempted to cut off our retreat. When, however, late on the 16th, some of our men came in contact with a detachment of the enemy near Cloyes, they momentarily checked its progress, and, as I have indicated, we succeeded in reaching Droue without loss.

That morning, the 17th, the weather was again very cold, a fog following the rain and sleet of the previous days. Somewhat later, however, snow began to fall. At Droue--a little place of about a thousand inhabitants, with a ruined castle and an ancient church--we breakfasted as best we could. About nine o'clock came marching orders, and an hour later, when a large number of our men were already on their way towards Saint Agil, our next halting-place, General Gougeard mounted and prepared to go off with his staff, immediately in advance of our rear-guard. At that precise moment, however, we were attacked by the Germans, whose presence near us we had not suspected.

It was, however, certainly known to some of the inhabitants of Droue, who, terrified by all that they had heard of the harshness shown by the Germans towards the localities where they encountered any resistance, shrank from informing either

Gougeard or any of his officers that the enemy was at hand. The artillery with which our rear was to be protected was at this moment on the little square of Droue. It consisted of a mountain battery under Sub-Lieutenant Gouesse of the artillery, and three Gatlings under Sub-Lieutenant De la Forte of the navy, with naval lieutenant Rodellec du Porzic in chief command. Whilst it was being brought into position, Colonel Bernard, Gougeard's chief of staff, galloped off to stop the retreat of the other part of our column. The enemy's force consisted of detachments of cavalry, artillery, and Landwehr infantry. Before our little guns could be trained on them, the Landwehr men had already seized several outlying houses, barns, and sheds, whence they strove to pick off our gutiners. For a moment our Mobilises hesitated to go forward, but Gougeard dashed amongst them, appealed to their courage, and then led them against the enemy.

Not more than three hundred yards separated the bulk of the contending forces, indeed there were some Germans in the houses less than two hundred yards away. Our men at last forced these fellows to decamp, killing and wounding several of them; whilst, thanks to Colonel Bernard's prompt intervention, a battalion of the 19th line regiment and two companies of the Foreign Legion, whose retreat was hastily stopped, threatened the enemy's right flank. A squadron of the Second Lancers under a young lieutenant also came to our help, dismounting and supporting Gougeard's Mobilises with the carbines they carried. Realizing that we were in force, the enemy ended by retreating, but not until there had been a good deal of fighting in and around the outlying houses of Droue.

Such, briefly, was the first action I ever witnessed. Like others, I was under fire for some time, being near the guns and helping to carry away the gunners whom the Germans shot from the windows of the houses in which they had installed themselves. We lost four or five artillerymen in that manner, including the chief officer, M. de Rodelleo du Porzic, whom a bullet struck in the chest. He passed away in a little cafe whither we carried him. He was, I believe, the last of his family, two of his brothers having previously been killed in action.

We lost four or five other officers in this same engagement, as well as a Breton chaplain of the Mobilises. Our total losses were certainly larger than Gougeard subsequently stated in his official report, amounting in killed and wounded, I think, to from 120 to 150 men. Though the officers as a rule behaved extremely well--some of them, indeed, splendidly--there were a few lamentable instances of cowardice. By Gougeard's orders, four were placed under arrest and court-martialled at the end of the retreat. Of these, two were acquitted, whilst a third was shot, and a fourth sentenced to two years' imprisonment in a fortress. [From the formation of the "Army of Brittany" until the armistice the total number of executions was eleven. They included one officer (mentioned above) for cowardice in presence of the enemy; five men of the Foreign Legion for murdering peasants; one Franc-titeur for armed robbery, and four men (Line and Mobile Guards) for desertion in presence of the enemy. The number would have been larger had it been possible to identify and punish those who were most guilty in the stampede of La Tuilerie during the battle of Le Mans.]

The enemy's pursuit having been checked, we eventually quitted Droue, but when we had gone another three miles or so and reached a village called Fontenelle, the Germans came on again. It was then about two o'clock in the afternoon, and for a couple of hours or so, whilst we continued our retreat, the enemy kept up a running cannonade, repeatedly endeavouring to harass our rear. We constantly replied to their fire, however, and steadily kept them off, losing only a few men before the dusk fell, when the pursuit ceased. We afterwards plodded on slowly--the roads being in a terrible condition--until at about half-past six o'clock we reached the village of Saint Agil, where the staff installed itself at Count de Saint-Maixent's stately renaissance chateau.

The weather was better on December 18, for, though it was extremely cold, the snow ceased falling. But we still had a formidable task before us. The roads, as I have said, were wretched, and at Saint Agil we had to contend with some terrible quagmires, across which we found it at first impossible to get our guns, ammunition-vans, and baggage train. It became necessary to lop and fell trees, and form with them a kind of bed over which our impedimenta might travel. Hour after hour went by amidst incessant labour. An ammunition waggon containing only half its proper load required the efforts of a dozen horses to pull it over that morass, whilst, as for the guns, each of the 12's required even more horses. It was three o'clock on the afternoon of the 18th when the last gun was got across. Three gun-carriages were broken during those efforts, but our men managed to save the pieces. Late in the operations the Germans again put in an appearance, but were held in respect by our Gatlings and mountain-guns. Half an hour, however, after our departure from Saint Agil, they entered the village.

In a very wretched condition, half-famished and footsore, we went on, through the sudden thaw which had set in, towards Vibraye, whose forest, full in those days of wild boars and deer, stretched away on our left. We were now in the department of the Sarthe, and, cutting across country in the direction of the Huisne, we at last reached the ancient little *bourg* of Connerre, on the high-road running (left of the river) towards Le Mans. There I took leave of our column, and, after buying a shirt and some socks, hastened to the railway station--a mile and a half distant-- hoping, from what was told me, that there might be some means of getting to Le Mans by train, instead of accompanying our men along the highway. At Connerre station I found a very good inn, where I at once partook of the best meal that I had eaten since leaving Le Mans, sixteen days previously. I then washed, put on my new shirt and socks, and went to interview the station-master. After a great deal of trouble, as I had a permit signed by Colonel Bernard, and wore an ambulance armlet, I was allowed to travel to Le Mans in a railway van. There was no regular service of trains, the only ones now running so far north being used for military purposes. I got to Le Mans a few hours before our column reached Yvre l'Eveque on the night of December 20, and at once sought a train which would convey me to Rennes, if not as far as Saint Malo. Then came another long, slow, dreary journey in a villainous wooden-seated third-class carriage. It was between ten and eleven o'clock in the morning when we reached Rennes. I still had about five-and-twenty francs in my pocket, and knowing that it would not cost me more than a quarter of that amount to get to Saint Malo, I resolved to indulge in a good *dejeuner* at the Hotel de France.

There was nobody excepting a few waiters in the long dining-room, but the tables were already laid there. When, however, I seated myself at one of them, the head-waiter came up declaring that I could not be accommodated, as the tables were reserved for *ces messieurs*. I was inquiring who *ces messieurs* might be, when some of them entered the room in a very swaggering manner. All were arrayed in stylish and brand-new uniforms, with beautiful boots, and looked in the pink of condition. They belonged, I found, to a free corps called the "Eclaireurs d'Ille-et-Vilaine," and their principal occupations were to mess together copiously and then stroll about the town, ogling all the good-looking girls they met. The corps never went to the front. Three or four weeks afterwards, when I again passed through Rennes--this second time with my father--Messieurs les Eclaireurs were still displaying their immaculate uniforms and highly polished boots amidst all the misery exhibited by the remnants of one of Chanzy's ***corps d'armee***.

Though I was little more than a boy, my blood fairly boiled when I was requested to give up my seat at table for these arrogant young fops. I went to complain at the hotel ***bureau***, but, being confronted there by the landlady instead of by the landlord, I did not express my feelings so strongly as I might have done. "Madame" sweetly informed me that the first ***dejeuner*** was entirely reserved for Messieurs les Eclaireurs, but that, if I would wait till the second ***dejeuner*** at noon, I should find ample accommodation. However, I was not inclined to do any such thing. I thought of all the poor, famished, shivering men whom I had left less than twenty-four hours previously, and some of whom I had more than once helped to buy bread and cheese and wine during our long and painful marches. They, at all events, had done their duty as best they could, and I felt highly indignant with the swaggering young bloods of Rennes, who were content to remain in their native town displaying their uniforms and enjoying themselves. Fortunately, such instances were very rare.

Returning to the railway station, I obtained something to eat at the refreshment-room, where I presently heard somebody trying to make a waiter understand an order given in broken French. Recognizing a fellow-countryman, I intervened and procured what he desired. I found that he was going to Saint Malo like myself, so we made the journey together. He told me that, although he spoke very little French, he had come to France on behalf of an English boot-making firm in order to get a contract from some of the military authorities. Many such people were to be found in Brittany, at Le Mans, at Tours, and elsewhere, during the latter period of the war. An uncle of mine, Frederick Vizetelly, came over, I remember, and interviewed Freyeinet and others on behalf of an English small-arm firm. I forget whether he secured a contract or not; but it is a lamentable and uncontrovertible fact that many of the weapons and many of the boots sold by English makers to the National Defence were extremely defective. Some of the American weapons were even worse than ours. As for the boots, they often had mere "composition soles," which were soon worn out. I saw, notably after the battle of Le Mans, hundreds--I believe I might say, without, exaggeration, thousands--of men whose boots were mere remnants. Some hobbled through the snow with only rags wrapped round their bleeding feet. On the other hand, a few of our firms undoubtedly supplied satisfactory boots, and it may have been so in the case of the traveller whom I met at Rennes.

A few days after my return to Saint Malo, my cousin, Montague Vizetelly, arrived there with a commission from the *Daily News* to join Chanzy's forces at Le Mans. Mr. Robinson, I was afterwards told, had put some questions about me to my brother Adrian, and, on hearing how young I was, had thought that I might not be equal to the occasion if a decisive battle between Prince Frederick Charles and Chanzy should be fought. My cousin-- then four-and-twenty years of age--was accordingly sent over. From that time nearly all my war letters were forwarded to the *Pall Mall Gazette*, and, as it happened, one of them was the first account of the great battle of Le Mans, from the French side, to appear in an English paper.

XI
BEFORE LE MANS

The War in various Regions of France--General Faidherbe--Battle of Pont-Noyelles--Unreliability of French Official News--Engagement of Nuits--Le Bourget Sortie--Battles of Bapaume and Villersexel--Chanzy's Plan of Operations--The Affair of Saint Calais--Wretched State of some of Chanzy's Soldiers--Le Mans and its Historical Associations--The Surrounding Country--Chanzy's Career--Positions of his Forces--Advance of Prince Frederick Charles--The first Fighting before Le Mans and its Result.

Whilst Chanzy was retreating on Le Mans, and there reorganizing and reinforcing his army, a variety of operations went on in other parts of France. After the German occupation of Amiens, Moltke instructed Manteuffel to advance on Rouen, which he did, afterwards despatching a column to Dieppe; the result being that on December 9 the Germans, for the first time, reached the sea-coast. Since December 3 Faidherbe had taken the chief command of the Army of the North at Lille. He was distinctly a clever general, and was at that time only fifty-two years of age. But he had spent eleven years in Senegal, organizing and developing that colony, and his health had been impaired by the tropical West African climate. Nevertheless, he evinced no little energy, and never despaired, however slender might be the forces under him, and however cramped his position. As soon as he had reorganized the army entrusted to his charge, he moved towards Amiens, and on December 23 and 24 a battle was fought at Pont-Noyelles, in the vicinity of that town. In some respects Faidherbe gained the advantage, but his success was a barren one, and his losses were far greater than those of the Germans, amounting, indeed, to 2300 men (apart from many deserters), whereas the enemy's were not more than a thousand. Gambetta, however, telegraphed to the Prefects that a great victory had been gained; and I remember that when a notice to that effect was posted at the town-hall of Saint Servan, everybody there became jubilant.

Most of our war-news, or, at least, the earliest intelligence of any important engagement, came to us in the fashion I have indicated, townsfolk constantly assembling outside the prefectures, subprefectures, and municipal buildings in order to read the day's news. At times it was entirely false, at others some slight success of the French arms was magnified into a victory, and a petty engagement became a pitched battle. The news in the French newspapers was usually very belated and often quite unreliable, though now and again telegrams from London were published, giving information which was as near to the truth as the many English war correspondents on both sides could ascertain. After the war, both Frenchmen and Germans admitted to me that of all the newspaper intelligence of the period there was nothing approaching in accuracy that which was imparted by our British correspondents. I am convinced, from all I heard in Paris, in Berlin, in Vienna, and elsewhere, during the two or three years which followed the war, that the reputation of the British Press was greatly enhanced on the Continent by the news it gave during the Franco-German campaign. Many a time in the course of the next few years did I hear foreigners inquire: "What do the London papers say?" or remark: "If an English paper says it, it must be true." I do not wish to blow the trumpet too loudly on behalf of the profession to which I belonged for many years, but what I have here mentioned is strictly true; and now that my days of travel are over, I should be glad to know that foreigners still hold the British Press in the same high esteem.

But, to return to my narrative, whilst the events I have mentioned were taking place in Normandy and Northern France, Gambetta was vainly trying to persuade Bourbaki to advance in the direction of Montargis. He also wished to reinforce Garibaldi; but the enmity of many French officers towards the Italian Liberator was so great that they would not serve with him. General von Werder was at this time covering the siege of Belfort and watching Langres. On December 18 there was an engagement at Nuits between some of his forces and those led by the French commander Cremer, who claimed the victory, but afterwards retreated towards Beaune. The French, however, were now able to re-occupy Dijon. On the 21st another sortie was made from Paris, this time on the north, in the direction of Le Bourget and Ville-Evrard. Ducrot was again in command, and 200,000 men were got together, but only 5000 were brought into action. There were a great many desertions, and no fewer than six officers of one brigade alone were court-martialled and punished for lack of courage. The affair appears to have been arranged in order to quiet the more reckless elements in Paris, who were for ever demanding "a great, a torrential sortie." In this instance, however, there was merely "much ado about nothing." The truth is, that ever since the Champigny affair both Trochu and Ducrot had lost all confidence.

On January 2 and 3, the French under Faidherbe, and the Germans under Goeben, fought a battle at Bapaume, south of Arras. The former were by far the more numerous force, being, indeed, as three to one, and Faidherbe is credited with having gained a victory. But, again, it was only a barren one, for although the Germans fell back, the French found it quite as necessary to do the same. About a week previously the 16th French Army Corps, with which Bourbaki had done little or nothing on the Loire, had been removed from Vierzon and Bourges to join the Army of the East, of which Bourbaki now assumed the chief command. The transport of the troops proved a very difficult affair, and there was great disorder and, again, many desertions. Nevertheless, on January 9, Bourbaki fought Werder at Villersexel, in the vicinity of Vesoul, Montbeliard, and Belfort. In this engagement there appear to have been serious mistakes on both sides, and though Bourbaki claimed a success, his losses were numerically double those of the Germans.

Meantime Chanzy, at Le Mans, was urging all sorts of plans on Gambetta and Freyeinet. In the first place he desired to recruit and strengthen his forces, so sorely tried by their difficult retreat; and in order that he might have time to do so, he wished Bourbaki to execute a powerful diversion by marching in the direction of Troyes. But Gambetta and Freyeinet had decided otherwise. Bourbaki's advance was to be towards the Vosges, after which he was to turn westward and march on Paris with 150,000 men. Chanzy was informed of this decision on and about January 5 (1871), and on the 6th he made a last attempt to modify the Government plan in order that Bourbaki's march might be directed on a point nearer to Paris. In reply, he was informed that it was too late to modify the arrangements.

With regard to his own operations, Chanzy's idea was to march towards the capital when his forces were reorganized. His bases were to be the river Sarthe, the town of Le Mans, and the railway-line running northward to Alencon. Thence he proposed to advance to some point on the river Eure between Dreux and Chartres, going afterwards towards Paris by such a route as circumstances might allow. He had 130,000 men near Le Mans, and proposed to take 120,000 with 350 field-pieces or machine-guns, and calculated that he might require a week, or to be precise eight days, to carry this force from Le Mans to Chartres, allowing for fighting on the way. Further, to assist his movements he wished Faidherbe, as well as Bourbaki, to assume the offensive vigorously as soon as he was ready. The carrying out of the scheme was frustrated, however, in part by the movements which the Government ordered Bourbaki to execute, and in part by what may be called the sudden awakening of Prince Frederick Charles, who, feeling more apprehensive respecting Bourbaki's movements, had hitherto, in a measure, neglected Chanzy's doings.

On December 22 Captain, afterwards General, de Boisdeffre [He was Chief of the French Staff during the famous Dreyfus Case, in which his name was frequently mentioned.] reached Le Mans, after quitting Paris in one of the balloons, and gave Chanzy certain messages with which Trochu had entrusted him. He brought nothing in writing, as what he had to communicate was considered too serious to be committed to paper. Yet both my father and myself could have imparted virtually the same information, which was but a ***secret de Polichinelle***. It concerned the date when the fall of Paris would become inevitable. We--my father and myself--had said repeatedly at Versailles and elsewhere that the capital's supply of food would last until the latter days of January, and that the city (unless in the meanwhile it were relieved) must then surrender. Authentic information to that effect was available in Paris before we quitted it in November. Of course Trochu's message to Chanzy was official, and carried greater weight than the assertions of journalists. It was to the effect that it would be necessary to negotiate a capitulation on January 20, in order to give time for the revictualling of the city's two million inhabitants. As it happened, the resistance was prolonged for another week or so. However, Boisdeffre's information was sufficiently explicit to show Chanzy that no time must be lost if Paris was to be saved.

Some German cavalry--probably the same men who had pursued Gougeard's column--showed themselves at Saint Calais, which is only some thirty miles north-east of Le Mans, as early as December 18, but soon retired, and no further advance of the enemy in that direction took place for several days. Chanzy formed two flying columns, one a division under General Jouffroy, and one a body of 4000 men under General Rousseau, for the purpose of worrying the enemy and keeping him at a distance. These troops, particularly those of Jouffroy, who moved towards Montoire and Vendome, had several small but none the less important engagements with the Germans. Prince Frederick Charles, indeed, realised that Jouffroy's operations were designed to ensure the security of Chanzy's main army whilst it was being recruited and reorganized, and thereupon decided to march on Le Mans and attack Chanzy before the latter had attained his object.

On Christmas Day a force of German cavalry, artillery, and infantry descended upon Saint Calais (then a town of about 3500 inhabitants), levied a sum of 17,000 francs, pillaged several of the houses, and ill-treated a number of the townsfolk. When some of the latter ventured to protest, pointing out, among other things, that after various little engagements in the vicinity several wounded Germans had been brought into the town and well cared for there, the enemy's commanding officer called them a pack of cowards, and flung them 2000 francs of his recent levy, to pay them, he said, for their so-called services. The affair was reported to Chanzy, who thereupon wrote an indignant letter to the German general commanding at Vendome. It was carried thither by a certain M. de Vezian, a civil engineer attached to Chanzy's staff, who brought back the following reply:

"Recu une lettre du General Chanzy. Un general prussien ne sachant pas ecrire une lettre de tel genre, ne saurait y faire une reponse par ecrit.

"Au quartier-general a Vendome, 28 Decembre 1870."

Signature (*illegible*).

It was, perhaps, a pity that Chanzy ever wrote his letter of protest. French generals were too much given to expressing their feelings in writing daring that war. Deeds and not words were wanted.

Meantime, the army was being slowly recruited. On December 13, Gambetta had issued--none too soon--a decree authorising the billeting of the men "during the winter campaign." Nevertheless, when Gougeard's troops returned to Yvree l'Eveque, they were ordered to sleep under canvas, like many other divisions of the army. It was a great mistake. In that severe weather--the winter was one of the coldest of the nineteenth century--the men's sufferings were very great. They were in need, too, of many things, new shoes, linen, great-coats, and other garments, and there was much delay in providing for their more urgent requirements. Thus the number of desertions was not to be wondered at. The commander-in-chief did his best to ensure discipline among his dispirited troops. Several men were shot by way of example. When, shortly before the battle of Le Mans, the 21st Army Corps crossed the Huisne to take up positions near Montfort, several officers were severely punished for riding in ambulance and baggage waggons instead of marching with their men.

Le Mans is not easily defended from an enemy advancing upon it from eastern, north-eastern, and south-eastern directions. A close defence is impossible by reason of the character of the country. At the time of which I write, the town was one of about 37,000 inhabitants. Very ancient, already in existence at the time of the Romans, it became the capital of Maine. William the Conqueror seized it, but it was snatched from his son, Robert, by Helie de La Fleche. Later, Geoffrey, the First of the Plantagenets, was buried there, it being, moreover, the birthplace of his son, our Henry II. In after years it was taken from Richard Coeur-de-Lion by Philip-Augustus, who assigned it, however, to Richard's widow, Queen Berengaria. A house in the town is wrongly said to have been her residence, but she undoubtedly founded the Abbaye de l'Epau, near Yvre l'Eveque, and was buried there. It was at Le Mans that King John of France, who surrendered to the Black Prince at Poitiers, was born; and in the neighbouring forest, John's grandson, Charles VI, first gave signs of insanity. Five times during the Anglo-French wars of the days of Henry V and Henry VI, Le Mans was besieged by one or another of the contending parties. The town again suffered during the Huguenot wars, and yet again during the Revolution, when the Vendeens seized it, but were expelled by Marceau, some 5000 of them being bayoneted on the Place de l'Eperon.

Rich in associations with the history of England as well as that of France, Le Mans, in spite of its accessibility--for railway lines coming from five different directions meet there--is seldom visited by our tourists. Its glory is its cathedral, strangely neglected by the numerous English writers on the cathedrals of France. Here are exemplified the architectural styles of five successive centuries, and, as Merimee once wrote, in passing from one part of the edifice to another, it is as if you passed from one to another religion. But the supreme features of the cathedral are its stained-glass windows, which include some of the very oldest in the world. Many years ago, when they were in a more perfect condition than they are now, Hucher gave reproductions of them in a rare folio volume. Here, too, is the tomb of Queen Berengaria of England, removed from the Abbaye de l'Epau; here, also, was formerly that of her husband's grandfather, Geoffrey Plantagenet. But this was destroyed by the Huguenots, and you must go to the museum to see all that remains of it--that is, the priceless enamel *plaque* by which it was formerly surmounted, and which represents Geoffrey grasping his sword and his azure shield, the latter bearing a cross and lions rampant--not the leoparded lions passant of his English descendants. Much ink has flowed respecting that shield during squabbles among heraldists.

Judging by recent plans of Le Mans, a good many changes have taken place there since the time of the Franco-German War. Various new, broad, straight streets have been substituted for some of the quaint old winding ones. The Pont Napoleon now appears to have become the Pont Gambetta, and the Place, des Minimes is called the Place de la Republique. I notice also a Rue Thiers which did not exist in the days when Le Mans was familiar to me as an old-world town. In this narrative I must, of course, take it as it was then, not as it is now.

The Sarthe, flowing from north to south, where it is joined by its tributary the Huisne, coming from the north-east, still divides the town into two unequal sections; the larger one, on the most elevated part of which stands the cathedral, being that on the river's left bank. At the time I write of, the Sarthe was spanned by three stone bridges, a suspension bridge, and a granite and marble railway viaduct, some 560 feet in length. The German advance was bound to come from the east and the south. On the east is a series of heights, below which flow the waters of the Huisne. The views range over an expanse of varying elevation, steep hills and deep valleys being frequent. There are numerous watercourses. The Huisne, which helps to feed the Sarthe, is itself fed by a number of little tributaries. The lowest ground, at the time I have in mind, was generally meadow-land, intersected here and there with rows of poplars, whilst the higher ground was employed for the cultivation of crops. Every little field was circumscribed by ditches, banks, and thick hedges.

The loftiest point of the eastern heights is at Yvre l'Eveque, which was once crowned by a renaissance chateau, where Henry of Navarre resided when he reduced Le Mans to submission. Northward from Yvre, in the direction of Savigne, stretches the high plateau of Sarge, which on the west slopes down towards the river Sarthe, and forms one of the most important of the natural defences of Le Mans. Eastward, from Yvre, you overlook first the Huisne, spanned at various neighbouring points by four bridges, but having much of the meadow-land in its valley cut up by little water-channels for purposes of irrigation--these making the ground additionally difficult for an attacking force to traverse. Secondly, you see a long plateau called Auvours, the possession of which must necessarily facilitate an enemy's operations. Following the course of the railway-line coming from the direction of Paris, you notice several pine woods, planted on former heaths. Still looking eastward, is the village of Champagne, where the slopes are studded with vines, whilst the plain is arable land, dotted over with clumps of chestnut trees. North-east of Champagne is Montfort, where Chanzy at first stationed the bulk of the 21st Army Corps under Jaures, this (leaving his flying columns on one side) being the most eastern position of his forces at the time when the German advance began. The right of the 21st Corps here rested on the Huisne. Its extreme left extended northward towards the Sarthe, but a division of the 17th Corps under General de Colomb guarded the Alencon (N.) and Conlie (N.W.) railway lines.

Confronted by the Huisne, the heights of Yvre and the plateaux of Sarge and Auvours, having, for the most part, to keep to the high-roads--for, bad as their state might be at that season, it was nothing compared with the condition of the many narrow and often deep lanes, whose high banks and hedges, moreover, offered opportunities for ambush--the Germans, it was obvious, would have a difficult task before them on the eastern side of Le Mans, even should they drive the 21st Corps from Montfort. The approach to the town is easier, however, on the south-east and the south, Here are numerous pine woods, but on going towards Le Mans, after passing Parigne-l'Eveque (S.E.) and Mulsanne (S.), the ground is generally much less hilly than on the east. There are, however, certain positions favourable for defence. There is high ground at Change, midway between the road from Saint Calais to Le Mans, *via* Yvre, and the road from Grand Luce to Le Mans *via* Parigne. Over a distance of eight miles, moreover, there extends--or extended at the time I refer to--a track called the Chemin des Boeufs, suitable for defensive purposes, with high ground at at least two points--Le Tertre Rouge, south-east of Le Mans, and La Tuilerie, south of the town. The line of the Chemin des Boeufs and the position of Change was at first entrusted by Chanzy to the 16th Corps, whose commander, Jaureguiberry, had his headquarters at the southern suburb of Pontlieue, an important point affording direct access to Le Mans by a stone bridge over the Huisne.

When I returned to Le Mans from Saint Servan in the very first days of January, Chanzy's forces numbered altogether about 130,000 men, but a very large proportion of them were dispersed in different directions, forming detached columns under Generals Barry, Curten, Rousseau, and Jouffroy. The troops of the two first-named officers had been taken from the 16th Corps (Jaureguiberry), those of Rousseau were really the first division of the 21st Corps (Jaures), and those of Jouffroy belonged to the 17th, commanded by General de Colomb. [The 16th and 17th comprised three divisions each, the 21st including four. The German Corps were generally of only two divisions, with, however, far stronger forces of cavalry than Chanzy disposed of.] It is a curious circumstance that, among the German troops which opposed the latter's forces at this stage of the war, there was a division commanded by a General von Colomb. Both these officers had sprung from the same ancient French family, but Von Colomb came from a Huguenot branch which had quitted France when the Edict of Nantes was revoked.

Chanzy's other chief coadjutors at Le Mans were Jaures, of whom I have already spoken, and Rear-Admiral Jaureguiberry, who, after the general-in- chief, was perhaps the most able of all the commanders. Of Basque origin and born in 1815, he had distinguished himself as a naval officer in the Crimean, Chinese, and Cochin China expeditions; and on taking service in the army under the National Defence, he had contributed powerfully to D'Aurelle's victory at Coulmiers. He became known among the Loire forces as the man who was always the first to attack and the last to retreat. [He looked somewhat older than his years warranted, being very bald, with just a fringe of white hair round the cranium. His upper lip and chin were shaven, but he wore white whiskers of the "mutton-chop" variety. Slim and fairly tall, he was possessed of no little nervous strength and energy. In later years he became Minister of Marine in the Waddington, the second Freycinet, and the Duclerc cabinets.]

Having referred to Chanzy's principal subordinates, it is fitting that I should give a brief account of Chanzy himself. The son of an officer of the First Empire, he was born at Nouart in the Argonne, and from his personal knowledge of that region it is certain that his services would have proved valuable during the disastrous march on Sedan, when, as Zola has rightly pointed out in "La Debacle," so many French commanding officers were altogether ignorant of the nature and possibilities of the country through which they advanced. Chanzy, however, like many others who figured among the Loire forces, had begun life in the navy, enlisting in that service when sixteen years of age. But, after very brief experience afloat, he went to the military school of St. Cyr, passed out of it as a sub-lieutenant in 1843, when he was in his twenty-first year, was appointed to a regiment of Zouaves, and sent to Algeria. He served, however, in the Italian campaign of 1859, became lieutenant-colonel of a line regiment, and as such took part in the Syrian expedition of 1860-61. Later, he was with the French forces garrisoning Rome, acquired a colonelcy in 1864, returned to Algeria, and in 1868 was promoted to the rank of general of brigade.

At the outset of the Franco-German War, he applied for active service, but the imperial authorities would not employ him in France. In spite of the associations of his family with the first Empire, he was, like Trochu, accounted an Orleanist, and it was not desired that any Orleanist general should have an opportunity to distinguish himself in the contemplated "march on Berlin." Marshal MacMahon, however, as Governor of Algeria, had formed a high opinion of Chanzy's merits, and after Sedan, anxious as he was for his country in her predicament, the Marshal, then a prisoner of war, found a means of advising the National Defence to make use of Chanzy's services. That patriotic intervention, which did infinite credit to Mac-Mahon, procured for Chanzy an appointment at the head of the 16th Army Corps, and later the chief command of the Second Loire Army.

When I first saw him in the latter days of 1870, he was in his fifty-eighth year, well built, and taller than the majority of French officers. His fair hair and fair moustache had become grey; but his blue eyes had remained bright, and there was an expression of quiet resolution on his handsome, well-cut face, with its aquiline nose and energetic jaw. Such, physically, was the general whom Moltke subsequently declared to have been the best that France opposed to the Germans throughout the war. I never once saw Chanzy excited, in which respect he greatly contrasted with many of the subordinate commanders. Jaureguiberry was sometimes carried away by his Basque, and Gougeard by his Celtic, blood. So it was with Jaures, who, though born in Paris, had, like his nephew the Socialist leader, the blood of the Midi in his veins. Chanzy, however, belonged to a calmer, a more quietly resolute northern race.

He was inclined to religion, and I remember that, in addition to the chaplains accompanying the Breton battalions, there was a chief chaplain attached to the general staff. This was Abbe de Beuvron, a member of an old noble family of central France. The Chief of the Staff was Major-General Vuillemot; the Provost-General was Colonel Mora, and the principal aides-de-camp were Captains Marois and de Boisdeffre. Specially attached to the headquarters service there was a rather numerous picked force under General Bourdillon. It comprised a regiment of horse gendarmes and one of foot gendarmes, four squadrons of Chasseurs d'Afrique, some artillery provided chiefly with mountain-guns, an aeronautical company under the brothers Tissandier, and three squadrons of Algerian light cavalry, of the Spahi type, who, with their flowing burnouses and their swift little Arab horses, often figured conspicuously in Chanzy's escort. A year or two after the war, I engaged one of these very men--he was called Saad--as a servant, and he proved most devoted and attentive; but he had contracted the germs of pulmonary disease during that cruel winter of 1870-71, and at the end of a few months I had to take him to the Val-de-Grace military hospital in Paris, where he died of galloping consumption.

The German forces opposed to Chanzy consisted of a part of the so-called "Armee-Abtheilung" under the Grand Duke of Mecklenburg, and the "Second Army" under Prince Frederick Charles of Prussia, the latter including the 3rd, 9th, 10th, and 13th Army Corps, and disposing of numerous cavalry and nearly four hundred guns. The Prince ascertained that the French forces were, in part, extremely dispersed, and therefore resolved to act before they could be concentrated. At the outset the Germans came down on Nogent-le-Rotrou, where Rousseau's column was stationed, inflicted a reverse on him, and compelled him (January 7) to fall back on Connerre--a distance of thirty miles from Nogent, and of less than sixteen from Le Mans. On the same day, sections of Jouffroy's forces were defeated at Epuisay and Poirier (mid-way between Le Mans and Vendome), and also forced to retreat. The French detachments (under Jouffroy, Curten, and Barry) which were stationed along the line from Saint Calais to Montoire, and thence to Saint Amand and Chateau-Renault--a stretch of some five-and-twenty miles--were not strong enough to oppose the German advance, and some of them ran the risk of having their retreat cut off. Chanzy realized the danger, and on the morning of January 8 he despatched Jaureguiberry to take command of all the troops distributed from the south to the south-east, between Chateau-du-Loir and Chateau-Renault, and bring them to Le Mans.

But the 10th German Corps was advancing in these directions, and, after an engagement with Barry's troops at Ruille, secured positions round La Chartre. This seriously threatened the retreat of the column under General Curten, which was still at Saint Amand, and, moreover, it was a further menace to Barry himself, as his division was distributed over a front of fourteen miles near Chateau-du-Loir. Jaureguiberry, however, entreated Barry to continue guarding the river Loir, in the hope of Curten being able to retreat to that point.

Whilst, however, these defensive attempts were being made to the south of Le Mans, the Germans were pressing forward on the north-east and the east, Prince Frederick Charles being eager to come in touch with Chanzy's main forces, regardless of what might happen on the Loir and at Saint Amand. On the north-east the enemy advanced to La Ferte Bernard; on the east, at Vance, a brigade of German cavalry drove back the French cuirassiers and Algerians, and Prince Frederick Charles then proceeded as far as Saint Calais, where he prepared for decisive action. One army corps was sent down the line of the Huisne, another had orders to advance on Ardenay, a third on Bouloire, whilst the fourth, leaving Barry on its left flank, was to march on Parigne-l'Eveque. Thus, excepting a brigade of infantry and one of cavalry, detached to observe the isolated Curten, and hold him in check, virtually the whole of the German Second Army marched against Chanzy's main forces.

Chanzy, on his side, now ordered Jaures (21st Corps) to occupy the positions of Yvre, Auvours, and Sarge strongly; whilst Colomb (17th Corps) was instructed to send General Paris's division forward to Ardenay, thus reducing Colomb's actual command to one division, as Jouffroy's column had previously been detached from it. On both sides every operation was attended by great difficulties on account of the very severe weather. A momentary thaw had been followed by another sudden frost, in such wise that the roads had a coating of ice, which rendered them extremely slippery. On January 9 violent snowstorms set in, almost blinding one, and yet the rival hosts did not for an hour desist from their respective efforts. At times, when I recall those days, I wonder whether many who have read of Napoleon's retreat from Moscow have fully realized what that meant. Amidst the snowstorms of the 9th a force of German cavalry attacked our extreme left and compelled it to retreat towards the Alencon line. Rousseau's column being in a dangerous position at Connerre, Colin's division of the 21st Corps was sent forward to support it in the direction of Montfort, Gougeard with his Bretons also advancing to support Colin. But the 13th German Corps attacked Rousseau, who after two engagements was driven from Connerre and forced to retreat on Montfort and Pont-de-Gennes across the Huisne, after losing in killed, wounded, and missing, some 800 of his men, whereas the enemy lost barely a hundred. At the same time Gougeard was attacked, and compelled to fall back on Saint-Mars-la-Bruyere.

But the principal event of the day was the defeat of General Paris's force at Ardenay by a part of the 3rd German Corps. The latter had a superiority in numbers, but the French in their demoralised condition scarcely put up a fight at all, in such wise that the Germans took about 1000 prisoners. The worst, however, was that, by seizing Ardenay, the enemy drove as it were a wedge between the French forces, hampering their concentration. Meantime, the 9th German Corps marched to Bouloire, which became Prince Frederick Charles's headquarters. The 10th Corps, however, had not yet been able to advance to Parigne l'Eveque in accordance with the Prince's orders, though it had driven Barry back on Jupilles and Grand Luce. The sole advantage secured by the French that day was that Curten managed to retreat from Chateau-Renault; but it was only on the night of the 10th, when he could be of little or no use to Chanzy, that he was able to reach Chateau-du-Loir, where, in response to Chanzy's urgent appeals, Jaureguiberry had succeeded in collecting a few thousand men to reinforce the troops defending Le Mans.

For four days there had been fighting on one and another point, from the northeast to the south of the town, the result being unfavourable to the French. Chanzy, it is true, was at this critical moment in bad health. According to one account which I heard at the time, he had had an attack of dysentery; according to another, he was suffering from some throat complaint, combined with violent neuralgic pains in the head. I do not think, however, that his ill-health particularly affected the issue, which depended so largely on the manner in which his plans and instructions were carried out. The strategy adopted by the Germans at Sedan and in the battles around Metz had greatly impressed the generals who commanded the French armies during the second period of the war. One might really say that they lived in perpetual dread of being surrounded by the enemy. If there was a lack of concentration on Chanzy's part, if he sent out one and another flying column, and distributed a considerable portion of his army over a wide area, it was precisely because he feared some turning movement on the part of the Germans, which might result in bottling him up at Le Mans.

The earlier instructions which Prince Frederick Charles forwarded to his subordinates certainly seem to indicate that a turning movement was projected. But after the fighting on January 9, when, as I have indicated, the 3rd German Army Corps penetrated wedge-like into the French lines, the Prince renounced any idea of surrounding Chanzy's forces, and resolved to make a vigorous frontal attack before they could be reinforced by any of the still outlying columns. In coming to this decision, the Prince may well have been influenced by the result of the recent fighting, which had sufficiently demonstrated the superiority of the German troops to show that, under the circumstances, a frontal attack would be attended with far less risk than if he had found himself faced by a really vigorous antagonist. Captain Hozier, whom I had previously seen at Versailles, was at this time acting as *Times* correspondent with the Prince's army, and, in subsequently reviewing the fighting, he expressed the opinion that the issue of the Prince's operations was never for a moment doubtful. Still, on all points but one, the French put up a fairly good defence, as I will now show.

XII
LE MANS AND AFTER

The real Battle of Le Mans begins (January 10)--Jouffroy and Paris are driven back--Gougeard's Fight at Champagne--The Breton Mobilises from Conlie--Chanzy's Determination--His Orders for January 11--He inspects the Lines--Paris driven from the Plateau of Auvours--Gougeard's gallant re-capture of the Plateau--My Return to Le Mans--The Panic at La Tuilerie--Retreat inevitable--Withdrawal of the French--Entry of the Germans--Street Fighting--German Exactions--My Escape from Le Mans--The French Retreat--Rear-Guard Engagements--Laval--My Arrest as a Spy--A Dramatic Adventure.

Some more snow fell on the morning of January 10, when the decisive fighting in front of Le Mans really began. On the evening of the 9th the French headquarters was still without news of Generals Curten, Barry, and Jouffroy, and even the communications with Jaureguiberry were of an intermittent character. Nevertheless, Chanzy had made up his mind to give battle, and had sent orders to Jaureguiberry to send Jouffroy towards Parigne-l'Eveque (S.E.) and Barry towards Ecommoy (S. of Le Mans). But the roads were in so bad a condition, and the French troops had been so severely tried, and were so ill-provided for, that several of the commander-in-chief's instructions could not be carried out.

Jouffroy at least did his best, and after a hard and tiring march from Grand Luce, a part of his division reached Parigne in time to join in the action fought there. But it ended disastrously for the French, one of their brigades losing as many as 1400 men, and the Germans taking altogether some 2000 prisoners. Jouffroy's troops then fell back to Pontlieue, the southern suburb of Le Mans, in a lamentable condition, and took care to place the Huisne between themselves and the Germans.

In the same direction Paris's demoralised, division, already worsted at Ardenay on the previous day, was driven from Change by the 3rd German Corps, which took no fewer than 5000 prisoners. It had now almost cut the French eastern and southern lines apart, threatening all direct communication between the 21st and the 16th French Corps. Nevertheless, it was in a dangerous position, having both of its flanks exposed to attack, one from Yvre and Auvours, and the other from Pontlieue and the Chemin des Boeufs, which last line was held by the 16th French Corps.

Meantime, Gougeard's Bretons had been engaged at Champagne, quite a close encounter taking place in the fields and on the vineyard slopes, followed by a house-to-house fight in the village streets. The French were at last driven back; but somewhat later, on the Germans retiring from Champagne, they reoccupied the place. The result of the day was that, apart from the somewhat hazardous success achieved by the 3rd German Corps, the enemy had gained no great advantage. His 13th Corps had made but little progress, his 9th had not been brought into action, and his 10th was as yet no nearer than Grand Luce. On the French side, Barry had at last reached Mulsanne, thus covering the direct southern road to Le Mans, Jaureguiberry being lower down at Ecommoy with some 9000 men of various arms and regiments, whom he had managed to get together. As for Curten's division, as it could not possibly reach the immediate neighbourhood of Le Mans in time for the fighting on the 11th, it received orders to march on La Suze, south-west of the imperilled town. During the 10th, moreover, Chanzy was strengthened by the welcome arrival of several additional field-pieces and a large number of horses. He had given orders to raise the Camp of Conlie, but instead of the forty or fifty thousand men, which at an earlier period it was thought that camp would be able to provide, he now only derived from it some 9000 ill-equipped, badly armed, and almost undrilled Breton Mobilises. [On the other hand, as I previously related, the camp had already provided the bulk of the men belonging to Gougeard's division.] They were divided into six battalions--one of which came from Saint Malo, the others from Rennes and Redon--and were commanded by a general named Lalande. They proved to be no accession of strength; they became, on the contrary, a source of weakness, and disaster, for it was their behaviour which eventually sealed the fate of the Second Loire Army.

But Chanzy, whatever his ailments might be, was personally full of energy and determination. He knew, moreover, that two new army corps (the 19th and the 25th) were being got ready to reinforce him, and he was still resolved to give battle and hold on for another four or five days, when he relied on compelling Prince Frederick Charles to retreat. Then, with his reinforced army, he hoped to march once more in the direction of Paris. Curiously enough, it was precisely on that critical day, January 10, that Gambetta sent Trochu a despatch by pigeon-post, telling him that on the 20th, at the latest, both Chanzy and Bourbaki would be moving on the capital, having between them over 400,000 men.

But if Chanzy's spirits did not fail him, those of his men were at a very low ebb indeed. He was repeatedly told so by subordinate commanders; nevertheless (there was something Napoleonic in his character), he would not desist from his design, but issued instructions that there was to be a resolute defence of the lines on the 11th, together with a determined effort to regain all lost positions. At the same time, the statements of the divisional generals respecting the low *morale* of some of the troops were not left unheeded, for a very significant order went forth, namely, that cavalry should be drawn up in the rear of the infantry wherever this might appear advisable. The inference was obvious.

Three divisions and Lalande's Breton Mobilises were to hold the south-eastern lines from Arnage along the track known as the Chemin des Boeufs, and to link up, as well as possible, with Paris's and Gougeard's divisions, to which fell the duty of guarding the plateau of Auvours and the banks of the Huisne. The rest of the 21st Corps (to which Gougeard's division belonged) was to defend the space between the Huisne and the Sarthe. Colomb's fragmentary force, apart from Paris's division, was still to cover Le Mans towards the north-east. Barry's men, on their expected arrival, were to serve as reserves around Pontlieue.

The morning of January 11 was bright. The snow had ceased falling, but lay some inches thick upon the ground. In order to facilitate the passage of troops, and particularly of military waggons, through the town, the Mayor of Le Mans ordered the inhabitants to clear away as much of this snow as possible; but it naturally remained undisturbed all over the countryside. Little had been seen of Chanzy on the two previous days, but that morning he mounted horse and rode along the lines from the elevated position known as Le Tertre Rouge to the equally elevated position of Yvre. I saw him there, wrapped in a long loose cloak, the hood of which was drawn over his kepi. Near him was his picturesque escort of Algerian Spahis, and while he was conversing with some officers I pulled out a little sketch-book which I carried, and tried to outline the group. An aide-de-camp who noticed me at once came up to inquire what I was doing, and I therefore had to produce the permit which, on returning to the front, I had obtained from the Chief of the Staff. It was found to be quite in order, and I went on with my work. But a few minutes later the general, having given his orders, gathered up his reins to ride away. As he slowly passed me, he gave me just one little sharp glance, and with a faint suspicion of a smile remarked, "I will look at that another time." The aide-de-camp had previously told him what my purpose was.

That day the 3rd German Corps again resumed the offensive, and once more drove Gougeard out of Champagne. Then the enemy's 9th Corps, which on January 10 had done little or nothing, and was therefore quite fresh, was brought into action, and made a resolute attack on the plateau of Auvours. There was a fairly long fight, which could be seen from Yvre. But the Germans were too strong for Paris's men, who at last disbanded, and came, helter-skelter, towards the bridge of Yvre in terrible confusion. Flight is often contagious, and Gougeard, who had fallen back from Champagne in fairly good order, feared lest his men should imitate their comrades. He therefore pointed two field-pieces on the runaways, and by that means checked their stampede.

Having established themselves at the farther end of the plateau, the Germans advanced very cautiously, constantly seeking cover behind the various hedges. General de Colomb, to whose command Paris's runaway division belonged, insisted, however, that the position must be retaken. Gougeard thereupon collected a very miscellaneous force, which included regular infantry, mobiles, mobilisés, and some of Charette's Volontaires de l'Ouest--previously known in Borne as the Pontifical Zouaves. Placing himself at the head of these men, he made a vigorous effort to carry out Colomb's orders. The French went forward almost at the charge, the Germans waiting for them from behind the hedges, whence poured a hail of lead. Gougeard's horse was shot under him, a couple of bullets went through his coat, and another--or, as some said, a splinter of a shell--knocked off his kepi. Still, he continued leading his men, and in the fast failing light the Germans, after repeated encounters, were driven back to the verge of the plateau.

That was told me afterwards, for at the moment I was already on my way back to Le Mans, which I wished to reach before it was absolutely night. On coming from the town early in the morning, I had brought a few eatables in my pockets, but they had soon been consumed, and I had found it impossible to obtain any food whatever at Yvre, though some of the very indifferent local wine was procurable. Thus I was feeling very hungry as I retraced my steps through the snow towards the little hostelry in the Rue du Gue de Maulny, where I had secured accommodation. It was a walk of some four or five miles, but the cold urged me on, and, in spite of the snow, I made the journey fairly rapidly, in such wise that little more than an hour later I was seated in a warm room in front of some steaming soup, answering all sorts of questions as to what I had seen during the day, and particularly whether *les notres* had gained a victory. I could only answer that the "Prussians" had taken Auvours, but that fighting was still going on, as Gougeard had gone to recapture the position. At the moment, indeed, that was the extent of my information. The landlord looked rather glum and his daughter somewhat anxious, and the former, shaking his head, exclaimed: "Voyez-vous, Monsieur l'Anglais, nous n'avons pas de chance-- pas de chance du tout! Je ne sais pas a quoi ca tient, mais c'est comme ca. Et, tenez, cela ne me surprendrait pas de voir ces sales Prussiens dans la ville d'ici a demain!" ["We have no luck, no luck at all. I don't know why, but there it is. And, do you know, it would not surprise me to see those dirty Prussians in the town between now and to-morrow."] Unfortunately for Le Mans and for France also, his forebodings were accurate. At that very moment, indeed, a great disaster was occurring.

Jaureguiberry had reached the southern suburb of Pontlieue at about nine o'clock that morning after a night march from Ecommoy. He had divided his miscellaneous force of 9000 men into three brigades. As they did not seem fit for immediate action, they were drafted into the reserves, so that their arrival was of no particular help that day. About eleven o'clock the 3rd German Corps, coming from the direction of Change, attacked Jouffroy's lines along the more northern part of the so-called Chemin des Boeufs, and, though Jouffroy's men fought fairly well, they could not prevent their foes from capturing the position of the Tertre Rouge. Still, the enemy gained no decisive success in this direction; nor was any marked result attained by the 13th German Corps which formed the extreme right of the attacking forces. But Prince Frederick Charles had sent orders to Voigts Rhetz, who was at Grand Luce, [A brigade of cavalry kept up communications between him and the 3rd Army Corps.] advance with the 10th Corps on Mulsanne, which the French had evacuated; and on reaching Mulsanne, the same general received instructions to come to the support of the 3rd Corps, which was engaged with Jouffroy's force. Voigts Rhetz's men were extremely fatigued; nevertheless, the 20th Division of Infantry, commanded by General Kraatz-Koschlau, went on towards the Chemin des Boeufs, following the direct road from Tours to Le Mans.

Here there was an elevated position known as La Tuilerie--otherwise the tileworks--which had been fortified expressly to prevent the Germans from bursting upon Le Mans from the direct south. Earth-works for guns had been thrown up, trenches had been dug, the pine trees, so abundant on the southern side of Le Mans, had been utilised for other shielding works, as well as for shelter-places for the defending force. Unfortunately, at the moment of the German advance, that defending force consisted of the ill-equipped, badly armed, and almost untrained Breton Mobilises, [There were just a few old soldiers among them.] who, as I have already related, had arrived the previous day from the camp of Conlie under the command of General Lalande. It is true that near these men was stationed an infantry brigade of the 6th Corps d'Armee, whose duty it was to support and steady them. They undoubtedly needed to be helped, for the great majority had never been in action before. Moreover, in addition to the infantry brigade, there were two batteries of artillery; but I fear that for the most part the gunners were little better than recruits. Exaggerated statements have been made respecting the quality of the firearms with which the Mobilises were provided. Many of the weapons were afterwards found to be very dirty, even rusty, but that was the result of neglect, which their officers should have remedied. It is true, however, that these weapons were for the most part merely percussion guns. Again, it has been said that the men had no ammunition, but that statement was certainly inaccurate. On the other hand, these Mobilises were undoubtedly very cold and very hungry--even as I myself was that day--no rations having been served to them until late in the afternoon, that is, shortly before they were attacked, at which moment, indeed, they were actually preparing the meal for which they had so long been waiting.

The wintry night was gathering round when Kraatz-Kosohlau found himself with his division before the position of La Tuilerie. He could see that it was fortified, and before attempting any further advance he fired a few shells. The Mobilises were immediately panic-stricken. They made no attempt at defence; hungry though they were, they abandoned even their pots and pans, and fled in the direction of Pontlieue, which formed, as it were, a long avenue, fringed with factories, textile mills, bleaching works, and so forth. In vain did their officers try to stop the fugitives, even striking them with the flats of their swords, in vain did Lalande and his staff seek to intercept them at the Rond Point de Pontlieue. Nothing could induce them to stop. They threw away their weapons in order to run the faster. At La Tuilerie not a gun was fired at the Germans. Even the infantry brigade fell back, without attempting to fight.

All this occurred at a moment when everybody thought that the day's fighting was over. But Jaureguiberry appeared upon the scene, and ordered one of his subordinates, General Lebouedeo, to retake the lost position. Lebouedeo tried to do so with 1000 tired men, who had been in action during the day, and failed. A second attempt proved equally futile. No effort apparently was made to secure help from Barry, who was at Arnage with 5000 infantry and two brigades of cavalry, and who might have fallen on the left flank of the German Corps. La Tuilerie was lost, and with it Le Mans was lost also.

I was quietly sipping some coffee and reading the local newspapers--three or four were published at Le Mans in those days--when I heard of that disastrous stampede. Some of the men had reached the town, spreading the contagion of fear as they came. Tired though I was, I at once went towards the Avenue de Fontlieue, where the excitement was general. Gendarmes were hurrying hither and thither, often arresting the runaways, and at other times picking up weapons and cartridge-cases which had been flung away. So numerous were the abandoned weapons and equipments that cartloads of them were collected. Every now and then an estafette galloped to or from the town. The civilians whom one met wore looks of consternation. It was evident, indeed, to everybody who knew how important was the position of La Tuilerie, that its capture by the Germans placed Le Mans in jeopardy. When the two attempts to retake it had failed, Jaureguiberry urged immediate retreat. This was rendered the more imperative by other events of the night and the early morning, for, inspirited by their capture of La Tuilerie, the Germans made fresh efforts in other directions, so that Barry had to quit Arnage, whilst Jouffroy lost most of his positions near the Chemin des Boeufs, and the plateau d'Auvours had again to be evacuated.

At 8 a.m. on January 12, Chanzy, after suggesting a fresh attempt to recover La Tuilerie, which was prevented by the demoralisation of the troops, was compelled to give a reluctant assent to Jaureguiberry's proposals of retreat. At the same time, he wished the retreat to be carried out slowly and methodically, and informed Gambetta that he intended to withdraw in the direction of Aleneon (Orne) and Pre-en-Pail (Mayenne). This meant moving into Normandy, and Gambetta pointed out that such a course would leave all Brittany open to the enemy, and enable him to descend without opposition even to the mouth of the Loire. Chanzy was therefore instructed to retreat on Laval, and did so; but as he had already issued orders for the other route, great confusion ensued, the new orders only reaching the subordinate commanders on the evening of the 12th.

From January 6 to 12 the French had lost 6000 men in killed and wounded. The Germans had taken 20,000 prisoners, and captured seventeen guns and a large quantity of army materiel. Further, there was an incalculable number of disbanded Mobiles and Mobilises. If Prince Frederick Charles had known at the time to what a deplorable condition Chanzy's army had been reduced, he would probably have acted more vigorously than he did. It is true that his own men (as Von Hoenig has admitted) were, generally speaking, in a state of great fatigue after the six days' fighting, and also often badly circumstanced in regard to clothing, boots, and equipments. [Even when the armistice arrived I saw many German soldiers wearing French sabots.] Such things cannot last for ever, and there had been little or no opportunity to renew anything since the second battle of Orleans early in December. In the fighting before Le Mans, however, the German loss in killed and wounded was only 3400--200 of the number being officers, whom the French picked off as often as possible.

On the morning of the 12th all was confusion at Pontlieue. Guns, waggons, horsemen, infantrymen, were congregated there, half blocking up the bridge which connects this suburb with Le Mans. A small force under General de Roquebrune was gallantly striving to check the Germans at one part of the Chemin des Boeufs, in order to cover the retreat. A cordon of gendarmes had been drawn up at the railway-station to prevent it from being invaded by all the runaways. Some hundreds of wounded men were allowed access, however, in order that they might, if possible, get away in one of the many trains which were being sent off as rapidly as possible. This service was in charge of an official named Piquet, who acted with the greatest energy and acumen. Of the five railway-lines meeting at Le Mans only two were available, that running to Rennes *via* Laval, and that running to Angers. I find from a report drawn up by M. Piquet a little later, that he managed to send off twenty-five trains, some of them drawn by two and three engines. They included about 1000 vans, trucks, and coaches; that is 558 vans laden with provisions (in part for the relief of Paris); 134 vans and trucks laden with artillery ***materiel*** and stores, 70 vans of ammunition, 150 empty vans and trucks, and 176 passenger carriages. On securing possession of the station, however, the Germans still found there about 200 vans and carriages, and at least a dozen locomotive engines. The last train left at 2.45 p.m. I myself got away (as I shall presently relate) shortly after two o'clock, when the station was already being bombarded.

General de Roquebrune having, at last, been compelled to withdraw from the vicinity of the Chemin des Boeufs, the Germans came on to the long avenue of Pontlieue. Here they were met by most of the corps of gendarmes, which, as I previously related, was attached to the headquarters-staff under General Bourdillon. These men, who had two Gatlings with them, behaved with desperate bravery in order to delay the German entry into the town. About a hundred of them, including a couple of officers, were killed during that courageous defence. It was found impossible, however, to blow up the bridge. The operation had been delayed as long as possible in order to facilitate the French retreat, and when the gendarmes themselves withdrew, there no longer remained sufficient time to put it into execution.

The first Germans to enter the town belonged to the 38th Brigade of Infantry, and to part of a cavalry force under General von Schmidt. After crossing the bridge of Pontlieue, they divided into three columns. One of them proceeded up the Rue du Quartier de Cavalerie in the direction of the Place des Jacobins and the cathedral. The second also went towards the upper town, marching, however, by way of the Rue Basse, which conducted to the Place des Halles, where the chief hotels and cafes were situated. Meantime, the third column turned to the left, and hastened towards the railway station. But, to their great amazement, their advance was repeatedly checked. There were still a number of French soldiers in the town, among them being Mobile Guards, Gendarmes, Franc-tireurs, and a party of Marine Fusiliers. The German column which began to ascend the Rue Basse was repeatedly fired at, whereupon its commanding officer halted his men, and by way of punishment had seven houses set on fire, before attempting to proceed farther. Nevertheless, the resistance was prolonged at various points, on the Place des Jacobins, for instance, and again on the Place des Halles. Near the latter square is--or was--a little street called the Rue Dumas, from which the French picked off a dozen or twenty Germans, so infuriating their commander that he sent for a couple of field-pieces, and threatened to sweep the whole town with projectiles.

Meantime, a number of the French who had lingered at Le Mans were gradually effecting their escape. Many artillery and commissariat waggons managed to get away, and a local notability, M. Eugene Caillaux--father of M. Joseph Caillaux who was French Prime Minister during the latter half of 1911, and who is now (Dec., 1913) Minister of Finances--succeeded in sending out of the town several carts full of rifles, which some of the French troops had flung away. However, the street-fighting could not be indefinitely prolonged. It ceased when about a hundred Germans and a larger number of French, both soldiers and civilians, had been killed. The Germans avenged themselves by pillaging the houses in the Rue Dumas, and several on the Place des Halles, though they spared the Hotel de France there, as their commander, Voigts Rhetz, reserved it for his own accommodation. Whilst the bombardment of a part of the lower town continued--the railway station and the barracks called the Caserne de la Mission being particularly affected--raids were made on the French ambulances, in one of which, on the Boulevard Negrier, a patient was barbarously bayoneted in his bed, on the pretext that he was a Franc-tireur, whereas he really belonged to the Mobile Guard. At the ambulance of the Ecole Normale, the sisters and clergy were, according to their sworn statements, grossly ill-treated. Patients, some of whom were suffering from smallpox, were turned out of their beds--which were required, it was said, for the German wounded. All the wine that could be found was drunk, money was stolen, and there was vindictive destruction on all sides.

The Mayor [The Prefect, M. Le Chevalier, had followed the army in its retreat, considering it his duty to watch over the uninvaded part of the department of the Sartha.] of Le Mans, M. Richard, and his two *adjoints*, or deputies, went down through the town carrying a towel as a flag of truce, and on the Place de la Mission they at last found Voigts Rhetz surrounded by his staff. The General at once informed the Mayor that, in consequence of the resistance of the town, it would have to pay a war-levy of four millions of francs (L160,000) within twenty-four hours, and that the inhabitants would have to lodge and feed the German forces as long as they remained there. All the appeals made against these hard conditions were disregarded during nearly a fortnight. When both the Mayor and the Bishop of Le Mans solicited audiences of Prince Frederick Charles, they were told by the famous Count Harry von Arnim--who, curiously enough, subsequently became German Ambassador to France, but embroiled himself with Bismarck and died in exile--that if they only wished to tender their humble duty to the Prince he would graciously receive them, but that he refused to listen to any representations on behalf of the town.

A first sum of L20,000 and some smaller ones were at last got together in this town of 37,000 inhabitants, and finally, on January 23, the total levy was reduced, as a special favour, to L80,000. Certain German requisitions were also to be set off against L20,000 of that amount; but they really represented about double the figure. A public loan had to be raised in the midst of continual exactions, which lasted even after the preliminaries of peace had been signed, the Germans regarding Le Mans as a milch cow from which too much could not be extracted.

The anxieties of the time might well have sufficed to make the Mayor ill, but, as a matter of fact, he caught small-pox, and his place had to be taken by a deputy, who with the municipal council, to which several local notabilities were adjoined, did all that was possible to satisfy the greed of the Germans. Small-pox, I may mention, was very prevalent at Le Mans, and some of the ambulances were specially reserved for soldiers who had contracted that disease. Altogether, about 21,000 men (both French and Germans), suffering from wounds or diseases of various kinds, were treated in the town's ambulances from November 1 to April 15.

Some thousands of Germans were billeted on the inhabitants, whom they frequently robbed with impunity, all complaints addressed to the German Governor, an officer named Von Heiduck, being disregarded. This individual ordered all the inhabitants to give up any weapons which they possessed, under penalty of death. Another proclamation ordained the same punishment for anybody who might give the slightest help to the French army, or attempt to hamper the German forces. Moreover, the editors, printers, and managers of three local newspapers were summarily arrested and kept in durance on account of articles against the Germans which they had written, printed, or published *before* Chanzy's defeat.

On January 13, which chanced to be a Friday, Prince Frederick Charles made his triumphal entry into Le Mans, the bands of the German regiments playing all their more popular patriotic airs along the route which his Royal Highness took in order to reach the Prefecture--a former eighteenth-century convent--where he intended to install himself. On the following day the Mayor received the following letter:

"Mr. Mayor,
"I request you to send to the Prefecture by half-past five o'clock this afternoon 24 spoons, 24 forks, and 36 knives, as only just sufficient for the number of people at table have been sent, and there is no means of changing the covers. For dinner you will provide 20 bottles of Bordeaux, 30 bottles of Champagne, two bottles of Madeira, and 2 bottles of liqueurs, which must be at the Prefecture at six o'clock precisely. The wine previously sent not being good, neither the Bordeaux nor the Champagne, you must send better kinds, otherwise I shall have to inflict a fine upon the town.
(Signed) "Von Kanitz."

This communication was followed almost immediately afterwards by another, emanating from the same officer, who was one of the Prince's aides-de-camp. He therein stated (invariably employing, be it said, execrable French) that the *cafe-au-lait* was to be served at the Prefecture at 8 a.m.; the *dejeuner* at noon; and the dinner at 7.30 p.m. At ten o'clock every morning, the Mayor was to send 40 bottles of Bordeaux, 40 bottles of Champagne, 6 bottles of Madeira, and 3 bottles of liqueurs. He was also to provide waiters to serve at table, and kitchen- and scullery-maids. And Kanitz concluded by saying: "If the least thing fails, a remarkable (*sic*) fine will be inflicted on the town."

On January 15 an order was sent to the Mayor to supply at once, for the Prince's requirements, 25 kilogrammes of ham; 13 kilos. of sausages; 13 kilos. of tongues; 5

dozen eggs; vegetables of all sorts, particularly onions; 15 kilos. of Gruyere cheese; 5 kilos. of Parmesan; 15 kilos. of best veal; 20 fowls; 6 turkeys; 12 ducks; 5 kilos. of powdered sugar. [All the German orders and requisitions are preserved in the municipal archives of Le Mans.] No wine was ever good enough for Prince Frederick Charles and his staff. The complaints sent to the town-hall were incessant. Moreover, the supply of Champagne, by no means large in such a place as Le Mans, gave out, and then came all sorts of threats. The municipal councillors had to trot about trying to discover a few bottles here and there in private houses, in order to supply the requirements of the Princely Staff. There was also a scarcity of vegetables, and yet there were incessant demands for spinach, cauliflowers, and artichokes, and even fruit for the Prince's tarts. One day Kanitz went to the house where the unfortunate Mayor was lying in bed, and told him that he must get up and provide vegetables, as none had been sent for the Prince's table. The Mayor protested that the whole countryside was covered with snow, and that it was virtually impossible to satisfy such incessant demands; but, as he afterwards related, ill and worried though he was, he could not refrain from laughing when he was required to supply several pounds of truffles. Truffles at Le Mans, indeed! In those days, too! The idea was quite ridiculous.

Not only had the demands of Prince Frederick Charles's staff to be satisfied, but there were those of Voigts Rhetz, and of all the officers lodging at the Hotel de France, the Hotel du Dauphin, the Hotel de la Boule d'Or and other hostelries. These gentlemen were very fond of giving dinners, and "mine host" was constantly being called upon to provide all sorts of delicacies at short notice. The cellars of the Hotel de France were drunk dry. The common soldiers also demanded the best of everything at the houses where they were billeted; and sometimes they played extraordinary pranks there. Half a dozen of them, who were lodged at a wine-shop in, I think, the Rue Dumas, broached a cask of brandy, poured the contents into a tub, and washed their feet in the spirituous liquor. It may be that a "brandy bath" is a good thing for sore feet; and that might explain the incident. However, when I think of it, I am always reminded of how, in the days of the Second Empire, the spendthrift Due de Gramont-Caderousse entered the. Cafe Anglais in Paris, one afternoon, called for a silver soup-tureen, had two or three bottles of champagne poured into it, and then made an unrepentant Magdalen of the Boulevards, whom he had brought with him, wash his feet in the sparkling wine. From that afternoon until the Cafe Anglais passed out of existence no silver soup-tureens were ever used there.

I have given the foregoing particulars respecting the German occupation of Le Mans--they are principally derived from official documents--just to show the reader what one might expect if, for instance, a German force should land at Hull or Grimsby and fight its way successfully to--let us say--York or Leeds or Nottingham. The incidents which occurred at Le Mans were by no means peculiar to that town. Many similar instances occurred throughout the invaded regions of France. I certainly do not wish to impute gluttony to Prince Frederick Charles personally. But during the years which followed the Franco-German War I made three fairly long stays at Berlin, putting up at good hotels, where officers--sometimes generals--often lunched and dined. And their appetites frequently amazed me, whilst their manners at table were repulsive. In those days most German officers were bearded, and I noticed that between the courses at luncheon and at dinner it was a common practice of theirs to produce pocket-glasses and pocket-combs, and comb their beards--as well as the hair on their heads--over the table. As for their manner of eating and the noise they made in doing so, the less said the better. In regard to manners, I have always felt that the French of 1870-71 were in some respects quite entitled to call their enemies "barbarians"; but that was forty-three years ago, and as time works wonders, the manners of the German military element may have improved.

In saying something about the general appearance of Le Mans, I pointed out that the town now has a Place de la Republique, a Gambetta Bridge, a Rue Thiers, and a statue of Chanzy; but at the period of the war and for a long time afterwards it detested the Republic (invariably returning Bonapartist or Orleanist deputies), sneered at Gambetta, and hotly denounced the commander of the Loire Army. Its grievance against Chanzy was that he had made it his headquarters and given battle in its immediate vicinity. The conflict having ended disastrously for the French arms, the townsfolk lamented that it had ever taken place. Why had Chanzy brought his army there? they indignantly inquired. He might very well have gone elsewhere. So strong was this Manceau feeling against the general--a feeling inspired by the sufferings which the inhabitants experienced at the time, notably in consequence of the German exactions--that fifteen years later, when the general's statue (for which there had been a national subscription) was set up in the town, the displeasure there was very great, and the monument was subjected to the most shameful indignities. [At Nouart, his native place, there is another statue of Chanzy, which shows him pointing towards the east. On the pedestal is the inscription; "The generals who wish to obtain the baton of Marshal of France must seek it across the Rhine"--words spoken by him in one of his speeches subsequent to the war.] But all that has passed. Nowadays, both at Auvours and at Pontlieue, there are monuments to those who fell fighting for France around Le Mans, and doubtless the town, in becoming more Republican, has become more patriotic also.

Before relating how I escaped from Le Mans on the day when the retreat was ordered, there are a few other points with which I should like to deal briefly. It is tolerably well known that I made the English translation of Emile Zola's great novel, "La Debacle," and a good many of my present readers may have read that work either in the original French or in the version prepared by me. Now, I have always thought that some of the characters introduced by Zola into his narrative were somewhat exceptional. I doubt if there were many such absolutely neurotic degenerates as "Maurice" in the French Army at any period of the war. I certainly never came across such a character. Again, the psychology of Stephen Crane's "Red Badge of Courage," published a few years after "La Debacle," and received with acclamations by critics most of whom had never in their lives been under fire, also seems to me to be of an exceptional character. I much prefer the psychology of the Waterloo episode in Stendhal's "Chartreuse de Parme," because it is of more general application. "The Red Badge of Courage," so the critics told us, showed what a soldier exactly felt and thought in the midst of warfare. Unlike Stendhal, however, its author had never "served." No more had Zola; and I feel that many of the pictures which novelists have given us of a soldier's emotions when in action apply only to exceptional cases, and are even then somewhat exaggerated.

In action there is no time for thought. The most trying hours for a man who is in any degree of a sensitive nature are those spent in night-duty as a sentry or as one of a small party at some lonely outpost. Then thoughts of home and happiness, and of those one loves, may well arise. There is one little point in connexion with this subject which I must mention. Whenever letters were found on the bodies of men who fell during the Franco-German War, they were, if this man was a Frenchman, more usually letters from his mother, and, if he was a German, more usually letters from his sweetheart. Many such letters found their way into print during the course of the war. It is a well-known fact that a Frenchman's cult for his mother is a trait of the national character, and that a Frenchwoman almost always places her child before her husband.

But what struck me particularly during the Franco-German War was that the anxieties and mental sufferings of the French officers were much keener than those of the men. Many of those officers were married, some had young children, and in the silent hours of a lonely night-watch their thoughts often travelled to their dear ones. I well remember how an officer virtually unbosomed himself to me on this subject one night near Yvre-l'Eveque. The reason of it all is obvious. The higher a man's intelligence, the greater is his sense of responsibility and the force of his attachments. But in action the latter are set aside; they only obtrude at such times as I have said or else at the moment of death.

Of actual cowardice there were undoubtedly numerous instances during the war, but a great deal might be said in defence of many of the men who here and there abandoned their positions. During the last months their sufferings were frequently terrible. At best they were often only partially trained. There was little cohesion in many battalions. There was a great lack of efficient non-commissioned officers. Instead of drafting regular soldiers from the ***depots*** into special regiments, as was often done, it might have been better to have distributed them among the Mobiles and Mobilises, whom they would have steadied. Judging by all that I witnessed at that period, I consider it essential that any territorial force should always contain a certain number of trained soldiers who have previously been in action. And any such force should always have the support of regulars and of efficient artillery. I have related how certain Breton Mobilises abandoned La Tuilerie. They fled before the regulars or the artillery could support them; but they were, perhaps, the very rawest levies in all Chanzy's forces. Other Breton Mobilises, on other points, fought very well for men of their class. For instance, no reproach could be addressed to the battalions of St. Brieuo, Brest, Quimper, Lorient, and Nantes. They were better trained than were the men stationed at La Tuilerie, and it requires some time to train a Breton properly. That effected, he makes a good soldier.

Respecting my own feelings during that war, I may say that the paramount one was curiosity. To be a journalist, a man must be inquisitive. It is a *sine qua non* of his profession. Moreover, I was very young; I had no responsibilities; I may have been in love, or have thought I was, but I was on my own, and my chief desire was to see as much as I could. I willingly admit that, when Gougeard's column was abruptly attacked at Droue, I experienced some trepidation at finding myself under fire; but firmness may prove as contagious as fear, and when Gougeard rallied his men and went forward to repel the Germans, interest and a kind of excitement took possession of me. Moreover, as I was, at least nominally, attached to the ambulance service, there was duty to be done, and that left no opportunity for thought. The pictures of the ambulances in or near Sedan are among the most striking ones contained in "La Debacle," and, judging by what I saw elsewhere, Zola exaggerated nothing. The ambulance is the truly horrible side of warfare. To see men lying dead on the ground is, so to say, nothing. One gets used to it. But to see them amputated, and to see them lying in bed suffering, often acutely, from dreadful wounds, or horrible diseases--dysentery, typhus, small-pox--that is the thing which tries the nerves of all but the doctors and the trained nurses. On several occasions I helped to carry wounded men, and felt no emotion in doing so; but more than once I was almost overcome by the sight of all the suffering in some ambulance.

When, on the morning of January 12, I heard that a general retreat had been ordered, I hesitated as to what course I should pursue. I did not then anticipate the street-fighting, and the consequent violence of the Germans. But journalistic instinct told me that if I remained in the town until after the German entry I might then find it very difficult to get away and communicate with my people. At the same time, I did not think the German entry so imminent as proved to be the case; and I spent a considerable time in the streets watching all the tumult which prevailed there. Now and again a sadly diminished battalion went by in fairly good order. But numbers of disbanded men hurried hither and thither in confusion. Here and there a street was blocked with army vans and waggons, whose drivers were awaiting orders, not knowing which direction to take. Officers and estafettes galloped about on all sides. Then a number of wounded men were carried in carts, on stretchers, and on trucks towards the railway-station. Others, with their heads bandaged or their arms in slings, walked painfully in the same direction. Outside the station there was a strong cordon of Gendarmes striving to resist all the pressure of a great mob of disbanded men who wished to enter and get away in the trains. At one moment, when, after quite a struggle, some of the wounded were conveyed through the mob and the cordon, the disbanded soldiers followed, and many of them fought their way into the station in spite of all the efforts of the Gendarmes. The *melee* was so desperate that I did not attempt to follow, but, after watching it for some time, retraced my steps towards my lodging. All was hubbub and confusion at the little inn, and only with difficulty could I get anything to eat there. A little later, however, I managed to tell the landlord--his name was Dubuisson--that I meant to follow the army, and, if possible, secure a place in one of the trains which were frequently departing. After stowing a few necessaries away in my pockets, I begged him to take charge of my bag until some future day, and the worthy old man then gave me some tips as to how I might make my way into the station, by going a little beyond it, and climbing a palisade.

We condoled with one another and shook hands. I then went out. The cannonade, which had been going on for several hours, had now become more violent. Several shells had fallen on or near the Caserne de la Mission during the morning. Now others were falling near the railway-station. I went my way, however, turned to the right on quitting the Rue du Gue-de-Maulny, reached some palings, and got on to the railway-line. Skirting it, I turned to the left, going back towards the station. I passed one or two trains, which were waiting. But they were composed of trucks and closed vans. I might perhaps have climbed on to one of the former, but it was a bitterly cold day; and as for the latter, of course I could not hope to enter one of them. So I kept on towards the station, and presently, without let or hindrance, I reached one of the platforms.

Le Mans being an important junction, its station was very large, in some respects quite monumental. The principal part was roofed with glass and suggested Charing Cross. I do not remember exactly the number of lines of metals running through it, but I think there must have been four or five. There were two trains waiting there, one of them, which was largely composed of passenger carriages, being crammed with soldiers. I tried to get into one carriage, but was fiercely repulsed. So, going to the rear of this train, I crossed to another platform, where the second train was. This was made up of passenger coaches and vans. I scrambled into one of the latter, which was open. There were a number of packing-cases inside it, but there was at least standing room for several persons. Two railway men and two or three soldiers were already there. One of the former helped me to get in. I had, be it said, a semi-military appearance, for my grey frieze coat was frogged, and besides, what was more important, I wore the red-cross armlet given me at the time when I followed Gougeard's column.

Almost immediately afterwards the train full of soldiers got away. The cannonade was now very loud, and the glass roof above us constantly vibrated. Some minutes elapsed whilst we exchanged impressions. Then, all at once, a railway official--it may have been M. Piquet himself--rushed along the platform in the direction of the engine, shouting as he went: "Depechez! Depechez! Sauvez-vous!" At the same moment a stray artilleryman was seen hastening towards us; but suddenly there came a terrific crash of glass, a shell burst through the roof and exploded, and the unlucky artilleryman fell on the platform, evidently severely wounded. We were already in motion, however, and the line being dear, we got fairly swiftly across the viaduct spanning the Sarthe. This placed us beyond the reach of the enemy, and we then slowed down.

One or two more trains were got away after ours, the last one, I believe, being vainly assailed by some Uhlans before it had crossed the viaduct. The latter ought then to have been blown up, but an attempt to do so proved ineffectual. We went on very slowly on account of the many trains in front of us. Every now and again, too, there came a wearisome stop. It was bitterly cold, and it was in vain that we beat the tattoo with our feet in the hope of thereby warming them. The men with me were also desperately hungry, and complained of it so bitterly and so frequently, that, at last, I could not refrain from producing a little bread and meat which I had secured at Le Mans and sharing it with them. But it merely meant a bite for each of us. However, on stopping at last at Conlie station--some sixteen or seventeen miles from Le Mans--we all hastily scrambled out of the train, rushed into a little inn, and almost fought like wild beasts for scraps of food. Then on we went once more, still very slowly, still stopping again and again, sometimes for an hour at a stretch, until, half numbed by the cold, weary of stamping our feet, and still ravenous, we reached the little town of Sille-le-Guillaume, which is not more than eight or nine miles from Conlie.

At Sille I secured a tiny garret-like room at the crowded Hotel de la Croix d'Or, a third-rate hostelry, which was already invaded by officers, soldiers, railway officials, and others who had quitted Le Mans before I had managed to do so. My comparatively youthful appearance won for me, however, the good favour of the buxom landlady, who, after repeatedly declaring to other applicants that she had not a corner left in the whole house, took me aside and said in an undertone: "listen, I will put you in a little *cabinet* upstairs. I will show you the way by and by. But don't tell anybody." And she added compassionately: "*Mon pauvre garcon*, you look frozen. Go into the kitchen. There is a good fire there, and you will get something to eat."

Truth to tell, the larder was nearly empty, but I secured a little cheese and some bread and some very indifferent wine, which, however, in my then condition, seemed to me to be nectar. I helped myself to a bowl, I remember, and poured about a pint of wine into it, so as to soak my bread, which was stale and hard. Toasting my feet at the fire whilst I regaled myself with that improvised *soupe-au-vin*, I soon felt warm and inspirited once more. Hardship sits on one but lightly when one is only seventeen years of age and stirred by early ambition. All the world then lay before me, like mine oyster, to be opened by either sword or pen.

At a later hour, by the light of a solitary guttering candle, in the little *cabinet* upstairs, I wrote, as best I could, an account of the recent fighting and the loss of Le Mans; and early on the following morning I prevailed on a railway-man who was going to Rennes to post my packet there, in order that it might be forwarded to England *via* Saint Malo. The article appeared in the *Pall Mall Gazette*, filling a page of that journal, and whatever its imperfections may have been, it was undoubtedly the first detailed account of the battle of Le Mans, from the French side, to appear in the English Press. It so happened, indeed, that the other correspondents with the French forces, including my cousin Montague Vizetelly of *The Daily News*, lingered at Le Mans until it was too late for them to leave the town, the Germans having effected their entry.

German detachments soon started in pursuit of the retreating Army of the Loire. Chanzy, as previously mentioned, modified his plans, in accordance with Gambetta's views, on the evening of January 12. The new orders were that the 16th Army Corps should retreat on Laval by way of Chassille and Saint Jean-sur-Erve, that the 17th, after passing Conlie, should come down to Sainte Suzanne, and that the 21st should proceed from Conlie to Sille-le-Guillaume. There were several rear-guard engagements during, the retreat. Already on the 13th, before the 21st Corps could modify its original line of march, it had to fight at Ballon, north of Le Mans. On the next day one of its detachments, composed of 9000 Mobilises of the Mayenne, was attacked at Beaumont-sur-Sarthe, and hastily fell back, leaving 1400 men in the hands of the Germans, who on their side lost only *nine*! Those French soldiers who retreated by way of Conlie partially pillaged the abandoned stores there. A battalion of Mobiles, on passing that way, provided themselves with new trousers, coats, boots, and blankets, besides carrying off a quantity of bread, salt-pork, sugar, and other provisions. These things were at least saved from the Germans, who on reaching the abandoned camp found there a quantity of military *materiel*, five million cartridges, 1500 cases of biscuits and extract of meat, 180 barrels of salt-pork, a score of sacks of rice, and 140 puncheons of brandy.

On January 14 the 21st Corps under Jaures reached Sille-le-Guillaume, and was there attacked by the advanced guard of the 13th German Corps under the Grand Duke of Mecklenburg. The French offered a good resistance, however, and the Germans retreated on Conlie. I myself had managed to leave Sille the previous afternoon, but such was the block on the line that our train could get no farther than Voutre, a village of about a thousand souls. Railway travelling seeming an impossibility, I prevailed on a farmer to give me a lift as far as Sainte Suzanne, whence I hoped to cut across country in the direction of Laval. Sainte Suzanne is an ancient and picturesque little town which in those days still had a rampart and the ruins of an early feudal castle. I supped and slept at an inn there, and was told in the morning (January 14) that it would be best for me to go southward towards Saint Jean-sur-Erve, where I should strike the direct highway to Laval, and might also be able to procure a conveyance. I did not then know the exact retreating orders. I hoped to get out of the way of all the troops and waggons encumbering the roads, but in this I was doomed to disappointment, for at Saint Jean I fell in with them again.

That day a part of the rear-guard of the 16th Corps (Jaureguiberry)--that is, a detachment of 1100 men with a squadron of cavalry under General Le Bouedec--had been driven out of Chassille by the German cavalry under General von Schmidt. This had accelerated the French retreat, which continued in the greatest confusion, all the men hastening precipitately towards Saint Jean, where, after getting the bulk of his force on to the heights across the river Erve, which here intersects the highway, Jaureguiberry resolved on attempting to check the enemy's pursuit. Though the condition of most of the men was lamentable, vigorous defensive preparations were made on the night of the 14th and the early morning of the following day. On the low ground, near the village and the river, trees were felled and roads were barricaded; while on the slopes batteries were disposed behind hedges, in which embrasures were cut. The enemy's force was, I believe, chiefly composed of cavalry and artillery. The latter was already firing at us when Jaureguiberry rode along our lines. A shell exploded near him, and some splinters of the projectile struck his horse in the neck, inflicting a ghastly, gaping wound. The poor beast, however, did not fall immediately, but galloped on frantically for more than a score of yards, then suddenly reared, and after doing so came down, all of a heap, upon the snow. However, the Admiral, who was a good horseman, speedily disengaged himself, and turned to secure another mount--when he perceived that Colonel Beraud, his chief of staff, who had been riding behind him, had been wounded by the same shell, and had fallen from his horse. I saw the Colonel being carried to a neighbouring farmhouse, and was afterwards told that he had died there.

The engagement had no very decisive result, but Schmidt fell back to the road connecting Sainte Suzanne with Thorigne-en-Charnie, whilst we withdrew towards Soulge-le-Bruant, about halfway between Saint Jean and Laval. During the fight, however, whilst the artillery duel was in progress, quite half of Jaureguiberry's men had taken themselves off without waiting for orders. I believe that on the night of January 15 he could not have mustered more than 7000 men for action. Yet only two days previously he had had nearly three times that number with him.

Nevertheless, much might be pleaded for the men. The weather was still bitterly cold, snow lay everywhere, little or no food could be obtained, the commissariat refraining from requisitioning cattle at the farms, for all through the departments for Mayenne and Ille-et-Vilaine cattle-plague was raging. Hungry, emaciated, faint, coughing incessantly, at times affected with small-pox, the men limped or trudged on despairingly. Their boots were often in a most wretched condition; some wore sabots, others, as I said once before, merely had rags around their poor frost-bitten feet. And the roads were obstructed by guns, vans, waggons, vehicles of all kinds. Sometimes an axle had broken, sometimes a horse had fallen dead on the snow, in any case one or another conveyance had come to a standstill, and prevented others from pursuing their route. I recollect seeing hungry men cutting steaks from the flanks of the dead beasts, sometimes devouring the horseflesh raw, at others taking it to some cottage, where the avaricious peasants, who refused to part with a scrap of food, at least had to let these cold and hungry men warm themselves at a fire, and toast their horseflesh before it. At one halt three soldiers knocked a peasant down because he vowed that he could not even give them a pinch of salt. That done, they rifled his cupboards and ate all they could find.

Experience had taught me a lesson. I had filled my pockets with ham, bread, hard-boiled eggs, and other things, before leaving Sainte Suzanne. I had also obtained a meal at Saint Jean, and secured some brandy there, and I ate and drank sparingly and surreptitiously whilst I went on, overtaking one after another batch of weary soldiers. However, the distance between Saint Jean and Laval is not very great. Judging by the map, it is a matter of some twenty-five miles at the utmost. Moreover, I walked only half the distance. The troops moved so slowly that I reached Soulge-le-Bruant long before them, and there induced a man to drive me to Laval. I was there on the afternoon of January 16, and as from this point trains were still running westward, I reached Saint Servan on the following day. Thus I slipped through to my goal, thereby justifying the nickname of L'Anguille--the Eel--which some of my young French friends had bestowed on me.

A day or two previously my father had returned from England, and I found him with my stepmother. He became very much interested in my story, and talked of going to Laval himself. Further important developments might soon occur, the Germans might push on to Chanzy's new base, and I felt that I also ought to go back. The life I had been leading either makes or mars a man physically. Personally, I believe that it did me a world of good. At all events, it was settled that my father and myself should go to Laval together. We started a couple of days later, and managed to travel by rail as far as Rennes. But from that point to Laval the line was now very badly blocked, and so we hired a closed vehicle, a ramshackle affair, drawn by two scraggy Breton nags. The main roads, being still crowded with troops, artillery, and baggage waggons, and other impedimenta, were often impassable, and so we proceeded by devious ways, amidst which our driver lost himself, in such wise that at night we had to seek a shelter at the famous Chateau des Bochers, immortalized by Mme. de Sevigne, and replete with precious portraits of herself, her own and her husband's families, in addition to a quantity of beautiful furniture dating from her time.

It took us, I think, altogether two days to reach Laval, where, after securing accommodation at one of the hotels, we went out in search of news, having heard none since we had started on our journey. Perceiving a newspaper shop, we entered it, and my father insisted on purchasing a copy of virtually every journal which was on sale there. Unfortunately for us, this seemed highly suspicious to a local National Guard who was in the shop, and when we left it he followed us. My father had just then begun to speak to me in English, and at the sound of a foreign tongue the man's suspicions increased. So he drew nearer, and demanded to know who and what we were. I replied that we were English and that I had previously been authorised to accompany the army as a newspaper correspondent. My statements, however, were received with incredulity by this suspicious individual, who, after one or two further inquiries, requested us to accompany him to a guard-house standing near one of the bridges thrown over the river Mayenne.

Thither we went, followed by several people who had assembled during our parley, and found ourselves before a Lieutenant of Gendarmes, on the charge of being German spies. Our denouncer was most positive on the point. Had we not bought at least a dozen newspapers? Why a dozen, when sensible people would have been satisfied with one? Such extensive purchases must surely have been prompted by some sinister motive. Besides, he had heard us conversing in German. English, indeed! No, no! He was certain that we had spoken German, and was equally certain of our guilt.

The Lieutenant looked grave, and my explanations did not quite satisfy him. The predicament was the more awkward as, although my father was provided with a British passport, I had somehow left my precious military permit at Saint Servan, Further, my father carried with him some documents which might have been deemed incriminating, They were, indeed, safe-conducts signed by various German generals, which had been used by us conjointly while passing, through the German lines after making our way out of Paris in November. As for my correspondent's permit, signed some time previously by the Chief of the Staff, I had been unable to find it when examining my papers on our way to Laval, but had consoled myself with the thought that I might get it replaced at headquarters. [The red-cross armlet which had repeatedly proved so useful to me, enabling me to come and go without much interference, was at our hotel, in a bag we had brought with us.] Could I have shown it to the Lieutenant, he might have ordered our release. As it happened, he decided to send us to the Provost Marshal. I was not greatly put out by that command, for I remembered the officer in question, or thought I did, and felt convinced that everything would speedily be set right.

We started off in the charge of a brigadier-otherwise a corporal--of Gendarmes, and four men, our denouncer following closely at our heels. My father at once pointed out to me that the brigadier and one of the men wore silver medals bearing the effigy of Queen Victoria, so I said to the former, "You were in the Crimea. You are wearing our Queen's medal."

"Yes," he replied, "I gained that at the Alma."

"And your comrade?"

"He won his at the Tohernaya."

"I dare say you would have been glad if French and English had fought side by side in this war?" I added. "Perhaps they ought to have done so."

"*Parbleu!* The English certainly owed us a **bon coup de main**, instead of which they have only sold us broken-down horses and bad boots."

I agreed that there had been some instances of the kind. A few more words passed, and I believe that the brigadier became convinced of our English nationality. But as his orders were to take us to the Provost's, thither we were bound to go. An ever increasing crowd followed. Shopkeepers and other folk came to their doors and windows, and the words, "They are spies, German spies!" rang out repeatedly, exciting the crowd and rendering it more and more hostile. For a while we followed a quay with granite parapets, below which flowed the Mayenne, laden with drifting ice. All at once, however, I perceived on our left a large square, where about a hundred men of the Laval National Guard were being exercised. They saw us appear with our escort, they saw the crowd which followed us, and they heard the cries, "Spies! German spies!" Forthwith, with that disregard for discipline which among the French was so characteristic of the period, they broke their ranks and ran towards us.

We were only able to take a few more steps. In vain did the Gendarmes try to force a way through the excited mob. We were surrounded by angry, scowling, vociferating men. Imprecations burst forth, fists were clenched, arms were waved, rifles were shaken, the unruly National Guards being the most eager of all to denounce and threaten us. "Down with the spies!" they shouted. "Down with the German pigs! Give them to us! Let us shoot them!"

A very threatening rush ensued, and I was almost carried off my feet. But in another moment I found myself against the parapet of the quay, with my father beside me, and the icy river in the rear. In front of us stood the brigadier and his four men guarding us from the angry citizens of Laval.

"Hand them over to us! We will settle their affair," shouted an excited National Guard. "You know that they are spies, brigadier."

"I know that I have my orders," growled the veteran. "I am taking them to the Provost. It is for him to decide."

"That is too much ceremony," was the retort. "Let us shoot them!"

"But they are not worth a cartridge!" shouted another man. "Throw them into the river!"

That ominous cry was taken up. "Yes, yes, to the river with them!" Then came another rush, one so extremely violent that our case seemed desperate.

But the brigadier and his men had managed to fix bayonets during the brief parley, and on the mob being confronted by five blades of glistening steel, its savage eagerness abated. Moreover, the old brigadier behaved magnificently. "Keep back!" cried he. "I have my orders. You will have to settle me before you take my prisoners!"

Just then I caught the eye of one of the National Guards, who was shaking his fist at us, and I said to him, "You are quite mistaken. We are not Germans, but English!"

"Yes, yes, *Anglais, Anglais*!" my father exclaimed.

While some of the men in the crowd were more or less incredulously repeating that statement, a black-bearded individual--whom I can, at this very moment, still picture with my mind's eye, so vividly did the affair impress me--climbed on to the parapet near us, and called out, "You say you are English? Do you know London? Do you know Regent Street? Do you know the Soho?"

"Yes, yes!" we answered quickly.

"You know the Lei-ces-terre Square? What name is the music-hall there?"

"Why, the Alhambra!" The "Empire," let me add, did not exist in those days.

The man seemed satisfied. "I think they are English," he said to his friends. But somebody else exclaimed, "I don't believe it. One of them is wearing a German hat."

Now, it happened that my father had returned from London wearing a felt hat of a shape which was then somewhat fashionable there, and which, curiously enough, was called the "Crown Prince," after the heir to the Prussian throne--that is, our Princess Royal's husband, subsequently the Emperor Frederick. The National Guard, who spoke a little English, wished to inspect this incriminating hat, so my father took it off, and one of the Gendarmes, having placed it on his bayonet, passed it to the man on the parapet. When the latter had read "Christy, London," on the lining, he once more testified in our favour.

But other fellows also wished to examine the suspicious headgear, and it passed from hand to hand before it was returned to my father in a more or less damaged condition, Even then a good many men were not satisfied respecting our nationality, but during that incident of the hat--a laughable one to me nowadays, though everything looked very ugly when it occurred--there had been time for the men's angry passions to cool, to a considerable extent at all events; and after that serio-comical interlude, they were much less eager to inflict on us the summary law of Lynch. A further parley ensued, and eventually the Gendarmes, who still stood with bayonets crossed in front of us, were authorized, by decision of the Sovereign People, to take us to the Provost's. Thither we went, then, amidst a perfect procession of watchful guards and civilians.

Directly we appeared before the Provost, I realized that our troubles were not yet over. Some changes had taken place during the retreat, and either the officer whom I remembered having seen at Le Mans (that is, Colonel Mora) had been replaced by another, or else the one before whom we now appeared was not the Provost-General, but only the Provost of the 18th Corps. At all events, he was a complete stranger to me. After hearing, first, the statements of the brigadier and the National Guard who had denounced us, and who had kept close to us all the time, and, secondly, the explanations supplied by my father and myself, he said to me, "If you had a staff permit to follow the army, somebody at headquarters must be able to identify you."

"I think that might be done," I answered, "by Major-General Feilding, who--as you must know--accompanies the army on behalf of the British Government. Personally, I am known to several officers of the 21st Corps-- General Gougeard and his Chief of Staff, for instance--and also to some of the aides-de-camp at headquarters."

"Well, get yourselves identified, and obtain a proper safe-conduct," said the Provost. "Brigadier, you are to take these men to headquarters. If they are identified there, you will let them go. If not, take them to the chateau (the prison), and report to me."

Again we all set out, this time climbing the hilly ill-paved streets of old Laval, above which the town's great feudal castle reared its dark, round keep; and presently we came to the local college, formerly an Ursuline convent, where Chanzy had fixed his headquarters.

In one of the large class-rooms were several officers, one of whom immediately recognized me. He laughed when he heard our story. "I was arrested myself, the other day," he said, "because I was heard speaking in English to your General Feilding. And yet I was in uniform, as I am now."

The Gendarmes were promptly dismissed, though not before my father had slipped something into the hand of the old brigadier for himself and his comrades. Their firmness had saved us, for when a mob's passions are inflamed by patriotic zeal, the worst may happen to the objects of its wrath.

A proper safe-conduct (which I still possess) was prepared by an aide-de-camp on duty, and whilst he was drafting it, an elderly but bright-eyed officer entered, and went up to a large circular stove to warm himself. Three small stars still glittered faintly on his faded cap, and six rows of narrow tarnished gold braid ornamented the sleeves of his somewhat shabby dolman. It was Chanzy himself.

He noticed our presence, and our case was explained to him. Looking at me keenly, he said, "I think I have seen you before. You are the young English correspondent who was allowed to make some sketches at Yvre-l'Eveque, are you not?"

"Yes, ***mon general***," I answered, saluting. "You gave me permission through, I think, Monsieur le Commandant de Boisdeffre."

He nodded pleasantly as we withdrew, then lapsed into a thoughtful attitude.

Out we went, down through old Laval and towards the new town, my father carrying the safe-conduct in his hand. The Gendarmes must have already told people that we were "all right," for we now encountered only pleasant faces. Nevertheless, we handed the safe-conduct to one party of National Guards for their inspection, in order that their minds might be quite at rest. That occurred outside the hospital, where at that moment I little imagined that a young Englishman--a volunteer in the Sixth Battalion of the Cotes-du-Nord Mobile Guards (21st Army Corps)--was lying invalided by a chill, which he had caught during an ascent in our army balloon with Gaston Tissandier. Since then that young Englishman has become famous as Field-Marshal Viscount Kitchener of Khartoum.

But the National Guards insisted on carrying my father and myself to the chief cafe of Laval. They would take no refusal. In genuine French fashion, they were all anxiety to offer some amends for their misplaced patriotic impulsiveness that afternoon, when they had threatened, first, to shoot, and, next, to drown us. In lieu thereof they now deluged us with punch *a la francaise*, and as the cafe soon became crowded with other folk who all joined our party, there ensued a scene which almost suggested that some glorious victory had been gained at last by invaded and unfortunate France.

XIII
THE BITTER END

Battues for Deserters--End of the Operations against Chanzy--Faidherbe's Battles--Bourbaki's alleged Victories and Retreat--The Position in Paris--The terrible Death Rate--State of the Paris Army--The Sanguinary Buzenval Sortie--Towards Capitulation--The German Conditions--The Armistice Provisions--Bourbaki's Disaster--Could the War have been prolonged?--The Resources of France--The general Weariness--I return to Paris--The Elections for a National Assembly--The Negotiations--The State of Paris--The Preliminaries of Peace--The Triumphal Entry of the Germans--The War's Aftermath.

We remained for a few days longer at Laval, and were not again interfered with there. A painful interest attached to one sight which we witnessed more than once. It was that of the many processions of deserters whom the horse Gendarmerie of the headquarters staff frequently brought into the town. The whole region was scoured for runaways, many of whom were found in the villages and at lonely farms. They had generally cast off their uniform and put on blouses, but the peasantry frequently betrayed them, particularly as they seldom, if ever, had any money to spend in bribes. Apart from those *battues* and the measures of all kinds which Chanzy took to reorganise his army, little of immediate import occurred at Laval. Gambetta had been there, and had then departed for Lille in order to ascertain the condition of Faidherbe's Army of the North. The German pursuit of Chanzy's forces ceased virtually at Saint Jean-sur-Erve. There was just another little skirmish at Sainte Melaine, but that was all. [I should add that on January 17 the Germans under Mecklenburg secured possession of Alengon (Chanty's original objective) alter an ineffectual resistance offered by the troops under Commandant Lipowski, who was seconded in his endeavours by young M. Antonin Dubost, then Prefect of the Orne, and recently President of the French Senate.] Accordingly my father and I returned to Saint Servan, and, having conjointly prepared some articles on Chanzy's retreat and present circumstances, forwarded them to London for the ***Pall Mall Gazette***.

The war was now fast drawing to an end. I have hitherto left several important occurrences unmentioned, being unwilling to interrupt my narrative of the fighting at Le Mans and the subsequent retreat. I feel, however, that I now ought to glance at the state of affairs in other parts of France. I have just mentioned that after visiting Chanzy at Laval (January 19), Gambetta repaired to Lille to confer with Faidherbe. Let us see, then, what the latter general had been doing. He was no longer opposed by Manteuffel, who had been sent to the east of France in the hope that he would deal more effectually than Werder with Bourbaki's army, which was still in the field there. Manteuffel's successor in the north was General von Goeben, with whom, on January 18, Faidherbe fought an engagement at Vermand, followed on the morrow by the battle of Saint Quentin, which was waged for seven hours amidst thaw and fog. Though it was claimed as a French victory, it was not one. The Germans, it is true, lost 2500 men, but the French killed and wounded amounted to 3500, and there were thousands of men missing, the Germans taking some 5000 prisoners, whilst other troops disbanded much as Chanzy's men disbanded during his retreat. From a strategical point of view the action at Saint Quentin was indecisive.

Turning to eastern France, Bourbaki fought two indecisive engagements near Villersexel, south-east of Vesoul, on January 9 and 10, and claimed the victory on these occasions. On January 13 came another engagement at Arcey, which he also claimed as a success, being congratulated upon it by Gambetta. The weather was most severe in the region of his operations, and the sufferings of his men were quite as great as--if not greater than-- those of Chanzy's troops. There were nights when men lay down to sleep, and never awoke again. On January 15,16, and 17 there was a succession of engagements on the Lisaine, known collectively as the battle of Hericourt. These actions resulted in Bourbaki's retreat southward towards Besancon, where for the moment we will leave him, in order to consider the position of Paris at this juncture.

Since the beginning of the year, the day of the capital's surrender had been fast approaching. Paris actually fell because its supply of food was virtually exhausted. On January 18 it became necessary to ration the bread, now a dark, sticky compound, which included such ingredients as bran, starch, rice, barley, vermicelli, and pea-flour. About ten ounces was allotted per diem to each adult, children under five years of age receiving half that quantity. But the health-bill of the city was also a contributory cause of the capitulation. In November there were 7444 deaths among the non-combatant population, against 3863 in November, 1869. The death-roll of December rose to 10,665, against 4214 in December the previous year. In January, between sixty and seventy persons died from small-pox every day. Bronchitis and pneumonia made an ever-increasing number of victims. From January 14 to January 21 the mortality rose to no less than 4465; from the latter date until January 28, the day of the capitulation, the figures were 4671, whereas in normal times they had never been more than 1000 in any week.

Among the troops the position was going from bad to worse. Thousands of men were in the hospitals, and thousands contrived to desert and hide themselves in the city. Out of 100,705 linesmen, there were, on January 1, no fewer than 23,938 absentees; while 23,565 units were absent from the Mobile Guard, which, on paper, numbered 111,999. Briefly, one man out of every five was either a patient or a deserter. As for the German bombardment, this had some moral but very little material effect. Apart from the damage done to buildings, it killed (as I previously said) about one hundred and wounded about two hundred persons.

The Government now had little if any confidence in the utility of any further sorties. Nevertheless, as the extremist newspapers still clamoured for one, it was eventually decided to attack the German positions across the Seine, on the west of the city. This sortie, commonly called that of Buzenval, took place on January 10, the day after King William of Prussia had been proclaimed German Emperor in Louis XIV's "Hall of Mirrors" at Versailles. [The decision to raise the King to the imperial dignity had been arrived at on January 1.] Without doubt, the Buzenval sortie was devised chiefly in order to give the National Guard the constantly demanded opportunity and satisfaction of being led against the Germans. Trochu, who assumed chief command, establishing himself at the fort of Mont Valerien, divided his forces into three columns, led by Generals Vinoy, Bellemare, and Ducrot. The first (the left wing) comprised 22,000 men, including 8000 National Guards; the second (the central column) 34,500 men, including 16,000 Guards; and the third (the right wing) 33,500 men, among whom were no fewer than 18,000 Guards. Thus the total force was about 90,000, the National Guards representing about a third of that number. Each column had with it ten batteries, representing for the entire force 180 guns. The French front, however, extended over a distance of nearly four miles, and the army's real strength was thereby diminished. There was some fairly desperate fighting at Saint Cloud, Montretout, and Longboyau, but the French were driven back after losing 4000 men, mostly National Guards, whereas the German losses were only about six hundred.

The affair caused consternation in Paris, particularly as several prominent men had fallen in the ranks of the National Guard. On the night of January 21, some extremists forced their way into the prison of Mazas and delivered some of their friends who had been shut up there since the rising of October 31. On the morrow, January 22, there was a demonstration and an affray on the Place de l'Hotel de Ville, shots being exchanged with the result that people were killed and wounded. The Government gained the day, however, and retaliated by closing the revolutionary clubs and suppressing some extremist newspapers. But four hours later Trochu resigned his position as Military Governor of Paris (in which he was replaced by General Vinoy), only retaining the Presidency of the Government. Another important incident had occurred on the very evening after the insurrection: Jules Favre, the Foreign Minister, had then forwarded a letter to Prince Bismarck.

The Government's first idea had been merely to surrender--that is to open the city-gates and let the Germans enter at their peril. It did not wish to negotiate or sign any capitulation. Jules Favre indicated as much when, writing to Bismarck, and certainly the proposed course might have placed the Germans--with the eyes of the world fixed upon them--in a difficult position. But Favre was no match for the great Prussian statesman. Formal negotiations were soon opened, and Bismarck so contrived affairs that, as Gambetta subsequently and rightly complained, the convention which Favre signed applied far more to France as a whole than to Paris itself. In regard to the city, the chief conditions were that a war indemnity of L8,000,000 should be paid; that the forts round the city should be occupied by the Germans; that the garrison--Line, Mobile Guard, and Naval Contingent (altogether about 180,000 men)--should become prisoners of war; and that the armament (1500 fortress guns and 400 field pieces) should be surrendered, as well as the large stores of ammunition. On the other hand, a force of 12,000 men was left to the French Government for "police duty" in the city, and the National Guards were, at Favre's urgent but foolish request, allowed to retain their arms. Further, the city was to be provisioned. In regard to France generally, arrangements were made for an armistice of twenty-one days' duration, in order to allow of the election of a National Assembly to treat for peace. In these arrangements Favre and Vinoy (the new Governor of Paris) were out-jockeyed by Bismarck and Moltke. They were largely ignorant of the real position in the provinces, and consented to very disadvantageous terms in regard to the lines which the Germans and the French should respectively occupy during the armistice period. Moreover, although it was agreed that hostilities should cease on most points, no such stipulation was made respecting the east of France, where both Bourbaki and Garibaldi were in the field.

The latter had achieved some slight successes near Dijon on January 21 and 23, but on February 1--that is, two days after the signing of the armistice--the Garibaldians were once more driven out of the Burgundian capital. That, however, was as nothing in comparison with what befell Bourbaki's unfortunate army. Manteuffel having compelled it to retreat from Besancon to Pontarlier, it was next forced to withdraw into Switzerland [Before this happened, Bourbaki attempted his life.] (neutral territory, where it was necessarily disarmed by the Swiss authorities) in order to escape either capture or annihilation by the Germans. The latter took some 6000 prisoners, before the other men (about 80,000 in number) succeeded in crossing the Swiss frontier. A portion of the army was saved, however, by General Billot. With regard to the position elsewhere, Longwy, I should mention, surrendered three days before the capitulation of Paris; but Belfort prolonged its resistance until February 13, when all other hostilities had ceased. Its garrison, so gallantly commanded by Colonel Denfert-Bochereau, was accorded the honours of war.

As I wrote in my book, "Republican France," the country generally was weary of the long struggle; and only Gambetta, Freycinet, and a few military men, such as Chanzy and Faidherbe, were in favour of prolonging it. From the declaration of war on July 15 to the capitulation of Paris and the armistice on January 28, the contest had lasted twenty-eight weeks. Seven of those weeks had sufficed to overthrow the

Second Empire; but only after another one-and-twenty weeks had the Third Republic laid down her arms. Whatever may have been the blunders of the National Defence, it at least saved the honour of France,

It may well be doubted whether the position could have been retrieved had the war been prolonged, though undoubtedly the country was still possessed of many resources. In "Republican France," I gave a number of figures which showed that over 600,000 men could have been brought into action almost immediately, and that another 260,000 could afterwards have been provided. On February 8, when Chanzy had largely reorganized his army, he, alone, had under his orders 4952 officers and 227,361 men, with 430 guns. That careful and distinguished French military historian, M. Pierre Lehautcourt, places, however, the other resources of France at even a higher figure than I did. He also points out, rightly enough, that although so large a part of France was invaded, the uninvaded territory was of greater extent, and inhabited by twenty-five millions of people. He estimates the total available artillery on the French side at 1232 guns, each with an average allowance of 242 projectiles. In addition, there were 443 guns awaiting projectiles. He tells us that the French ordnance factories were at this period turning out on an average 25,000 chassepots every month, and delivering two million cartridges every day; whilst other large supplies of weapons and ammunition were constantly arriving from abroad. On the other hand, there was certainly a scarcity of horses, the mortality of which in this war, as in all others, was very great. Chanzy only disposed of 20,000, and the remount service could only supply another 12,000. However, additional animals might doubtless have been found in various parts of France, or procured from abroad.

But material resources, however great they may be, are of little avail when a nation has practically lost heart. In spite, moreover, of all the efforts of commanding officers, insubordination was rampant among the troops in the field. There had been so many defeats, so many retreats, that they had lost all confidence in their generals. During the period of the armistice, desertions were still numerous. I may add, that if at the expiration of the armistice the struggle had been renewed, Chanzy's plan-- which received approval at a secret military and Government council held in Paris, whither he repaired early in February--was to place General de Colomb at the head of a strong force for the defence of Brittany, whilst he, Chanzy, would, with his own army, cross the Loire and defend southern France.

Directly news arrived that an armistice had been signed, and that Paris was once more open, my father arranged to return there, accompanied by myself and my younger brother, Arthur Vizetelly. We took with us, I remember, a plentiful supply of poultry and other edibles for distribution among the friends who had been suffering from the scarcity of provisions during the latter days of the siege. The elections for the new National Assembly were just over, nearly all of the forty-three deputies returned for Paris being Republicans, though throughout the rest of France Legitimist and Orleanist candidates were generally successful. I remember that just before I left Saint Servan one of our tradesmen, an enthusiastic Royalist, said to me, "We shall have a King on the throne by the time you come back to see us in the summer." At that moment it certainly seemed as if such would be the case. As for the Empire, one could only regard it as dead. There were, I think, merely five recognized Bonapartist members in the whole of the new National Assembly, and most of them came from Corsica. Thus, it was by an almost unanimous vote that the Assembly declared Napoleon III and his dynasty to be responsible for the "invasion, ruin, and dismemberment of France."

The Assembly having called Thiers to the position of "Chief of the Executive Power," peace negotiations ensued between him and Bismarck. They began on February 22, Thiers being assisted by Jules Favre, who retained the position of Minister of Foreign Affairs, mainly because nobody else would take it and append his signature to a treaty which was bound to be disastrous for the country. The chief conditions of that treaty will be remembered. Germany was to annex Alsace-Lorraine, to receive a war indemnity of two hundred million pounds sterling (with interest in addition), and secure commercially "most favoured nation" treatment from France. The preliminaries were signed on February 26, and accepted by the National Assembly on March 1, but the actual treaty of Frankfort was not signed and ratified until the ensuing month of May.

Paris presented a sorry spectacle during the weeks which followed the armistice. There was no work for the thousands of artisans who had become National Guards during the siege. Their allowance as such was prolonged in order that they might at least have some means of subsistence. But the unrest was general. By the side of the universal hatred of the Germans, which was displayed on all sides, even finding vent in the notices set up in the shop-windows to the effect that no Germans need apply there, one observed a very bitter feeling towards the new Government. Thiers had been an Orleanist all his life, and among the Paris working-classes there was a general feeling that the National Assembly would give France a king. This feeling tended to bring about the subsequent bloody Insurrection of the Commune; but, as I wrote in "Republican France," it was precisely the Commune which gave the French Royalists a chance. It placed a weapon in their hands and enabled them to say, "You see, by that insurrection, by all those terrible excesses, what a Republic implies. Order, quietude, fruitful work, are only possible under a monarchy." As we know, however, the efforts of the Royalists were defeated, in part by the obstinacy of their candidate, the Comte de Chambord, and in part by the good behaviour of the Republicans generally, as counselled both by Thiers and by Gambetta.

On March 1, the very day when the National Assembly ratified the preliminaries of peace at Bordeaux, the Germans made their triumphal entry into Paris. Four or five days previously my father had sent me on a special mission to Bordeaux, and it was then that after long years I again set eyes on Garibaldi, who had been elected as a French deputy, but who resigned his seat in consequence of the onerous terms of peace. Others, notably Gambetta, did precisely the same, by way of protesting against the so-called "Devil's Treaty." However, I was back in Paris in time to witness the German entry into the city. My father, my brother Arthur, and myself were together in the Champs Elysees on that historical occasion. I have related elsewhere [In "Republican France."] how a number of women of the Paris Boulevards were whipped in the Champs Elysees shrubberies by young roughs, who, not unnaturally, resented the shameless overtures made by these women to the German soldiery. There were, however, some unfortunate mistakes that day, as, for instance, when an attempt was made to ill-treat an elderly lady who merely spoke to the Germans in the hope of obtaining some information respecting her son, then still a prisoner of war. I remember also that Archibald Forbes was knocked down and kicked for returning the salute of the Crown Prince of Saxony. Some of the English correspondents who hurried to the scene removed Forbes to a little hotel in the Faubourg St. Honore, for he had really been hurt by that savage assault, though it did not prevent him from penning a graphic account of what he witnessed on that momentous day.

The German entry was, on the whole, fairly imposing as a military display; but the stage-management was very bad, and one could not imagine that Napoleon's entry into Berlin had in any way resembled it. Nor could it be said to have equalled the entry of the Allied Sovereigns into Paris in 1814. German princelings in basket-carriages drawn by ponies did not add to the dignity of the spectacle. Moreover, both the Crown Prince of Saxony and the Crown Prince of Germany (Emperor Frederick) attended it in virtually an *incognito* manner. As for the Emperor William, his councillors dissuaded him from entering the city for fear lest there should be trouble there. I believe also that neither Bismarck nor Moltke attended, though, like the Emperor, they both witnessed the preliminary review of troops in the Bois de Boulogne. The German occupation was limited to the Champs Elysees quarter, and on the first day the Parisians generally abstained from going there; but on the morrow--when news that the preliminaries of peace had been accepted at Bordeaux had reached the capital--they flocked to gaze upon ***nos amis les ennemis***, and greatly enjoyed, I believe, the lively music played by the German regimental bands. "Music hath charms," as we are all aware. The departure of the German troops on the ensuing evening was of a much more spectacular character than their entry had been. As with their bands playing, whilst they themselves sang the "Wacht am Rhein" in chorus, they marched up the Champs Elysees on their way back to Versailles, those of their comrades who were still billeted in the houses came to the balconies with as many lighted candles as they could carry. Bivouac fires, moreover, were burning brightly here and there, and the whole animated scene, with its play of light and shade under the dark March sky, was one to be long remembered.

The Franco-German War was over, and a new era had begun for Europe. The balance of power was largely transferred. France had again ceased to be the predominant continental state. She had attained to that position for a time under Louis XIV, and later, more conspicuously, under Napoleon I. But in both of those instances vaulting ambition had o'er-leapt itself. The purposes of Napoleon III were less far-reaching. Such ideas of aggrandisement as he entertained were largely subordinated to his desire to consolidate the *regime* he had revived, and to ensure the continuity of his dynasty. But the very principle of nationality which he more than once expounded, and which he championed in the case of Italy, brought about his ruin. He gave Italy Venetia, but refused her Rome, and thereby alienated her.

Further, the consolidation of Germany--from his own nationalist point of view--became a threat to French interests. Thus he was hoist chiefly by his own *petard*, and France paid the penalty for his errors.

The Franco-German War was over, I have said, but there came a terrible aftermath--that is, the rising of the Commune, some of the introductory features of which were described by me in "Republican France." There is only one fairly good history of that formidable insurrection in the English language--one written some years ago by Mr. Thomas March. It is, however, a history from the official standpoint, and is consequently one-sided as well as inaccurate in certain respects. Again, the English version of the History of the Commune put together by one of its partisans, Lissagaray, sins in the other direction. An impartial account of the rising remains to be written. If I am spared I may, perhaps, be privileged to contribute to it by preparing a work on much the same lines as those of this present volume. Not only do I possess the greater part of the literature on the subject, including many of the newspapers of the time, but throughout the insurrection I was in Paris or its suburbs.

I sketched the dead bodies of Generals Clement Thomas and Lecomte only a few hours after their assassination. I saw the Vendome column fall while American visitors to Paris were singing, "Hail, Columbia!" in the hotels of the Rue de la Paix. I was under fire in the same street when a demonstration was made there. Provided with passports by both sides, I went in and out of the city and witnessed the fighting at Asnieres and elsewhere. I attended the clubs held in the churches, when women often perorated from the pulpits. I saw Thiers's house being demolished; and when the end came and the Versailles troops made their entry into the city, I was repeatedly in the street-fighting with my good friend, Captain Bingham. I recollect sketching the attack on the Elysee Palace from a balcony of our house, and finding that balcony on the pavement a few hours later when it had been carried away by a shell from a Communard battery at Montmartre. Finally, I saw Paris burning. I gazed on the sheaves of flames rising above the Tuileries. I saw the whole front of the Ministry of Finances fall into the Rue de Rivoli. I saw the now vanished Carrefour de la Croix Rouge one blaze of fire. I helped to carry water to put out the conflagration at the Palais de Justice. I was prodded with a bayonet when, after working in that manner for some hours, I attempted to shirk duty at another fire which I came upon in the course of my expeditions. All that period of my life flashes on my mind as vividly as Paris herself flashed under the wondering stars of those balmy nights in May.

My father and my brother Arthur also had some remarkable adventures. There was one occasion when they persuaded a venturesome Paris cabman to drive them from conflagration to conflagration, and this whilst the street-fighting was still in progress. Every now and then, as they drove on, men and women ran eagerly out of houses into which wounded combatants had been taken, imagining that they must belong to the medical profession, as nobody else was likely to go about Paris in such a fashion at such a moment. Those good folk forgot the journalists. The service of the Press carries with it obligations which must not be shirked. Journalism has become, not merely the chronicle of the day, but the foundation of history. And now I know not if I should say farewell or ***au revoir*** to my readers. Whether I ever attempt a detailed account of the Commune of Paris must depend on a variety of circumstances. After three-and-forty years "at the mill," I am inclined to feel tired, and with me health is not what it has been. Nevertheless, my plans must depend chiefly on the reception given to this present volume.

www.bookjungle.com *email: sales@bookjungle.com fax: 630-214-0564 mail: Book Jungle PO Box 2226 Champaign, IL 61825*

The Codes Of Hammurabi And Moses
W. W. Davies

QTY

The discovery of the Hammurabi Code is one of the greatest achievements of archaeology, and is of paramount interest, not only to the student of the Bible, but also to all those interested in ancient history...

Religion **ISBN:** *1-59462-338-4* Pages:132
MSRP *$12.95*

The Theory of Moral Sentiments
Adam Smith

QTY

This work from 1749. contains original theories of conscience amd moral judgment and it is the foundation for systemof morals.

Philosophy **ISBN:** *1-59462-777-0* Pages:536
MSRP *$19.95*

Jessica's First Prayer
Hesba Stretton

QTY

In a screened and secluded corner of one of the many railway-bridges which span the streets of London there could be seen a few years ago, from five o'clock every morning until half past eight, a tidily set-out coffee-stall, consisting of a trestle and board, upon which stood two large tin cans, with a small fire of charcoal burning under each so as to keep the coffee boiling during the early hours of the morning when the work-people were thronging into the city on their way to their daily toil...

Childrens **ISBN:** *1-59462-373-2* Pages:84
MSRP *$9.95*

My Life and Work
Henry Ford

QTY

Henry Ford revolutionized the world with his implementation of mass production for the Model T automobile. Gain valuable business insight into his life and work with his own auto-biography... "We have only started on our development of our country we have not as yet, with all our talk of wonderful progress, done more than scratch the surface. The progress has been wonderful enough but..."

Biographies/ **ISBN:** *1-59462-198-5* Pages:300
MSRP *$21.95*

www.bookjungle.com email: sales@bookjungle.com fax: 630-214-0564 mail: Book Jungle PO Box 2226 Champaign, IL 61825

The Art of Cross-Examination
Francis Wellman

QTY

I presume it is the experience of every author, after his first book is published upon an important subject, to be almost overwhelmed with a wealth of ideas and illustrations which could readily have been included in his book, and which to his own mind, at least, seem to make a second edition inevitable. Such certainly was the case with me; and when the first edition had reached its sixth impression in five months, I rejoiced to learn that it seemed to my publishers that the book had met with a sufficiently favorable reception to justify a second and considerably enlarged edition. ..

Reference   ISBN: *1-59462-647-2*   Pages:412 MSRP *$19.95*

On the Duty of Civil Disobedience
Henry David Thoreau

QTY

Thoreau wrote his famous essay, On the Duty of Civil Disobedience, as a protest against an unjust but popular war and the immoral but popular institution of slave-owning. He did more than write—he declined to pay his taxes, and was hauled off to gaol in consequence. Who can say how much this refusal of his hastened the end of the war and of slavery ?

Law   ISBN: *1-59462-747-9*   Pages:48 MSRP *$7.45*

Dream Psychology Psychoanalysis for Beginners
Sigmund Freud

QTY

Sigmund Freud, born Sigismund Schlomo Freud (May 6, 1856 - September 23, 1939), was a Jewish-Austrian neurologist and psychiatrist who co-founded the psychoanalytic school of psychology. Freud is best known for his theories of the unconscious mind, especially involving the mechanism of repression; his redefinition of sexual desire as mobile and directed towards a wide variety of objects; and his therapeutic techniques, especially his understanding of transference in the therapeutic relationship and the presumed value of dreams as sources of insight into unconscious desires.

Psychology   ISBN: *1-59462-905-6*   Pages:196 MSRP *$15.45*

The Miracle of Right Thought
Orison Swett Marden

QTY

Believe with all of your heart that you will do what you were made to do. When the mind has once formed the habit of holding cheerful, happy, prosperous pictures, it will not be easy to form the opposite habit. It does not matter how improbable or how far away this realization may see, or how dark the prospects may be, if we visualize them as best we can, as vividly as possible, hold tenaciously to them and vigorously struggle to attain them, they will gradually become actualized, realized in the life. But a desire, a longing without endeavor, a yearning abandoned or held indifferently will vanish without realization.

Self Help   ISBN: *1-59462-644-8*   Pages:360 MSRP *$25.45*

www.bookjungle.com email: sales@bookjungle.com fax: 630-214-0564 mail: Book Jungle PO Box 2226 Champaign, IL 61825

QTY

☐ **The Rosicrucian Cosmo-Conception Mystic Christianity** by *Max Heindel* ISBN: *1-59462-188-8* **$38.95**
The Rosicrucian Cosmo-conception is not dogmatic, neither does it appeal to any other authority than the reason of the student. It is: not controversial, but is: sent forth in the, hope that it may help to clear... New Age/Religion Pages 646

☐ **Abandonment To Divine Providence** by *Jean-Pierre de Caussade* ISBN: *1-59462-228-0* **$25.95**
"The Rev. Jean Pierre de Caussade was one of the most remarkable spiritual writers of the Society of Jesus in France in the 18th Century. His death took place at Toulouse in 1751. His works have gone through many editions and have been republished... Inspirational/Religion Pages 400

☐ **Mental Chemistry** by *Charles Haanel* ISBN: *1-59462-192-6* **$23.95**
Mental Chemistry allows the change of material conditions by combining and appropriately utilizing the power of the mind. Much like applied chemistry creates something new and unique out of careful combinations of chemicals the mastery of mental chemistry... New Age Pages 354

☐ **The Letters of Robert Browning and Elizabeth Barret Barrett 1845-1846 vol II** ISBN: *1-59462-193-4* **$35.95**
by *Robert Browning* and *Elizabeth Barrett* Biographies Pages 596

☐ **Gleanings In Genesis (volume I)** by *Arthur W. Pink* ISBN: *1-59462-130-6* **$27.45**
Appropriately has Genesis been termed "the seed plot of the Bible" for in it we have, in germ form, almost all of the great doctrines which are afterwards fully developed in the books of Scripture which follow... Religion/Inspirational Pages 420

☐ **The Master Key** by *L. W. de Laurence* ISBN: *1-59462-001-6* **$30.95**
In no branch of human knowledge has there been a more lively increase of the spirit of research during the past few years than in the study of Psychology, Concentration and Mental Discipline. The requests for authentic lessons in Thought Control, Mental Discipline and... New Age/Business Pages 422

☐ **The Lesser Key Of Solomon Goetia** by *L. W. de Laurence* ISBN: *1-59462-092-X* **$9.95**
This translation of the first book of the "Lernegton" which is now for the first time made accessible to students of Talismanic Magic was done, after careful collation and edition, from numerous Ancient Manuscripts in Hebrew, Latin, and French... New Age/Occult Pages 92

☐ **Rubaiyat Of Omar Khayyam** by *Edward Fitzgerald* ISBN:*1-59462-332-5* **$13.95**
Edward Fitzgerald, whom the world has already learned, in spite of his own efforts to remain within the shadow of anonymity, to look upon as one of the rarest poets of the century, was born at Bredfield, in Suffolk, on the 31st of March, 1809. He was the third son of John Purcell... Music Pages 172

☐ **Ancient Law** by *Henry Maine* ISBN: *1-59462-128-4* **$29.95**
The chief object of the following pages is to indicate some of the earliest ideas of mankind, as they are reflected in Ancient Law, and to point out the relation of those ideas to modern thought. Religiom/History Pages 452

☐ **Far-Away Stories** by *William J. Locke* ISBN: *1-59462-129-2* **$19.45**
"Good wine needs no bush, but a collection of mixed vintages does. And this book is just such a collection. Some of the stories I do not want to remain buried for ever in the museum files of dead magazine-numbers an author's not unpardonable vanity..." Fiction Pages 272

☐ **Life of David Crockett** by *David Crockett* ISBN: *1-59462-250-7* **$27.45**
"Colonel David Crockett was one of the most remarkable men of the times in which he lived. Born in humble life, but gifted with a strong will, an indomitable courage, and unremitting perseverance... Biographies/New Age Pages 424

☐ **Lip-Reading** by *Edward Nitchie* ISBN: *1-59462-206-X* **$25.95**
Edward B. Nitchie, founder of the New York School for the Hard of Hearing, now the Nitchie School of Lip-Reading, Inc, wrote "LIP-READING Principles and Practice". The development and perfecting of this meritorious work on lip-reading was an undertaking... How-to Pages 400

☐ **A Handbook of Suggestive Therapeutics, Applied Hypnotism, Psychic Science** ISBN: *1-59462-214-0* **$24.95**
by *Henry Munro* Health/New Age/Health/Self-help Pages 376

☐ **A Doll's House: and Two Other Plays** by *Henrik Ibsen* ISBN: *1-59462-112-8* **$19.95**
Henrik Ibsen created this classic when in revolutionary 1848 Rome. Introducing some striking concepts in playwriting for the realist genre, this play has been studied the world over. Fiction/Classics/Plays 308

☐ **The Light of Asia** by *sir Edwin Arnold* ISBN: *1-59462-204-3* **$13.95**
In this poetic masterpiece, Edwin Arnold describes the life and teachings of Buddha. The man who was to become known as Buddha to the world was born as Prince Gautama of India but he rejected the worldly riches and abandoned the reigns of power when... Religion/History/Biographies Pages 170

☐ **The Complete Works of Guy de Maupassant** by *Guy de Maupassant* ISBN: *1-59462-157-8* **$16.95**
"For days and days, nights and nights, I had dreamed of that first kiss which was to consecrate our engagement, and I knew not on what spot I should put my lips..." Fiction/Classics Pages 240

☐ **The Art of Cross-Examination** by *Francis L. Wellman* ISBN: *1-59462-309-0* **$26.95**
Written by a renowned trial lawyer, Wellman imparts his experience and uses case studies to explain how to use psychology to extract desired information through questioning. How-to/Science/Reference Pages 408

☐ **Answered or Unanswered?** by *Louisa Vaughan* ISBN: *1-59462-248-5* **$10.95**
Miracles of Faith in China Religion Pages 112

☐ **The Edinburgh Lectures on Mental Science (1909)** by *Thomas* ISBN: *1-59462-008-3* **$11.95**
This book contains the substance of a course of lectures recently given by the writer in the Queen Street Hall, Edinburgh. Its purpose is to indicate the Natural Principles governing the relation between Mental Action and Material Conditions... New Age/Psychology Pages 148

☐ **Ayesha** by *H. Rider Haggard* ISBN: *1-59462-301-5* **$24.95**
Verily and indeed it is the unexpected that happens! Probably if there was one person upon the earth from whom the Editor of this, and of a certain previous history, did not expect to hear again... Classics Pages 380

☐ **Ayala's Angel** by *Anthony Trollope* ISBN: *1-59462-352-X* **$29.95**
The two girls were both pretty, but Lucy who was twenty-one who supposed to be simple and comparatively unattractive, whereas Ayala was credited, as her Bombwhat romantic name might show, with poetic charm and a taste for romance. Ayala when her father died was nineteen... Fiction Pages 484

☐ **The American Commonwealth** by *James Bryce* ISBN: *1-59462-286-8* **$34.45**
An interpretation of American democratic political theory. It examines political mechanics and society from the perspective of Scotsman James Bryce Politics Pages 572

☐ **Stories of the Pilgrims** by *Margaret P. Pumphrey* ISBN: *1-59462-116-0* **$17.95**
This book explores pilgrims religious oppression in England as well as their escape to Holland and eventual crossing to America on the Mayflower, and their early days in New England... History Pages 268

www.bookjungle.com email: sales@bookjungle.com fax: 630-214-0564 mail: Book Jungle PO Box 2226 Champaign, IL 61825

QTY

The Fasting Cure by *Sinclair Upton* **ISBN:** *1-59462-222-1* **$13.95**
In the Cosmopolitan Magazine for May, 1910, and in the Contemporary Review (London) for April, 1910, I published an article dealing with my experiences in fasting. I have written a great many magazine articles, but never one which attracted so much attention... *New Age/Self Help/Health Pages 164*

Hebrew Astrology by *Sepharial* **ISBN:** *1-59462-308-2* **$13.45**
In these days of advanced thinking it is a matter of common observation that we have left many of the old landmarks behind and that we are now pressing forward to greater heights and to a wider horizon than that which represented the mind-content of our progenitors... *Astrology Pages 144*

Thought Vibration or The Law of Attraction in the Thought World **ISBN:** *1-59462-127-6* **$12.95**
by *William Walker Atkinson* *Psychology/Religion Pages 144*

Optimism by *Helen Keller* **ISBN:** *1-59462-108-X* **$15.95**
Helen Keller was blind, deaf, and mute since 19 months old, yet famously learned how to overcome these handicaps, communicate with the world, and spread her lectures promoting optimism. An inspiring read for everyone... *Biographies/Inspirational Pages 84*

Sara Crewe by *Frances Burnett* **ISBN:** *1-59462-360-0* **$9.45**
In the first place, Miss Minchin lived in London. Her home was a large, dull, tall one, in a large, dull square, where all the houses were alike, and all the sparrows were alike, and where all the door-knockers made the same heavy sound... *Childrens/Classic Pages 88*

The Autobiography of Benjamin Franklin by *Benjamin Franklin* **ISBN:** *1-59462-135-7* **$24.95**
The Autobiography of Benjamin Franklin has probably been more extensively read than any other American historical work, and no other book of its kind has had such ups and downs of fortune. Franklin lived for many years in England, where he was agent... *Biographies/History Pages 332*

Name
Email
Telephone
Address
City, State ZIP

☐ Credit Card   ☐ Check / Money Order

Credit Card Number
Expiration Date
Signature

Please Mail to: Book Jungle
                  PO Box 2226
                  Champaign, IL 61825
or Fax to: 630-214-0564

ORDERING INFORMATION

web: www.bookjungle.com
email: sales@bookjungle.com
fax: 630-214-0564
mail: Book Jungle PO Box 2226 Champaign, IL 61825
or PayPal to sales@bookjungle.com

Please contact us for bulk discounts

DIRECT-ORDER TERMS

20% Discount if You Order Two or More Books
Free Domestic Shipping!
Accepted: Master Card, Visa, Discover, American Express

www.ingramcontent.com/pod-product-compliance
Lightning Source LLC
Chambersburg PA
CBHW080537170426
43195CB00016B/2592